Selected Unpublished Papers of **Jacob A. Arlow**
Conversations with the Unconscious

Nancy R. Goodman and Kim L. Kleinman highlight the path Jacob Arlow forged to help us all have "conversations with the unconscious". The papers themselves are gems of Arlow's thinking about the unconscious fantasy compromise formation, the creative mind and the process of listening and interpreting in psychoanalysis. These previously unpublished papers add to his already large tome of work and ignite interest in going back to read his published papers. We discover the timelessness of Jacob Arlow's profound impact on modern psychoanalysis—theory and practice. Many of the papers sound like contemporary concepts about space for thinking and understanding what is so painful to know. The reader will also be able to delve deeply in the primary concepts of compromise formation, conflict, and repression which were involved with Arlow's way of working. Kim Kleinman and Nancy Goodman chose papers for their commentaries related to their interests. Goodman selected papers on topics she finds central such as listening, importance of metaphor, psychoanalysis and film, and the use of one's subjectivity. In her introductory essay she asks that the split so many hold between Kleinian thought and Arlowian thought be mended in order to maintain a concept of a unitary mind full of terrains of unconscious fantasy linked to instinct, trauma, and creativity. She states that our "as/if" divisions between schools of psychoanalysis is defensive against experience of the full brunt of "finding unconscious fantasy" in all of its presentations. Kim Kleinman is particularly interested in issues related to training, education, and Kleinian ideas of phantasy in relation to Arlow's ideas about fantasy. In her introduction, Kim writes about a particular aspect of these papers which is Arlow's developmental perspectives—fantasy evolves over time.

Arlene Kramer Richards offers a chapter about how she came to know Arlow—in her psychoanalysis as she speaks to an early childhood memory. The reader can feel the analysis taking place, especially the dialogue and interaction as Arlow and Richards work together exploring, agreeing, and disagreeing. Kim and Nancy also include a chapter of an interview of Arlene and Arnold Richards about Jacob Arlow. It is a magnificent treat to read the interview as they review their memories of and knowledge about Jacob Arlow.

The book as a whole is fascinating and compelling in reading the newly discovered papers and learning about the place of Arlow in psychoanalysis and his foundational thinking about the ubiquitous presence of unconscious fantasy in the mind and in culture.

IPBooks

Nancy R. Goodman, PhD, is a training and supervising analyst with the Contemporary Freudian Society, Washington DC, and the IPA. She is faculty in the Wuhan, China Training Program. Many publications reflect her interest in unconscious fantasy, trauma, sadomasochism, and symbolizing. Publications include edited volumes: *Finding Unconscious Fantasy in Narrative, Trauma, and Body Pain: A Clinical Guide* (2017) (with Paula Ellman); *The Power of Witnessing: Reflections, Reverberations, and Traces of the Holocaust* (2012) (with Marilyn Meyers). Nancy is founder and Director of www.virtualpsychoanalyticmuseum.org with IPBooks. She maintains a psychoanalytic practice in Bethesda, Maryland.

Kimberly L. Kleinman MS, LCSW is a Life Cycle Training and Supervising Analyst. She has co-edited *From Cradle to Couch, Essays in Honor Sylvia Brody* and *The Plumsock Papers: Giving New Analysts a Voice*. She has taught developmental approaches to understanding therapy in various institutes including the Contemporary Freudian Society and the Harlem Family Institute as well as in China.

SELECTED UNPUBLISHED PAPERS OF JACOB A. ARLOW

Selected Unpublished Papers of Jacob A. Arlow

Conversations with the Unconscious

Nancy R. Goodman, PhD

Kimberly L. Kleinman, MS, LCSW

IPBOOKS.net
International Psychoanalytic Books

International Psychoanalytic Books (IPBooks)
New York • IPBooks.net

Selected Unpublished Papers of Jacob A. Arlow: Conversations with the Unconscious

Published by IPBooks, Queens, NY
Online at: www.IPBooks.net

ISBN: 978-1-949093-95-7

Contents

Chapter 1

Following the Stream of Unconscious Fantasy: Reading Arlow

Nancy R. Goodman, PhD

Arlow's writings about the constant stream of unconscious fantasy in the mind (at all times) and his writing about listening in expansive ways during sessions (to his patients and to himself) have been significant guideposts for development of psychoanalytic thinking and practice. The psychoanalytic listening instrument of psychoanalysis has been tuned by his work. Reading Arlow fosters belief in the creativity of mind when metaphor evolves to communicate depths of anxiety, pain, and the underlying unconscious fantasy. It is knowing the importance of the unconscious fantasy and how to listen for the symbolic communications revealing layers of meaning which makes reading Arlow so intriguing, stimulating, and useful

The invitation to review a trove of unpublished articles by Jacob A. Arlow

Kim Kleinman and Nancy Goodman are contacted by Arnold Richards, publisher of IPBooks, to be editors for a book presenting unpublished papers of Jacob Arlow and a paper by Arlene Kramer Richards about her analysis with

Arlow.[1] As the project developed, we added an interview of Arlene Kramer Richards and Arnold Richards to answer questions about Arlow and their understanding of his work. We read the 30 articles sent to us deciding to each choose favorites for individual commentaries.

Nancy Goodman's choices of articles by subject matter.

You will see my interests in my choices of subjects—metaphor, listening, enactments, time, models in the analyst's mind, compromise formations, the primal scene, transference and countertransference, and the intersubjective conversation. Another major interest of mine is the psychoanalytic study of film in which scenes are produced similar to the way the mind in psychoanalytic sessions produces unconscious scenes holding symbolic meaning. Whether in film or in sessions, these scenes relate to particular unconscious processes and often to traumatic events. Arlow's paper on the film *Blow-Up* became one of my favorites being so full of symbolic repetitions of the primal scene, voyeurism, and contempt. It is an intense and delightful experience to claim articles, to read them closely, and to comment on them for others. I recommend this format, that we designed, for those wanting to feel close to knowledge creation of favored authors.

Jacob A. Arlow and the unconscious fantasy

Jacob A. Arlow's understanding of the presence of unconscious fantasy in the mind and descriptions of ways to listen in psychoanalytic treatment for

---

1 We subsequently discovered a few published versions of the papers which are indicated in the volume.

the patient's unconscious fantasy material are primary guides for schools of psychoanalytic study in the United States and around the world. His prolific writing, training of analysts, supervising and teaching bring therapeutic action to psychoanalytic treatments providing deep understanding and help to patients in emotional pain. Many concepts belonging to Ego Psychoanalysis intersect with his idea of a continuous flow of unconscious fantasy influence. The compromise formation of wish and fear so often resulting in symptomatology can be unraveled to free patients only when the unconscious dimensions are revealed and articulated, especially when identified in the transference. Arlow teaches us to attend to the meaning that is conveyed as patients and analysts develop metaphor. It is through metaphor that we find a way to communicate the affects and unconscious scenes associated with unconscious fantasies. I see Arlow working as an artist believing that the blank screen/canvas in the analytic room will become a gallery of images being discovered through a particular kind of listening involving imagination—the analyst's and the patient's.

As I read these discovered papers I could clearly see the depth of mind conveyed through Arlow's writing about unconscious fantasy. His belief in the instinctual underpinnings beginning in childhood is evident as is his articulation of the unconscious fantasy function he identifies. This function makes fantasy at all moments, producing layers of derivatives in compromise formations that relate to the original unconscious fantasy. Daydreams and myths of the individual and of society also are productions of the psyche reaching back to the more fundamental original fantasy with all of its human wishes and longings and terrors. In my close reading of my chosen articles, I could see up close the huge significance of Arlow's thinking which appears in his already large tome of published work. Arlow is masterful in bringing the reader of the paper into how his mind is working and how he is discovering the unconscious fantasies in session.

In *Fantasy, Myth, and Reality: Essays in Honor of Jacob A. Arlow, MD* (1988)

Harold Blum states:

> Jacob A. Arlow is renowned throughout the psychoanalytic world. His accomplishments are so great, his thinking so profound, his writings so prolific that monographs could be written on Jacob Arlow in each of his several roles: theoretician, researcher, clinician, teacher, lecturer, discussant. (p.3)

Yale Kramer, in the same volume, remarks that psychoanalysts might be uncomfortable with quantities but in reference to Arlow uses the phrase "an astonishing vitality" as he reports the presence of over 140 papers and presentations, most making major contributions to psychoanalysis especially understanding unconscious fantasy along with his legacy of teaching and supervising (p. 10).

The Power of Metaphor: Arlow's film screens

Psychoanalysis is based on the idea that the mind is layered and that it is a liberating journey to find, discover, and understand the underlying forces that develop inhibitions, pain and suffering. Psychoanalysts have the belief that once the layers are known and felt, growth and creativity can take place. In keeping with the communication power of metaphor I begin to build my metaphor for his work by first thinking of his famous metaphor of one film screen with different films playing on the front and back showing how fantasy accompanies the manifest story.

> Unconscious daydreaming is a constant feature of mental life. It is an ever-present accompaniment of conscious experience. What is consciously apperceived and experienced is the result of the interaction

between the data of experience and unconscious fantasying as mediated by various functions of the ego. (Arlow, 1969, p. 22)

As I see it, Arlow is speaking of depth of mind being birthed by a psychic facility for the operation of what he calls an unconscious fantasying function.

Psychoanalysts can notice much in Arlow's descriptions. He is being playful; he is providing us with a communication we can recall and find meaningful through his imagery; he is prodigiously free associating to his life's work as a psychoanalyst and as a member of a family and culture. The blank screen as a location for projections during analytic sessions has been a meme throughout the history of psychoanalysis and here, Arlow extends it into an internal constant, not only an aspect of the psychoanalytic clinical situation. In his view, there are multiple observations taking place and this is a guide to how the psychoanalytic approach views knowledge. But, the simultaneous films metaphor is not a final rendition, because we know from his work that the story appearing behind current perceptions also has history and has gone through elaborations over time. According to Arlow, the original unconscious fantasy is from the infantile, an outcropping from instinctual pressures *a la* Freud's reality principle. Pleasure is preserved through unconscious fantasy and from these beginnings, Arlow sees the mind developing versions of these deep beginning fantasies through symbolic equivalences and reworking of early compromises. It is the compromise formations with harsh superego presence that produce terrible pain and symptoms including distortions, somatic compromises, and restrictions in ability to love and to live. Full revealing of compromise formations is crucial to psychoanalytic therapeutic effect and becomes unraveled with identification of the powerful multiply determined unconscious fantasies.

Nancy Goodman's metaphor for Arlow's work

Reading his metaphor invites me to develop my own. Indeed it is this desire to create that Arlow has brought to his patients, his writings, and to psychoanalysis—the belief in the communication promise of metaphor. The image that keeps recurring as I think about and write about Arlow is the image of a stream, not quite a river, but a stream with a summertime flow over rocks and some vegetation growing on the sides near the banks. Arlow is watching over this scene inviting all students of psychoanalysis to observe, to be moved emotionally by the landscape, and to receive and transform, to be able to speak of meaning. I need to explain that this image is definitely overdetermined by my experience of a year of living with the COVID 19 epidemic and feeling the stream to both dry up and become arid and to flood and almost drown in a rush creating dangerous waters. Arlow would help us find a way to comprehend what is being communicated from the stream of the other's mind and from his own mind. I want to honor the constant flow of the unconscious so central to Arlow's thinking and want to make it rather calm and non-life claiming. Death is too close these days. However, when there is a stream, the flow of water can turn churning and violent with fast moving currents downstream. I know the unconscious holds storms of all kinds. In other words, my metaphor to capture Arlow's thinking is not static, is not a moment, but is about movement and swirling and passage of time because it is within time that change and transformations take place. Receiving the wisdom of Jacob Arlow and the streaming unconscious fantasy formation he acknowledges, what he calls the fantasying function, produces the feel of always being at a shoreline to witness the depth of meaning and the place of the moving unconscious fantasy as it is felt and perceived over a lifetime.

What I notice most in these unpublished papers: the unconscious is everywhere

Reading Arlow brings awareness that the unconscious is everywhere. While Freud taught us that to listen for parapraxis, jokes, body symptoms, dreams, primal scenes, and screen memories helps decipher the hidden parts of the mind exerting pressures and causing pain and distortions, Arlow expands with his own vision. Arlow constructs a model in which the unconscious is always active arising from instincts of early childhood and being reorganized especially by superego mandates. This is what is available in each paper. One can also hear the evolution of ideas taking place. For example, in the papers I studied, I could hear Arlow working out ideas about identification with patients and empathy producing awakenings within the analyst. He addressed this in writing about enactments, listening techniques, the creating of interpretations, and what he called the unique special conversation. There are times when his language is formal and clear as he describes compromise formations involved in the symptoms of his patients and the recognition of repetitions of compromises throughout the free associative process of sessions especially when entering the transference. The structural theory is the explanatory model for Arlow because the unconscious is involved at all levels of development of ego, id, and superego, with continual intermingling of the forces of each.

One of the great pleasures for me, was to hear his respect for his patients. As he put it, the analyst must listen and receive the patient's psychic reality and not assume intellectual understanding—keep listening. There is depth at all times. I think some critics that he is speaking of high level fantasies that are not deep fantasies is a complete misreading. He is listening to the stories, the myth making of his patients built on the past, the early sometimes inchoate unconscious fantasies, and highly structured fantasies influencing the more surface material.

Let's not idealize: Areas in need of revision–female development and splits in theories of unconscious fantasy

Admiring the contributions of a major psychoanalytic writer and thinker can lead to a kind of blind idealization. I take up here some areas where Arlow and his way of thinking need revision including listening for the feminine and integrating thinking about unconscious fantasy among various schools of thought.

—listening for the feminine

One example regarding the patriarchal thinking regarding women is in an article where Arlow reports a patient who dreams of something getting larger and swollen and is anxious. He interprets her concerns as being about the erection of the penis. I was waiting for the interpretation of her concerns about her own genital becoming aroused. He does not mention the arousal of her clitoris, labia, internal changes of her vagina, nor of her breasts. I thought he had abandoned her at this point. He also does not give room for association to the swelling body of pregnancy.

Without recognition of the feminine body, there is negation of the unconscious fantasies that are part of the psychic representations of the female and her compromises; i.e., her wishes and fears. Understanding of female, received attention and thus depth of understanding by many women psychoanalysts writing about primary femininity and female genital anxieties including my study group on the topic which read articles, conducted clinical research, and published (Basseches, et.al., 1996). These are precisely the issues that have been taken up by the new writings about female development in which his patient, Arlene Kramer Richards has been such an innovator. Arlene Kramer Richards clearly identifies with the profound understanding of the

8

unconscious relayed from her analyst, Jacob Arlow, and has gone on to grow psychoanalysis with her important writing on recognition of the female genital, including the little girls knowledge of internal sensations, the influence of feminism on psychoanalysis, and all fantasized compromises arising from female genital anxieties (Richards, 1992, 2020).

—need for healing of splits between theories: the fullness of understanding unconscious fantasy

In the background of my own enthusiasm at being able to rummage through these found papers, has been the disquieting question I have about how to bring together unconscious fantasy of Arlowians and the unconscious fantasy of Kleinians. Writing my introduction to these works by Arlow provides me with the opportunity to address this divide in psychoanalytic thinking. The divide can be observed throughout our psychoanalytic literature when perusing the references listed in articles. There is a split in referencing Klein's work on unconscious phantasy and referencing Arlow's work on unconscious fantasy. When schools of psychoanalysis are so divided in theory, it weakens our power to help patients, we are refusing to listen to some area of the mind as we claim only one to be valid. When Arlow does mention Klein it is often to contrast his thinking from hers and to question the existence of early fantasy, the infant fantasy that is so alive for Kleinians. There is an attitude of "we do not have to consider that". I often hear my Kleinian colleagues derogate Arlow stating he only is speaking about daydreams, hardly the essence of deep profound unconscious dimensions of the mind. He is written off as if his unconscious fantasying function of the mind does not offer profound capacities for clinical work to hear the deepest aspects of psychic functioning.

9

The "as/if" only one theory

There is an "as if" quality to the divisions in thinking about unconscious fantasy in that each theoretical school tends to think it is the only one, as if any additional exploration of the concept were false—as if only one could be true. Different schools even spell the word differently with a "ph" or an "f" influencing a belief in a divide rather than opportunity to enhance understanding. In our review of writing on finding unconscious fantasy, Paula Ellman and I (Ellman and Goodman, 2017), invited psychoanalysts from differing theoretical orientations and geographic locations to write about finding unconscious fantasy in clinical work. In our collection of chapters, we found that all analysts were expressing belief that unconscious fantasy was at the core of psychic life regardless of the spelling. Some included mainly Arlow or Klein in their reference list and some included both. In his compilation of writings on unconscious fantasy from the continent, Ricardo Steiner (2003) includes articles with both fantasy and phantasy, all grounded in Freud's premise that unconscious fantasy is an outcropping from instinctual life being confronted with frustrations of reality, the reality principle. His review of the concept is replete in historic foundations but as he puts it, is only a review of ideas from the Continent, i.e., not North America, not a mention of Arlow.

This is another aspect of the "as-if" –there is only one geographic area or institutional place for unconscious fantasy–"as if" theories touching would ignite destruction of all that a group is thinking about in the deep mind. It is "as if" there cannot be more than one knowledge base about unconscious fantasy/phantasy, the central concept in psychoanalysis. "As if" schools of thought cannot inter-inform to give fuller meaning to working hypotheses and working clinical listening.

Psychoanalysts understand the affects and object relations which relate to difference so often leading to sadomasochism inferring that someone must submit and fuse with another (Bass, 2000; Basseches, Ellman, and Goodman,

2013; Novick, J. & Novick, K. K. 1996). A component of sadomasochism is that it functions as a fetish to deny the terrors of difference (Goodman, 2013). When this happens in our theoretical world, the primitive fears of difference require representation in order to mend the split, the unsymbolized terrors about destruction.

Bringing theories together to have a model of the unitary mind: Giving up the either/or

Reading these discovered papers of Arlow highlights for me our psychoanalytic need to bring theories together and to de-fetishize one theory when it is used to block knowledge of another. The unconscious mind with primitive and sophisticated unconscious fantasies, perceptions, wishes, fears, and affects benefits from acknowledging difference in ways that can enhance thinking in order to enable integration and understanding of the unconscious and the multiple ways that finding unconscious fantasy can be claimed in our offices to help bring about revelations and transformations. In his descriptive frontispiece blurb for "Finding Unconscious Fantasy" (Ellman and Goodman, 2017), David Bell noted the need in psychoanalysis to heal the wounds of splits in what he terms, "clinic-theoretic bifurcation" of concepts.

> The editors in their scholarly introduction, foreground a tension in psychoanalysis that takes its origin at the earliest beginnings of our discipline—a kind of clinic-theoretic bifurcation between the concepts of "trauma" and "unconscious fantasy". The editors are to be congratulated on having done much to this split and in so doing show how different ways of thinking can enrich each other."

We set out to heal the split between trauma and unconscious fantasy that existed in psychoanalytic theory by switching focus to a function. We focused on "finding" the unconscious fantasy including the unconscious traumatic fantasy and reviewed theoretical writings on trauma and the unconscious fantasy. I propose that highlighting how trauma and unconscious fantasy have a continuous influence on the mind makes for a theory of a unitary mind, a psyche where the dead places of trauma exist side by side with the living mind of fantasy creation (Goodman, 2012). That is, that trauma and unconscious fantasy dynamically co-exist and influence psychic representations becoming symbolized.

The need for overarching concepts and functions to bring together theories of unconscious fantasy

The major question concerning unconscious fantasy is how we can have a more complete model of the mind with layers of unconscious able to be recognized with two major theories (and more) of unconscious fantasy so they can augment each other. Or, does either/or have to spin on and on weakening our capacities to fully think about unconscious fantasy? Reading the work of the International Psychoanalytic Association study of the concept of phantasy/fantasy shows the ability to consider similarities and differences in conceptual understanding across continents and across individual thinkers (Bohleber, et.al., 2015). I was impressed at their conclusions that, in fact, Kleinian conceptualizations and Arlowian conceptualizations have much in common.

> For Freud unconscious phantasies can only be partially known. They are to be inferred from the derivatives of the unconscious itself. Kleinians agree that, while unconscious phantasies must be inferred from the patient's clinical material, their existence is independent of

the inference. Arlow thinks similarly on this matter. He speaks of an unconscious fantasy function. The stream of inner stimulation is organized by fantasy thinking. (2015, p. 727)

The Unitary Mind Built on the function of "finding unconscious fantasy"

With the idea of "finding unconscious fantasy", Ellman and Goodman (2017) emphasize the process by which layers of the mind and their relation to unconscious fantasy, particularly core fantasies, are discovered in narrative, trauma and body pain. This offers an approach to follow to reveal all fantasy dimensions and their derivatives, no matter what named by various psychoanalytic groups. Using the idea of the "field", the functional concept of "finding unconscious fantasy" opens our psychoanalytic field to contain the unconscious through the use of varying overarching concepts. Fitting with the idea of "finding" is the contemporary view, developing among psychoanalytic schools of thought, that the mind has a readiness to make unconscious fantasy—that this is the fabric of the mind. This is similar to an idea that the mind is ready to make words, to organize around language, the instinctive mental capacity for language. The idea of readiness for unconscious fantasy can function as an umbrella concept for specific views of unconscious fantasy functioning. With this new conceptualization about the mind, Kleinian view of fantasy and Arlowian view of fantasy and others (and more to come), can be brought together as approaches for mapping out the psychic fullness of receiving and making unconscious fantasy. This view of the psyche as having capacity to create the scene, the story with the feel, from infancy on gives an opportunity to bring together the knowledge from Klein and Isaacs about the infantile unconscious and the continuous stream of the unconscious over time described by Arlow.

In my descriptions of the "Finding Theater" (2017), I present the idea of working within the metaphor of an internal theater where there are multiple stages upon which various unconscious scenes are being played out—all at once. I also proposed that there could be the principles of psychoanalytic schools on stages offering lighting and music of particular styles—and all providing access to unconscious fantasy that has been ready to be made since infancy and can be found. As I read the to-be-published here, articles by Arlow, I found my thinking of the overlap of theories and the specificity of each as profoundly helpful for psychoanalysts to help patients. The destruction of either/or thinking can be dissolved while acknowledging that the deep mind of unconscious fantasy is continually being discovered. From dialogue with my many colleagues across continents, I take in and absorb the promise of possibility in facing the unconscious psychic realities of theory and of the individual mind, including my own. Seeing the overlaps along with the differences brings about the alpha function needed to think and make knowledge. If the various worlds of thought cannot meet, we have weakened our efforts leaving dead places in our minds, the unthinkable. Arlow's intent to recognize the power of metaphor and belief in listening helps ensure further attempts to fully communicate about unconscious fantasy and the creative mind.

References

Basseches, H., Ellman, P., Elmendorf, S., Fritsch, E., Goodman, N., Helm, F., & Rockwell, S. (1996). Hearing what cannot be seen: A Psychoanalytic research group's inquiry into female sexuality. *Journal of the American Psychoanalytic Association* 44S: 511-528.

Bass, A. (2000). *Difference and Disavowal: The Trauma of Eros.* Stanford: Stanford University Press.

Basseches, H. I., Ellman, P. L. & Goodman, N. R. (2013). *Battling the Life and Death Forces of Sadomasochism: Clinical Perspectives.* London: Karnac.

Blum H. P., 1988. A Tribute to Jacob A. Arlow, M.D. In Blum, H. P., Kramer, Y., Richards, A.K., Richards, R. D. (Eds.) *Fantasy, Myth, and Reality: Essays in Honor of Jacob A. Arlow, M.D,* Madison, Ct.: International Universities Press., pp. 3-9.

Bohleber, W., Jimenez, J. P., Scarfone, D., Varvin, S., and Zysman, S. (2016). Unconscious phantasy and its conceptualizations: An attempt at conceptual integration. *International Journal of Psychoanalysis*, 96, 705-730.

Ellman, P. L. and Goodman, N. R. (2017). *Finding Unconscious Fantasy in Narrative, Trauma, and Body Pain: A Clinical Guide.* New York: Routledge.

Goodman, N. R. (2012). The power of witnessing. In N. R. Goodman and M. Meyers (Eds.) *The Power of Witnessing: Reflections, Reverberations, and Traces of the Holocaust—trauma, psychoanalysis, and the living mind.* pp. 3-26. New York: Routledge..

Goodman, N. R., (2013). Sailing with Mr. B. through waters of "hurting love" in Basseches, H. I.; Ellman, P. L., Goodman, N. R., (Eds.) *Battling the Life and Death Forces of Sadomasochism: Clinical Perspectives.* pp.95-110. London: Karnac.

Goodman, N. R., (2017). The "Finding Theater": a schema for finding unconscious fantasy in P. L. Ellman and N. R. Goodman (Eds.) *Finding*

Unconscious Fantasy in Narrative, Trauma, and Body Pain: A Clinical Guide. pp.22-34. New York: Routledge.

Kramer, Y. (1988). In the Visions of the Night: Perspectives on the Work of Jacob A. Arlow. In Blum, H. P., Kramer, Y., Richards, A.K., Richards, R. D. (Eds.) *Fantasy, Myth, and Reality: Essays in Honor of Jacob A. Arlow, M.D,* Madison, Ct.: International Universities Press.,. pp. 9-41.

Novick, J. & Novick, K. K. (1996). *Fearful Symmetry: The Development and Treatment of Sadomasochism.* Northvale, N.J.: Jason Aronson.

Richards, A. K. (1992). The influence of sphincter control and genital sensation in body image, and gender identity. *Psychoanalytic Quarterly* 61:331-351.

Richards, A. K. (1992). The influence of sphincter control and genital sensation in body image, and gender identity. *Psychoanalytic Quarterly* 61:331-351.

Richards, A.K. (2020). Rage and Creativity: How Second Generation Feminist Thought Collective Influenced Psychoanalysis in L. Spira (Ed.) *Rage and Creativity: How Feminism Sparked Psychoanalysis.* pp. 3-20. New York: IPBooks.

Steiner, R. (Ed.). 2003. *Unconscious Phantasy.* London: Karnac.

Chapter 2

J. A. Arlow as a Developmentalist

Kimberly Kleinman, LCSW

This volume contains many papers that were prepared to be delivered in person on panels, symposia or meetings. As a result many of these papers can be easily understood by new as well as experienced psychoanalytic scholars. Amongst the many areas of interest Arlow discussed, the one that fascinated me is his approach to developmental theory. I see him as a Developmental Psychoanalyst. In his paper on Technique in this book, he tells us that he remembers when he first read Anna Freud's *The Ego and Mechanisms of Defense*, (1937). It was in his last year of training. In his paper in this book entitled "Training for Psychoanalysis and Psychotherapy" he tells us that "Psychoanalysis is a developmental psychology. He states it is "...of utmost importance that analysts be fully versed in the many vicissitudes of development and impingements on development." (p. 290 in this book)

Arlow goes on to say that structural theory is by nature a developmental theory.

"By introducing the structural theory, which emphasizes the role of the ego in integrating and resolving the contradictions among the various elements in conflict, Freud made it possible to explore in greater detail the factors, inherent or experiential, that determine the ego's capacity to effect appropriate compromise formations. The implications of structural concepts for developmental theory and the understanding of unconscious fantasy were enormous." (p. 234 in this book)

Arlow also described development as non-linear: "In fact, the various phases of functional development overlap and merge subtly one into the other (page 238 in this book?)." He acknowledges that drive theory can give the impression that psychosexual stages are discrete and sequential. He frequently refutes this when he describes the use of the growing understanding of development provided by researchers and clinicians. Coates (1977) and Rona Knight (2020) have focused on the issue of conceptualizing development in a non-linear way and might be surprised to know that Arlow apparently agrees with them.

Arlow has a positive reaction to the increase in knowledge about development. He describes it as a practical necessity. He cautions against a simplistic view of developmental trauma. The analyst whose sole therapeutic function is to provide a holding environment so that development can resume leaves out the explication of the patient's conflict. Furthermore, transference is a derivative of fantasy, not a reproduction of an actual relationship. In short, the analyst's role as the interpreter of fantasy is reinforced by the avalanche of observational and analytic data about early childhood available to us now.

Although Arlow was trained during an era that there were tremendous splits between child analysts and adult analysts. He apparently was against accepting clinicians who had child only training as psychoanalysts. This makes it even more interesting that Arlow wrote about play and how the concept of play applied to his patients in 1987. Child analysts have also seen his work as relevant to theirs. A search in Pep-web.org shows that 8 child analysts cited his article; "Trauma, Play, and Perversion" that was published in the *Psychoanalytic Study of the Child*(42:31-44.) One of his earliest works; "Masturbation and Symptom Formation"; *J. Amer. Psychoanal. Assn.*, 1:45-58 includes 5 references to papers published in the Psychoanalytic Study of the Child and a reference to Anna Freud. A Pep-web.org search indicates that there are five articles (spanning 1959 to 2020 about adolescence or child development that cite this 1953 paper. The papers in this volume also reflect an inclusive approach, using child and adult psychoanalytic literature to understand the mind.

Training For Psychoanalysis and Psychotherapy in this volume is about Arlow's view about psychoanalytic education. He advocates exposing candidates to the work of experienced analysts, and he emphasizes the importance of information about development. I think Arlow's work could provide an early model for the importance of an integrated child, adolescent and adult training.

Since the papers in this volume are later papers, it is of interest to see how Arlow knits together later theory about PreOedipal trauma, early development and his earlier modern conflict theory. Arlow's synthetic mind was clearly not a closed mind.

References

Coates, S.W. (1997). Is It Time to Jettison the Concept of Developmental Lines?. *Gender and Psychoanal.*, 2(1):35-53

Knight, Rona, (2020) Turning Psychoanalysis On its Head: Examining Historical Theories of Child Development. Presentation at the ACP Conference.

Chapter 3

A Pre-Oedipal Screen Memory in Analysis

Arlene Kramer Richards

As an ego psychologist working in mid-twentieth century New York Jacob Arlow was part of a theoretical group that advocated being as impersonal and non-self-revealing as possible. The clinical theory of the day was that the analyst should be a blank screen on which the analysand could project feelings that came from his own past, wishes and fears that were biologically pre-programmed and free of cultural influence. Interpersonal and intersubjective issues were to be avoided in favor of structural or intra-psychic conflict. That theory was rejected by those who objected that a two person model was more descriptive of the patterns of interaction that caused so many patients psychic stress. Reading those theorists who advocated a self psychological, object-relational, inter-personal, or relational model left me perplexed. Who were they talking about? My experience with an ego psychologist did not fit with the austere therapy they were writing about. I want to convey some flavor of that experience in gratitude for what I was given in a five time a week psychoanalysis on the couch by an eminent ego psychologist: Jacob Arlow.

My analysis with Jacob Arlow began with a rejection and a misunderstanding. I had wanted to be analyzed by Edith Jacobson, but she said she had no time for me. So I decided to ask Dr. Arlow after reading his paper on the Bar Mitzvah. I called for an appointment, he agreed to see me the following week. I went to his office on Central Park South in New York. It was in an apartment building. Elegant neighborhood but no doorman. The waiting room had frowzy brown tweed armchairs, a brown carpet and a magazine stand. It was cozy but well worn. He came out to meet me, showed me the closet for my coat, gestured toward the toilet and ushered me into his office. One step down and we were in his office, in the sunken living room, a fashion of the decade before. The office furniture was not much better. He sat himself down behind a huge desk. He pointed to a smaller chair facing the desk.

He asked why I was there. I told him that I had been depressed for a long time and had known that I needed and wanted treatment, but had not had the money for it until now. I had worked since my marriage to put my husband through medical school, internship, and residency . Now that he had established a practice in New York and I was working and in graduate school, I needed to get more understanding of my depression and to become able to do my doctoral dissertation. I knew that part of my immediate need had to do with my son's approaching bar mitzvah and that I was happy to have read his paper to understand why I felt this as a loss rather than an achievement.

I also told him that I had felt rejected by Dr. Jacobson. And I said that I had heard from my husband, whose teacher he had been. that he was a great analyst. He said that he could not remember that. I said that then I would have to wonder what my husband was really doing on those evenings when he told me that he had a class with Dr. Arlow. I laughed. He laughed. I thought we both understood that he had been trying to be a blank screen, not impeded by a prior relationship. Laughing together felt good.

He took a careful history, then talked about fee and about times. I was able to come in the middle of the day so the fee that was low for him, $25.00/session, and would take all of my salary at the time, was mutually agreeable. My husband could support our family by then and my graduate school status provided a tuition of $50.00/ year for our children as well as health insurance for all of us.

Early in the analysis I told him of a memory that I thought was important. I was 14 months old. I knew the date because it was at my cousin Zangwill's first birthday and I was two months older than he was. I was in my baby walker. It was a contraption that had a seat supported on a frame that had wheels in its four bottom corners. It enabled a baby to walk while it supported her weight. Someone took me out of the walker and put Zangwill in it so he could walk. I vividly recalled the intense rage that impelled me to walk on my own to get over to him to get my walker back. That image remained with me. Dr. Arlow listened to this anecdote, I thought, with satisfaction. I thought he heard it as a castration and penis envy story. But I was sure it was a real memory. The rage felt intense and real. I could feel it in my body as we talked.

We talked about that screen memory several times in the course of the analysis. The connection between the rage and my protective attitude toward younger males gave me a whole new sense of myself and my very early wish to be a mother. It partially explained why I had a baby when I was still a teen. I was intent on protecting a young male from my rage.

The rage also co-determined my early choice of career as an elementary school teacher, a choice which was far below what would have been available to me at that time with my education and talents. And it made sense of choosing someone to marry who needed my support.

Later, it co-determined my choice to work with young black boys who were having difficulty learning how to read. And it affected my transference toward my analyst so that I resisted any interpretation that reminded me that I had once been weak and needy as all infants are weak and needy. It made me ready to believe that every intervention was a put-down even when I recognized it as an attempt to understand me.

Much of the time I resisted his understandings of what I was saying. We argued vigorously. I hated it that he thought he knew more about me than I did. I experienced humiliation at some of the things he said. But often I would think about those things after the sessions and would have to admit to myself that they did make sense. I experienced myself as a specimen to be studied rather than a self who studied others. It was painful, but helpful.

I recalled another important memory early in the analysis.

As a young adolescent I had loved going to my father's fabric store and office. He was a textile converter, buying unfinished cotton fabric and having it dyed and finished to sell in small lots to custom shirt-makers, to department store home sewing departments, and to young designers. The beauty of the colors, textures and patterns fascinated me. Seeing and meeting the young designers was exciting. I would do anything the staff wanted: I swept the floors. I fetched coffee, I filed invoices, I addressed envelopes. It was way more exciting than school.

One day my father called me into his office. He said that he had heard that I really wanted to work there. He said that the business was for his son. The best I could ever be there was a book-keeper. I went home crushed. My mother said: "Then he will have to pay for you to go to college." He did and I did.

The trauma had reawakened the old trauma of having my walker given to a younger boy. My response was similar. I worked hard at an excellent school. I loved the University of Chicago. I got a lot out of it. My rage fueled my work. Now I realize that it was an example of what Freud called "nachtraglichkeit". The later event reawakened the old memory and changed how I saw the meaning of it.

Through all of this Dr. Arlow was patient. I was aware that he was working on a clay sculpture during our sessions, but I never complained or saw this as interfering with the analytic work. I never even mentioned it. It seemed to me at the time that doing that was helping him to keep quiet and listen to me rather than overwhelm me with his point of view. I now think that I was protecting him as well.

Towards the end of the analysis Dr. Arlow asked me whether he could use some of my case material in a paper he was writing. I readily agreed, but said that I needed to ask my husband if he would mind that. He thought it better to say no. I came back to analysis saying that my husband did not want that material published. When the paper was published I recognized that a parapraxis of mine was the basis for part of his paper. I had always thought that my brother was ten and a half years younger than me. But he was really eight and a half years younger. The paper specifically excluded people who had siblings less that ten and a half years younger than they were. Yet it also described some of the dynamics resulting from fantasies of having killed siblings. Such a fantasy had co-determined all of my feelings about younger males and caused me to want to nurture and protect them.

One day during my analysis I rode my bicycle to my session. I brought it into the waiting room with me. Coming out of the session I saw that I had a flat tire. I had no tools with me to change the tire. Worse yet I had no money. Dr. Arlow offered to lend me money to get home. I chose to walk the bike back but felt gratitude and support for his offer. I thought how far we were from that initial blank screen idea. He was on my side. He really wanted me to feel better.

All of this led to a sense that I did not have to feel guilty for my mother's miscarriages and dead babies. Having relieved my guilt, I was able to conceive a thesis, design relevant research and write that dissertation in a few months. It provided evidence for the hypothesis that language structures were developed before imitation of the structures could take place.

Years after the analysis I thought that I would write a paper about female genital anxieties because I had observed that analysts attributed female rage towards males as penis envy. But it seemed to some analysts that women resented discrimination against females, lower pay for equal work, discrimination in acceptance in graduate and professional schools, and a double standard of morality. I had observed in myself, my friends and my women patients a strange fear of being intruded on at night when their husbands were away.

Observing my own babies' pleasure at having the genital wiped when being diapered and at having it touched while being bathed made me think that genital pleasure was important to girls as well as boys. Girls have something to lose, pleasure. We have something to fear, genital pain. And something genital to look forward to, babies. The proliferation of attention to the sensation of the whole vulva area rather than just the clitoris and vagina in the culture of that time contributed to my thinking that contrary to the idea that females were depressed by loss of a fantasy penis, females valued their source of pleasure and feared losing it.

I suggested to a mentor, Dr. Brenner, that he was wrong in thinking that female depression was based on loss of the penis, and that fear of loss of the source of their own pleasure created anxiety. Anxiety and fearfulness seemed to me to be important for women as well as for men. To his credit, and to my lasting gratitude, he said: "Gather the evidence and write a paper about that."

I sent a draft of that paper to Dr. Arlow. He sent back a three page response. He said that the idea was so radical and so contrary to all analytic theory that I would have to gather years of evidence and write a whole book about it if I was to get any credence. I thought he was trying to protect me from rejection. I published it anyway.

It is only now that I am writing this that it seems to me that much of what is patronizing and denigrating in the way men "protect" women is sincerely meant as protection. My father really wanted me to become a lady of leisure rather than investing in a difficult commercial enterprise. My analyst wanted to protect me from being denigrated by colleagues. Both made me angry. And the anger fueled ambition. I am grateful for the chance to have become tougher and more independent that each of them provided in his own way.

I continue to use walking and other physical exercise to contain anger, rage and other negative affects. The memory or fantasy of my walk towards Cousin Zangwill and my walker has served as an adaptive means of regaining a sense of control of myself and the world around me. That, combined with the sense that I could and would protect the young and weak gave me a feeling of power that has sustained me through some difficult times.

My gratitude for what I got from analysis has motivated a life spent being an analyst myself. I consider Dr. Arlow the best friend I ever had or could have. His work with me gave me a life of meaning and satisfaction that is the best life I could have had.

Chapter 4

Interview with Arlene Kramer Richards and Arnold Richards about Jacob Arlow November 2020.

by Nancy Goodman and Kim Kleinman

Nancy: We want to talk with you about these discovered archival papers and about Jacob Arlow in general. I am wondering if you can comment on how these papers were discovered. Because it is very exciting to have this new trove of papers for people to read.

Arnie: Well that's my story.

Arlene: Yes, tell it

Arnie: Jack Arlow died. The papers were collected by his son. And he has been collecting stuff until today. That's how we got all of the papers. We got them from Michael Arlow, who has been in charge of going through all of his papers. And recently what we have done is that he shredded all of the clinical papers and has sent me all of the psychoanalytic stuff as well as some correspondence, letters, memoirs, and so forth. So that is how we got them. They came from his son Michael.

Arlene: They were stored in his house.

Arnie: Yes, they were stored in Jack's house. Michael is a chemist and he lives in Michigan. I guess near Ann Arbor, somewhere around there. And so that is who he is. Jack had four sons, one of them died. Michael is retired He has worked for the government and so forth and that is another story. Another son is a lawyer who became a judge. And one lives in Portland and one lives in Seattle. So those are the four sons and one son died of AIDS.

Arnie: And Michael has always had an ambivalent relationship with his father but he has been very positive about his intellectual legacy and he has done a lot, a lot of work in collecting all of these papers and sending them to me and to Tamar. So that is the story. And without him we wouldn't have all of these papers.

Nancy: For me it is an honor to be a part of this project.

Kim: For me as well.

Arnie: It is a very important project because he was a very important contributor to psychoanalysis.

Arlene: Yes,

Nancy: So I can think of another question which is: What do you consider the roots of Arlow's thinking, his thinking which pervades psychoanalysis, so much so that I don't think people even realize that when they are reading clinical papers and they are reading discussions in the contemporary world that the basic ideas are from Arlow about unconscious fantasy . But where did his ideas come from?

Arnie: I think Arlene can answer that but before she does you know that Auden said that Freud became a climate of opinion in his poem about Freud's death. Yes, climate of opinion, W.H. Auden, a very famous quote. And I would say that Arlow became a climate of psychoanalysis, theoretical and clinical practice. Go ahead Arlene.

Arlene: This is a very important question and I asked it of him once when I was in analysis with him because I was reading Ella Freeman Sharpe, who had a very important role in British psychoanalysis and who at the time was not read in the US at all. I was interested in her work because of H.D and literary tradition in England and how the literary crowd really introduced Freudian thought into England. And of course the Standard Edition was translated by a member of the Bloomsbury set and Ella Freeman Sharpe came out of that. So when I discovered this thinking about unconscious fantasy and how important it was and how she considered it the keystone of psychoanalytic work I said, "Hey, this is a concurrent view (at the time I thought it was a concurrent view) that you have had about unconscious fantasy." And he got furious, furious, and said that it is not the same thing at all. "They spell it with a 'Ph', I spell it with an "F", He said "I hadn't read her." I think he had. "And besides her view of unconscious fantasy begins with infancy and mine has to do with the Oedipal period. Very different."

Nancy: Wow. So?

Arlene: I wasn't there to argue theory with him. (Laughs.) I went on to talk about what it meant to me and why it was important and so on.

Kim: Now the way people think about phantasy with a 'Ph' and fantasy with an 'F' is daydreaming and phantasy with a "Ph' is unconscious phantasy. That is the difference between the British interpretation of those two words, And it is something that we hear frequently about Arlow, that he is about daydreams and not about.... I don't know if it is an oversimplification because he spelled fantasy with an 'F' but maybe you can say something about that. About Arlow, and that it is not about daydreams and we can for the record correct that misunderstanding.

Arlene: Well, I think that daydreams and night dreams are not different for Arlow. That in fact dreaming and all of the products of the mind are in fact motivated by unconscious fantasy. Jokes, by unconscious fantasy, slips of the tongue, night dreams, daydreams, unconscious fantasy structures all of these products of the mind, poetry...

Arnie: And unconscious fantasy effects perception and cognition night and day. That is Arlow's fundamental belief.

Arlene: Um hum.

Nancy: Yes, and it is profound and it has a major effect on my thinking and work with patients that the unconscious fantasy is always there in in some form.

Arlene: Um um

Nancy: And in our own minds as we listen. Is 'F' and 'Ph'...it is such a shame, as if there really were a difference, rather than the question of how are they different, how are they the same, how did that come about? The war about it I think needs to be mended and I think maybe writing about these new papers and rethinking together about how to present Arlow may be will be helpful. I know in writing about unconscious fantasy Arlow was not the only person who wrote "F." Pontalis wrote "F,"

Arnie": Pontalis?

Nancy: Yes, Pontalis.

Arnie: He wrote "F." I didn't know that.

Arlene: Um hum

Nancy: So Arlow himself had this split about "they are this and I am that.".

Arlene: Very strongly defended.

Arnie: It's political

Arnie: Them vs us. The Kleinians versus the Freudians and the Brits versus the Americans.

Arlene: Yes

Arnie: And that always impacts on the ways we think about theory and practice.

Nancy: There is this book by Ricardo Steiner, *Unconscious Phantasy,* and it is really very good. He writes from a lot of the famous European papers. But he says in the introduction that he is only writing from the European thinking on unconscious phantasy so he doesn't have to confront the rich thinking of so many writers in America.

Arlene: Yeah.

Arnie: But that wasn't his only contribution or his only central idea. I am sure you see that there are others, other than unconscious fantasy that were important to him.

Nancy: Well, what else comes to your mind?

Arnie: Well, in terms of pluralism and comparative psychoanalysis, he thinks that what is essential in theories of psychoanalysis is the theory of pathogenesis. Freudians had one theory of pathogenesis, the importance of the ambivalence conflicts of childhood, theory of self-psychology had another theory of pathogenesis, the empathic failures in childhood; Kleinians had another theory of pathogenesis about pathological object relationships. So each theory had their own theory of pathogenesis which determines how they view the patient and the mind.

Nancy: So how would you describe Arlow's theory of pathogenesis?

Arnie: I would say it is the centrality of the ambivalence conflicts of childhood. That is his theory of pathogenesis, that's what is central. And the centrality of the of the conflict about libidinal and aggressive wishes in childhood and how they impact on the important relationships in childhood, including the Oedipus complex. I think that is where Arlow stands.

Nancy: Well in the papers that I was reading there are a few things that strike me the most. The ever-present attention to unconscious fantasy. If you listen to Arlow listening, he is listening for the evolution of a story in the mind of the patient. He absolutely believes there is a story that is causing the symptoms, that is causing the pain. And the second thing is his use of compromise formation.

Arnie: He is looking for what he calls the "red thread" when he listens to a patient and I think the red thread is the manifestation of the unconscious fantasy that appears in the material.

Nancy: I like this idea of the red thread.

Arnie: You listen to the material and you listen…I know that he has some dramatic examples where he says that this comes up, and it is coming up again and how it relates with each other, and that is the way he works. But certainly he is a great listener.

Kim: Yeah.

Arlene Um hum. I think an important part of that is that it is listening for repetition.

Kim: How the patient starts the session, and then whatever they say, such as "There was a lot of traffic…" And then they are talking about something else and something else. The same conflict that they start the session with is the same conflict throughout the session and you look for the thread that binds them all.

Arlene: And that can be very upsetting to the patients.

Kim: Right.

Arlene: To see those associations in a very incontrovertible pattern. When you point out the pattern it becomes so clear

SELECTED UNPUBLISHED PAPERS OF JACOB A. ARLOW

Arnie: A subset of this thread idea is that the transference is also a red thread in the clinical situation. The thing about the transference is that it comes up again and again and again. The way I like to put it is "Wherever you look you see it," And that is what makes it transference .

Nancy: It can be upsetting as Arlene is describing to shake things up. "Oh my god, look at all of that." I think it can also be very gratifying to be so understood. There is a clarity. There's a clarity.

Arlene: Um hum

Nancy: :And it is right there. It is right there all of the time.

Arnie: Yes, Because the analyst is providing meaning for your madness.
(Everyone Laughs)

Arnie: Structure for your inchoate ideas. And that ultimately can be very reassuring.

Nancy: Is this your phrase, Arnie? Meaning for your madness?

Arnie: Yes, I just made it up on the spot.

Nancy: I love it.
(Everyone Laughs.)

Arnie: The therapist provides meaning for the patient's madness. I like it. I like it.

Nancy: I like it a lot.

Arlene: That is very good. Yeah.

Nancy: I really like it.

Arlene: Laughs.

Nancy: You will have to make a journal issue out of that topic. The other thing that really appeals to me in Arlow's listening papers is that he talks about listening to himself.

Arlene: Yes,

Nancy: And he is very honest about it. He has this idea that there is a spontaneous aspect to giving interpretation that sounds so contemporary.

Arlene: Uh huh.

Nancy: His unconscious listening to the patient's unconscious. He doesn't use the term reverie but he is talking about what people would call his reverie.

Arlene: Um hum.

Nancy: I don't know how others received it when he spoke in this way? Do you know?

Arlene: With awe.

Arnie: His account of his illness was very interesting.

Arlene: Awe. When he gave a paper everyone was in awe.

Arnie: And his supervisees were certainly very impressed. But he did have a problem, He did not suffer fools gladly.

Arlene: No.

Arnie: When he had a supervisee who he thought was stupid he let them know that. And so there are some supervisees that I have spoke to that didn't like him at all.

Arnie: You knew that, didn't you Arlene?

Arlene: Well sometimes there were people who absolutely could not get along with him in analysis. They absolutely could not be analyzed by him.
Arnie: Do you have any idea of what was involved there?

Arlene: Well, I can only imagine but I have to say that he was very opinionated and very certain of himself. It took a certain amount of a sense of humor to let him get away with things like that and not to fight about them beyond a certain level. (Laughs.) I think for example at one time he gave a paper at New York Psychoanalytic and a patient was before me. His hour was before mine. It was the next day after the paper. The patient stormed out. And when I came into my session Dr. Arlow was talking about how I was making fun of him for something and I couldn't figure out what was going on here. It turned out…I hadn't even been at that paper. I didn't even go to that meeting. I had no idea what had gone on. And so he was interpreting and interpreting and interpreting something that to me was mysterious. I think it was a reaction to what had happened the hour before. He was still continuing on and on that hobby horse and I was totally lost. So what I am trying to say is that he was a human being.

Arnie: There were very smart analysands who had a lot of difficulty with Jack. Because the thing about Jack was that he could listen to a session and identify the operative unconscious fantasy. Now Arlene and I have a theory, it is called the Richards and Richards theory of therapeutic technique. Do you know our theory? Our theory is that a theoretician develops a theory to counter their own anti-therapeutic proclivities. So Jack was capable of recognizing patient's unconscious fantasies very early on. So what does he stress in his theory? He says "Wait for the evidence." As if he is reminding himself that you really have to wait for the evidence even through you may be sure you know what is going on.

Nancy: Well that is something that has been with us since Freud. Freud could feel that he heard right what had been repressed, but he didn't take care of the relationship that had to develop to uncover and to let that become therapeutic. I guess it is difficult to know so quickly, to be so smart, because that really isn't everything.

Arnie: And I would say, in terms of Freud, the difference between the Wolf Man and the Rat Man...I think in the Wolf Man he jumped to conclusions and gave the Wolf Man interpretations before the evidence. I think with the Rat Man he waited for the evidence more. Would you agree with that Arlene?

Arlene: Yes. And he was more restrained in his final understanding. It is not just that he waited for the evidence but also that he didn't come to such absolute conclusions.

Arnie: Yeah, you are right.

Nancy: Well the way we are talking about it there is a certain view of the analyst as the one who knows.

Arlene: Um hum,.

Nancy: And the patient as the one who doesn't know. It sounds a bit authoritarian in its set-up.

Arlene: Very.

Arnie: He (Arlow) comes by it honestly given his political background. He came from an authoritarian background where those in charge knew everything. They were right and that was his mindset that he brought, that he had developed before he became an analyst. He brought that to psychoanalysis. That is my opinion, my own personal view of the impact of his politics on his practice.

Nancy: I hear all of these human elements but I really do idealize his eyes and his ear to hear the unconscious unfolding and to use metaphor to explain it. It is very powerful. I can't imagine anyone being an analyst or ever being a patient who would not recognize that there is a search in the mind for the metaphor story.

Arlene: Um hum,

Arnie: Arlene, would you like to say more about metaphor and Scharp and Arlow and that whole centrality of metaphor?

Arlene: Yes, that is something really that is in every aspect...In the paper about comics, about Superman and all that; the paper about the Bar Mitzvah ritual and all of that, he developed and he thought through and used metaphor in every instance. In my own work I think I have been very influenced by that, but I think being a different person and having a different character and having had the experience of having had his view, it seems to me that the metaphor allows interpretations that do not contradict what the patient says. It is still a bird singing in a tree; but, it is also springtime. The metaphor idea, and teaching a patient to think in metaphors, or think through what the metaphor implies, enables interpretations to be taken not as demeaning but what the patient immediately thought, the bird, but still adding the deeper understanding of the springtime. That the bird is the metaphor for the springtime. So it is not what the patient said was fake or superficial and what I say is deeper, It is that you need the bird. Without the bird you could never get to the springtime. What the patient says and what the patient has to teach enables the analyst to understand.

Arnie: But isn't it a matter of the fact that words are not always what they seem.

Arlene: What do you mean?

Arnie: There is meaning behind the words. There is more to the words than what the words say. There is an underlying message. (Laughs.) Again, it is a message in the madness. Words are not always what they seem, skim milk masquerades as cream.

Kim: So even if something feels like a rationalization, the rationalization is still an expression of the unconscious metaphor.

Arlene: Yes.

Arnie: Right.

Nancy: So this is essentially a belief in a creative mind.

Arlene: Creative mind..

Arnie: Oh, a creative mind. Yes. Yes. Well that is a whole theme of a psychoanalyst as artist.

Nancy: In this time of COVID we hear, at least I hear, of people experiencing time in a different way. They don't know what day it is, what month it is, what is happening. They feel out of time, it is confusing. Arlow wrote a lot about perceptions of time.

Arlene: Yeah.

Nancy: And there are fantasies. It isn't only a perception which is worthy in its own right but there are fantasies which are attached to experiences of time. As I say that, I realize I want to interpret more for my patients, what it means to them, what their madness is, Arnie. Laughs.

Arlene: (laughs). And I think of his metaphor of a movie screen....

Arnie: Arlene, you read my mind. (Laughs.)

Arlene: Laughs.

Arnie: I was about to say that there are two screens and the projector.

Arlene: Yes.

Nancy: It is beautiful.

Arlene: Yes. And it was at thanksgiving.

Arlene: That was so important.

Kim: What was the first paper you both read of Arlow's?

Arlene: Yeah I remember. It was the Bar Mitzvah paper. That was the first one I read. I read it because just at the time I was wanting to start analysis, I was wanting to start it partly because I experienced my son's upcoming Bar Mitzvah as a loss.

Arlene: A loss of my connection with him in that he would be joining the men. He would become a man, no longer really my child in the same sense. And I needed to mourn this. And I thought it was crazy because I was very happy that he was able to reach this milestone and that he was doing so well with his speech that he was writing and all that. Why should I be so sad? I thought there is something going on in my mind that I am not really in touch with. And Arnie suggested that I read that paper. Do you remember?

Arnie: No. I don't remember that at all. What I remember, and I have to look up the year, is when I read the Arlow and Brenner book about the structural model. Do you remember when that was written? What year? I have to look it up.

Kim: I just looked it up: 1964.

Arlene: 1964, Yes.

Arnie: And I am not sure I read it... Because I was just starting analytic training. That was my first year of analytic training in 64. Before that I had read the Brenner book *The Introduction to Psychoanalysis,* which is the first book of theirs that I read. That I read in Medical School between '54 and 5'8, and this I read in '64. So that is my...

Kim: It is $16.95 on Amazon right now.

Arlene: Laughs.

Arnie: Oh, that's a lot.

Arlene: Yeah.

Arnie: It is one of those books. Yeah.

Nancy: Arnie, was that the first that you read of Arlow?

Arlene: Yeah.

Nancy: And were classes filled with Arlow papers? Or not?

Arnie: Oh, you mean in analytic training?

Nancy: Yeah.

Arlene: In analytic training, were a lot of? . . .

Arnie: No, no. Well that is a whole other story.

Kim: Okay.

Arnie: Do you know that story?

Kim: Let's hear.

Arnie: When I was in analytic training from '65 to '69. Right? What you read was Freud, Freud, and more Freud. And Arlow complained to the E.C. that you are reading too much of Freud.

Arlene: The Educational Committee.

Arnie: To the Educational Committee that you are reading too much of Freud and not enough of contemporary theory.

Arlene: Right.

Arnie: Like me. And Charlie. So they had a big meeting and they voted him down so then he went off to teach more at Columbia and Downstate then at New York. So that is another bit of educational history.

Kim: So that was in his unpublished papers he wrote about how he feels that you don't teach the history of medicine to medical students.

Arlene: Um hum.

Arnie: Right, right.

Kim: You don't teach outdated theories in medical school.

Arnie: Good. So that is what he believed.

Nancy: So he very much believed in himself.

Arlene: Oh yeah, he believed in himself, absolutely.

Arnie: Yeah, there is no question about it.

Kim: (Laughs.)

Arnie: Yes. That was part of him.

Nancy: So what else did you read in training? I am interested now.

Arlene: Hum.

Arnie: What?

Arlene: What else did you read in training?

Arnie: Well, almost everything was by Freud. I am hard put to . . . Well, not everything was by Freud. We read Edith Jacobson. We read Hartmann. We read Kris. We read Loewenstein. And did we read maybe something of Fenichel. And I don't think we read very much written after the forties. That's what we read. We read the past.

Nancy: Was Klein mentioned?

Arlene: Never.

Arnie: Klein was an anathema. She was only mentioned to be put down. And that had a profound effect on the American Psychoanalytic Association because the whole question with certification, you had to get certified. But as Ruth Eissler said, "We don't need to be certified. This is only for California and the Kleinians. That is why we have to make sure they are Kosher.

Nancy: I want to come back to the beautiful metaphor of the two screens and the films on both sides.

Arlene: Um hum.

Nancy: Once you know that metaphor and you read it in his writing, you never forget it. It just is a very powerful metaphor of wondering that whatever is on the front screen, there is a back screen. There is a parallel story.

Arlene: Um hum.

Arnie: Good way to put it.

Nancy: I think it is one of the great metaphors of psychoanalysis.

Arlene: Um hum.

Arnie: Yes.

Arlene: Because it makes the unconscious so much less mysterious and so much less a challenge to consciousness.

Arnie: And the centrality of the transference.

Kim: One question that I have in my mind is that when Arlow talks about his theory of transference, you know he briefly refers to it, it sounds like to my contemporary ears he is addressing Klein's ideas about projective identification. What makes me think of it is that it makes the theory of the unconscious less mysterious and his description of the patient is projecting and that we resonate in some way personally with content that the patient brings into the office and it helps us understand the patient. His way of describing it sounds less mysterious than projective identification but it also very much sounds like he is addressing the idea of projective identification in his writing.

Arlene: Yes.

Kim: Did he publicly admit he read Klein or would that have been a secret?

Arnie: His suggestion is that you have to give importance to your own unconscious fantasy.

Kim: Yes.

Arnie: As well as...You can't let yourself get off the hook.

Kim: Um hum.

Arnie: And he believed that. And he practiced that. And you have to be exquisitely honest with yourself if you are going to expect the patient to be honest with themselves.

Arlene: Hum.

Arnie: You have to acknowledge what is going on in your mind in order to be able to understand and get the patient to acknowledge what is going on in theirs.

Kim: Oh wow, so he would actually talk about his own thoughts?

Arnie: So that is what is going on in the session, Arlene?

Arlene: Yes, often it was very painful, on both sides.

Arnie: Right.

Kim: But he would talk about his own thoughts, his own experiences.

Arlene: No, no, no, no. He wouldn't say them as his own thoughts, he would say them as reality.

Kim: Okay. (Laughs.)

Arnie: His view of reality, right?

Arlene: No, he would say them as if they were real.

Arnie: Real, okay.

Kim: I don't want to put you on the spot, but can you give an example?

Arlene: There was a movie, something about a Cuckoo?

Arnie: One Flew Over the Cuckoo's Nest.

Arlene: Yes, One Flew Over the Cuckoo's Nest.

Arnie: You remember Nurse Rachet?

Kim: Yes.

Arlene: Yeah. It was about mental hospitals and the terrible treatment in them and all of that.

Arnie: Yes.

Arlene: And he thought that when I mentioned that movie that that was an attack on him. That this was negative transference. And he was sure it was negative transference. And I thought it had a very different meaning, that I was saying it. I thought it had to do with my unsureness about my own perceptions. And he insisted on his view because that was the reality, it was negative. I was saying something negative about a doctor.

Arnie: About the profession. About his profession.

Arlene: That's his view. We never really resolved it but it always stuck with me as a kind of negative example of what could happen if you thought that the analyst's perception was reality.

Nancy: That is a great example of when the analyst is taking the role of certainty in the interpretation.

Arlene: Um hum. ''

Kim: Sometimes I do that too.

Arlene: Yeah, I think we all are prone to do that.

Kim: And then some patients go along with it, some patients like it, some patients fight about it and tell me what they are hearing that I am not hearing.

Arlene: I fought a lot. In fact much of the analysis consisted of fighting.

Arnie: Those are the best analyses.

Arlene: Much of the time it was about that.

Nancy: So you taught him a lot.

Kim: I was thinking the same thing. (Laughs.)

Arlene (Laughs.)

Arnie: The analytic couple that fights together stays together.

Kim: Laughs. So do you think that he changed his position over time, that he fought less with his patients or he always did?

Arlene: I mean it was very painful to do all this fighting around. It was not calm or soothing or pleasant. It was not pleasant.

Arnie: I don't know if Arlene will agree. I think that there was a profound change in Arlow when he started with his ability to uncover unconscious fantasy from the material, even before the patient knew it. That gave him this authoritarian, not authoritarian but knowledgeable position in the analytic situation. But later on in life he wrote about analysis as a conversation.

Nancy: Yes, yes.

Arnie: And a conversation is between two people, and not where one knows everything and the other does not. So I think that made a big difference. I think he…we may want to say he mellowed, whatever, whatever). And of course the other change that occurred is that he had less and less use for the members of his profession and he only would supervise and teach social workers. Was that correct?

Arlene: Yes.

Arnie: And he thought they were the smartest or the most able to learn psychoanalysis.

Arnie: He became very much less impressed with titles and professional standing.

Nancy: You know it is interesting because I think Melanie Klein also has a reputation for pushing the interpretation,

Arnie: Oh, definitely.

Nancy: And it is making me wonder what is it about being in touch with unconscious fantasy that creates such aggression in some people. I don't know if our conversation would convince people that they want to read Arlow. I want to convince people of how helpful it is to be aware of the continuous stream of unconscious that is creative, that is meaningful.

Arlene: I think that that is true, and it is important, and I think it is also important to see that you too can write a paper. You too can move on. To not idealize or overidealize people in the past because that inhibits creativity. To see that they were like us, flawed human beings, doing the best they can, and contributing one new thing or two new things that change everybody's view on what is going on.

Nancy: Yes, yes, that it doesn't shut down further growth,

Arlene: Yeah.

Nancy: Because of idealization. And that happens all the time.

Arlene: Yes.

Nancy: That you become an acolyte, not a creator.

Arlene: That is something he did not want to have happen to his work or to him.

Kim: Another question that I thought about is about training. People at Tavistock emphasize removing one's resistance to seeing the unconscious as a cornerstone of training. They feel that that is really what training is about. Arlow felt that there was information that people needed in order to become an analyst. It wasn't just about your resistance to the unconscious had to be lifted but that you actually needed information Beginners should be supplied with that information. So I am going to assume that of course he felt that they should learn the structural theory.

Arlene: Yes,

Kim: How do you think he would put into words that candidates needed to learn theory?

Arlene: I think it was for him a constant exploration.

Kim: Okay,

Arlene: That things were never the thing you need to know.

Kim: Ah.

Arlene: That they were always a moving target. The more you know the more you can think of something else.

Arnie: That you are always learning. And he was always learning.

Arlene: And that was why he didn't even use words like "ego" and "superego" and certainly not "projective identification." Not any of those words because he felt that the reified concepts, the things you *must* think, dampened the possibility of creativity.

Kim: So. there were never things that he would say: "Oh, don't read that."? Like you should read everything, would that be fair?

Arlene: No.

Kim: There were things he thought you shouldn't read?

Arlene: He thought you shouldn't read Klein, for example. He thought when I read Ella Freedman Sharpe that was a mistake.

Kim: What a shame.

Nancy: Well the continent doesn't read Arlow.

Kim: And how do we build a bridge?

Arlene: Yeah.

Arnie: Well that is another story.

Arlene: Yes,

Arnie: And it is a complicated story. I am sure you know his quote, "The id, ego, and superego does not exist in a patient's mind, it only exists in a psychoanalytic textbook."

Kim: I love that.

Arnie: Yes, very important quote.

Nancy: But this rift between rich writing and understanding of the unconscious on the Continent, in the United States, the fact that there isn't communication about it, and many of my friends who are studying Klein say, "Oh, but Arlow only talks about daydreams. That's the difference." Which isn't true, there is great depth in Arlow's writing about unconscious fantasy. So . . .

Arnie: Well but the political divide begins in France not in England. And the epitome of this is André Green, who looked down on the Americans. Do you remember that meeting of the American Psychoanalytic Association where he was on a panel with Ted Jacobs?

Arnie: Do you remember that? And he said about . .

Arlene: Jacobs said something about the patient saw his tie and was finding some meaning in the tie that he was wearing, that the analyst was wearing and André Green said, "We are not interested in haberdashery."

Arnie: Well, you know. Laughs. So ever since then they have not looked favorably on American psychoanalysis and American psychoanalysts. Now the issue with England and the Kleinians, I am not sure what drove that. I think it may have been, and this just came to my mind at this moment, it may have had to do with the rivalry between Melanie Klein and Anna Freud. Right? And Anna Freud had very strong connections with the United States because she was connected with Ruth Eissler and Dora Hartmann and Romy Greenson and they supported her.

Arlene: Literally They supported her economically.

Arnie: Economically. So she had a very strong connection. She had a very ,very strong connection with the United States. And so England remained divided between the Anna Freudians and the Kleinians and the middle group. And so I think they identified the connection between the Anna Freudians and the Americans.

Arlene: I think that is important and I think also we have to remember that Freud himself was very anti-American.

Arnie: Yes. He looked down on them. And he said to Jung, "We are bringing them the plague." You know that quote? He said that we were bringing them the plague. And he thought that psychoanalysis would be destroyed in the United States because all they were interested in was money He certainly did not have much hope for psychoanalysis

Nancy: And so the split now...I think it would be quite wonderful if our introduction to this book could help invite a mending of this split. The work of Arlow, the work of Klein, the work of the contemporary Kleinians, it is all trying to understand this very central and important place in the mind of unconscious fantasy.

Arlene: Exactly.

Nancy: And we are losing out if you have to cordon off one literature versus another literature. There is something that curtails really full understanding.

Arlene Um hum.

Arnie: But there is another issue that was very important to the Europeans and that was that Arlow and Brenner were against "child only analysts." The effort to make child analysis...You know, you can become a member of the IPA if you were just a child analyst. I think Arlow and Brenner were some of the most vocal opponents to that idea. And there they were also against Anna Freud. Because Anna Freud wanted you to be able to become an analyst if you just treated children.

Nancy: This was a very useful discussion.

Arnie: I think so. I learned a lot.

Arlene: Good.

Chapter 5

Transference as Defense

Jacob A. Arlow, MD

Commentary: Nancy R. Goodman, PhD

A link to Freud's writing on transference is immediately made as Arlow describes his choice of title for this essay on a very particular type of defense that can be overlooked in analytic process. Throughout the chapter there are theoretical discussions and compelling clinical material showing what happens when the transference is not seen as arising from an identified context for the patient and in the process of the session. It is actually fun to read Arlow's definition of transference and outlining of the history of this "defining feature" (a term from Freud reiterated by Arlow) of psychoanalysis. Freud taught beginning analysts to "keep one's eye" on the transference and stated that "every conflict has to be fought out in the sphere of transference" (1912, p. 104). He goes on to relate the salience of transference interpretation in the writings of Strachey and Klein showing the solidarity of thinking among the different schools. One also learns that for Arlow it is the replacement of the more primitive superego with an introjected "beneficent agent" of cure that brings about change reconstituting the superego.

The reader can surmise that Arlow has depth of knowledge of the beginnings of psychoanalytic thought and then feels no qualms to add to what came before. He expands the view of interpreting defense by defining what is most important in bringing psychoanalytic cure to the patient –being able to hear when the move to the transference wish and fear is the sidetrack, is the defense. He wants analysts to see how this takes place and to use it in their interpreting. He cites Blum as an advocate who tells us that transference analysis is essential, but that extra-transference interpretations and genetic reconstructions are also important. At this point in his career he tells us he is mainly conducting supervisions and consultations and has begun to notice what he calls analytic listening becoming not a listening to the material but listening for the material—the transference. This makes him have disquietude about truly understanding the full mind and unconscious processes taking place. Throughout multiple clinical examples, he convincingly demonstrates how and why shifts to the transference are being used defensively often for the patients to remove themselves from very powerful emerging affects. The unconscious meaning of these moves will be missed if only transference is listened for and considered the only valid place of attention. Arlow listens carefully. He hears the context and the details of the stream of associations of the patient. In doing so, he catches the context, such as recollections of childhood humiliations and painful fantasies, which then lead to a transference sidetrack. Arlow pulls the patient back to the context which he so much at that moment is scared to acknowledge. In other words, the defenses of old are present asking to be noticed and addressed so that the compromises that are in place can be known and reconsidered. For example, he says to a patient: "You switched from talking about your brothers to talking about me…in order to avoid facing how angry you were at your brothers." The patient then has more abundant associations about his murderous rage. Arlow postulates that when there is increasing intensity of drive derivatives toward primary objects, transference may defensively arise as a compromise formation. He becomes concerned that he is belaboring the point but reminds himself that he keeps hearing case presentations looking solely at transference. He is determined to bring attention to a wider field of understanding.

Transference as Defense

Jacob A. Arlow, MD

O riginally I had intended to entitle this communication "The Dynamics of Transference," until I saw this was precisely the title that Freud used in introducing the subject. Perhaps no subject in psychoanalysis has been as thoroughly explored and examined as the subject of transference. For Freud, transference was one of the defining qualities of psychoanalysis. The analysis of the transference in the therapeutic situation was and remains the central technical imperative, as enunciated by Freud. He made this clear on many occasions. "Finally," he said, "every conflict has to be fought out in the sphere of transference." (Freud, 1912a, p. 104). To the beginning analyst, he advised, in effect, do not worry about being able to make the correct interpretation of material. That happens automatically and with little effort. The important thing is to keep one's eye on the transference. (1912b) Furthermore, he added, "One does not communicate any interpretation until a dependable transference has developed... the first stage of treating consists of attaching him [the patient] to the treatment and to the person of the physician. To assure this, one need do nothing but allow him time." (, p.) In characteristic fashion, Freud summed up his attitude on the subject in an epigram when he stated: "For when all is said and done, it is impossible to destroy anyone in absentia or in effigy." (Freud, 1912a, p. 108)

Although much has changed in the course of time in psychoanalysis, the basic influence of the ideas of Freud's just described have persisted. Teaching about the transference remains fundamentally unchanged as regards the course of the psychoanalytic process. Characteristically, psychoanalytic treatment is divided into three phases. The first or opening phase is a preliminary one. During this time, the analyst learns of the nature of the patient's difficulty. For the most part, the analyst is instructed to do whatever possible to strengthen and to further the transference attachment. In this connection, Freud stated: "When . . . the treatment has attained mastery over the patient . . . the whole of his illness' new production is concentrated upon a single point, his relation to the doctor . . . all of the patient's symptoms have abandoned their original meaning and have taken on a new sense which lies in relation to the transference; for only such symptoms have persisted as are capable of undergoing such transformation." (1916-1917, p. 144) The final phase of treatment consists of the resolution of the transference.

Freud was very explicit that everything had to be focused on the person of the physician, but the extreme picture of the nature of the transference neurosis just quoted is not quite accurate, and one notes that Freud abandoned the term "transference neurosis" after 1922. Nevertheless, these teachings established a tradition of technique which has been followed to this day in most quarters, in effect, that everything has to be focused on the person of the physician. It was Freud's view that analysis depends essentially on the formation and resolution of an artificial illness, the transference neurosis, and this led one wag, critical of psychoanalysis, to say "Psychoanalysis is the disease for which it claims to be the cure."

The primacy of transference interpretation culminated in what is perhaps today the most oft-quoted epigram concerning psychoanalytic technique. I am referring to the statement by Strachey (1934) to the effect that only transference interpretations are mutative. In this connection, I observed that, to Strachey, "the essential interpretations in the course of treatment are those that deal with the clarification of the transference relationship, interpretations that distinguish between the analyst with his objective, reasonable attitude of helpfulness and the harsh, destructive, archaic Superego. In the course of the analysis, the patient, bit by bit, piece by piece, introjects the calm, non-judgmental, understanding analyst and reconstitutes him as a good object within the Superego. The new good object based on the image of the psychoanalyst replaces the earlier, more primitive Superego of the patient, the Superego that had been the pathogenic agent, the cause of the patient's suffering. By way of contrast, the introjected, reasonable analyst, reconstituted within the Superego, becomes the beneficent agent of cure." (Arlow, 1981, p. 502) This view of the primacy of transference interpretation remained relatively unchallenged, even by those whose theoretical frame of reference differed widely from Strachey's or Melanie Klein's.

A direct challenge to this point of view, however, was made by Blum in 1983 in his paper on "The Position and Value of Extra-transference Interpretation." With appropriate caution, he stated: "Extra-transference interpretation refers to interpretation that is relatively outside the analytic transference relationship. Although interpretive resolution of the transference neurosis is the central area of analytic work, transference is not the sole or whole focus of interpretation, or the only effective 'mutative' interpretation or always the most significant interpretation. Extra-transference interpretation has a position and a value which is not simply ancillary, preparatory and supplementary to transference interpretation. Transference analysis is essential, but extra-transference interpretation, including genetic interpretation and reconstruction, is also necessary, complementary and synergistic." (p. 615) To date it would appear that hardly anyone else has challenged the one-sided, technically exclusive view of the centrality of transference interpretation.

Several things drew my attention to these issues. Of late, my work has consisted mainly of consulting, supervising and conducting clinical seminars for graduate analysts. Repeatedly I observed how exclusive concentration on possible transference derivatives skewed the way analysts listened to their patients. As a result, an artificial insensitivity seemed to impose itself upon the discourse in the psychoanalytic situation. Often analysts permit outlandish statements and bizarre connections that would never have escaped comment in ordinary conversation to go by without notice or comment as the analysts prospect instead for transference material. They are not listening to the material; they are listening for material, transference material. At a workshop on technique I heard a case presentation, in which consideration of some of the patient's most painful experiences was bypassed and attention was focused on some rather trivial transference issue. During the discussion, no one took issue with this obvious misplacement of interest. It was this experience that impelled me to take a closer look at the role of transference interpretation. Unfortunately, because of confidentiality considerations, it is not possible for me to reproduce here the details of the aforementioned presentation.

The case dramatized for me the issue of how analysts approach the transference and understand its precise dynamic configuration in the course of a patient's associations. When analysts talk about transference, they are not always referring to the same thing. Analysts differ widely as to what constitutes transference, how it originates, and the purpose it serves. Strictly speaking, the word transference derives from two Latin words meaning to carry over or carry across. Freud coined the term early in the history of psychoanalysis when he entertained very concretistic concepts concerning libidinal cathexes. At that time the discharge aspect of the drive cathexis was paramount. What happens in the process of transference, he said, is that the cathexis vested in the mental representation of the original, the primary object of the libido, is transferred and becomes vested in the mental representation of the analyst. Accordingly, consciously and unconsciously, the patient begins to direct the same impulses and wishes towards the person of the analyst as he had previously directed toward the infantile imago. The patient's thoughts and behavior towards the analyst constitute later-day recapitulations of the childhood wishes. In this sense, Freud felt that the transference recapitulated the patient's early history but, because of repression, repetition had replaced recollection. Accordingly, it became the responsibility of the therapist to help the patient to recall, or to reconstruct his past if remembering is not possible.

It is these considerations, I believe, that led to an intensification of the tendency towards exclusive preoccupation with the transference. Supposedly the transference constitutes a living record of the forgotten past, but what is often overlooked in the process is the fact that the manifest transference constitutes a defensively distorted set of derivative representations of the unconscious conflict as organized into some form of compromise fantasy. It is not necessarily a recapitulation of actual events of the past. This is what I hope to demonstrate in the course of this paper. Returning to the historical influence on transference repetition, what happened was that transference came to be seen in a somewhat different light. Focus centered on the repetition of a set of early interpersonal reactions, repetitively relived with subsequent important individuals. Put in technical terms, transference came to be regarded as a transposition of a set of early object relations onto subsequent objects. It was history repeating itself.

It is not unusual to hear case reports in which the complicated interactions between the patient and a parent were described as being subsequently repeated with the analyst, but in the recounting there is no mention of the underlying unconscious conflicts which shape the interactions. It was as if history was being repeated without any reference to the notion that the complicated interpersonal reactions constituted the derivative compromise expressions of persistent unconscious conflicts. When transference is presented one-sidedly in this light, the process of pathogenesis is reduced to the effects of a set of untoward, deleterious interpersonal relations, a kind of harmful conditioning by insensitive or malignant caretakers. Such an approach may eventuate in concepts that the role of the analyst is to be a "'real'" person whose empathic, caring concern and sensitivity serve as the basic elements in therapeutic progress. One of the consequences of such an approach is that transference becomes regarded primarily as a recapitulation of the individual's history and accordingly omits the role of the drives or of unconscious fantasies.*

What is lost in these conceptualizations is the defensive compromise aspect of the transference. If, as psychoanalysts, we espouse a deterministic view of the functioning of the human mind, then all human interactions have a certain dimension of transference to them. The transferences that concern us, however, are those that grow out of pathogenic conflicts, failed compromises which bring the patients to treatment. These are the transferences that we deal with in the course of therapy. From this point of view, the concept of transference in the therapeutic situation is closely linked with our theory of pathogenesis. Briefly stated, this is how I view how transference develops.

After a certain period of time, perhaps during the ages between three and six, the vicissitudes of the individual's experience are metaphorically apprehended in a series of unconscious fantasies that are typical, idiosyncratic, for that individual. They represent the ways in which the individual tried to resolve the many conflicting influences, both internal and external, and the vicissitudes of fate in terms of the leading constellation of forces. These constellations create the mental set on the basis of which the individual tends to perceive, interpret and respond to events and stimuli. They take the form of unconscious fantasies which exert a persistent influence on mental functioning. The unconscious fantasy itself is an amalgam of various tendencies. The existence of the fantasy, like any unconscious process, is inferred from its derivative manifestations as they occur in the context of the patient's associations. They are compromise formations which may be adaptive and beneficial, or failed compromise formations which may be maladaptive and painful. In the latter case, pathology eventuates. On the basis of the persistent pressure of the unconscious fantasy system, the neurotic individual misperceives, misinterprets and misresponds to stimuli and events.

Nunberg (1925) pointed out that this is the dilemma that confronts the patient as he enters treatment. Consciously, the patient wishes to be relieved of the consequences of the persistent pathogenic, unconscious fantasies. Unconsciously, he/she wishes to involve the analyst as a player in an unconscious scenario which is a derivative representation of the fantasy wishes. The patient attempts to foist upon the analyst a leading role in such a scenario, and he/she misperceives, misinterprets and misresponds to the analyst in keeping with this unconscious fantasy. This is the transference that concerns us in the treatment situation. It also constitutes the dynamics of the neurotic interactions with other individuals that take place outside of the treatment situation. These concepts of the origin of the transference have been described briefly, and therefore simplistically, but they may serve as the basis for our discussion of how transference phenomena emerge in the course of treatment, even in the course of a single session.

What I hope to demonstrate is that, as we observe the stream of the patient's associations, paying attention to the context and the contiguity of the individual elements, we frequently note the following taking place. As the patient presents derivatives of some unconscious conflict and as these representations become increasingly clear in meaning, that is, come closer to being connected with the original object, at that point there is a shift and, instead of the primary object being the subject of the patient's wishes, the analyst is substituted for the object. The derivative expressions of the wish remain the same. Sometimes the meaning of the sequence of associations is so obvious and the introduction of the analyst so unrealistically intrusive that the defensive function of the shift of primary object can hardly be denied.

A simple but clear-cut example. It is taken from the analysis of a case worker in her 30s, whose past history is particularly striking. Her father was a paranoid schizophrenic who had never been hospitalized. Her mother was at best a borderline personality. The home situation was chaotic, primarily because of the father's uncontrolled, aggressive and sexual behavior. Perforce the patient mastered several techniques for controlling her fears and her anger.

At one point in the treatment the patient was disturbed when one of her clients, a young boy, had assaulted his teacher. This reminded her of the violence at home. She remembered shaking with fright as a child when her parents would fight. She spoke of living in a torture chamber and recalled a particular fight occasioned by her wanting to go away to college, which her father opposed. She spoke of a colleague whom she sometimes fantasies marrying but feels that this will never be. "Just imagine," she said, "my wedding announcement will appear in the *New York Times,* Miss so and so, the daughter of two psychotic parents, was married, etc., etc." She had been looking through the *New York Times* marriage announcements and had been feeling depressed. She then spoke more about how her parents had ruined her life.

At this point there was a sudden change in the stream of her associations. The patient said, "I have an idea that I would like to tear you apart. I wish I had a sledge hammer and I could smash everything in this room to pieces. It makes me think of all the obsessional business I went through when I first came to your office years ago. Shall I push the couch in this direction or that direction? It took me a long time to get over it."

The inappropriate interposition of the analyst as the object of the patient's fury at this moment in her associations can only be understood in terms of a defensive displacement onto the analyst of her murderous rage against her parents. It will come as no surprise that the patient's first association at the beginning of the following session was "I felt that coming here was like stepping into a boxing ring with you."

The defensive displacement of the patient's destructive rage from her parent onto the analyst can hardly be denied in this instance. The shift of her aggression towards the analyst is evidence of the patient's need to somehow spare her parents, a feeling of concern, guilt or other elements of which the patient is not aware. Focusing one-sidedly on the transference and disregarding how it emerges in the context of the defensive needs of the patient may transform the therapeutic process into a stilted, intellectualized and dehumanized experience.

In the example which follows one may observe how concentration on transference may serve to sever the material from its contextual setting and thereby deprive the analyst of an opportunity to demonstrate the genetic roots of the transference. This material was taken from a study concerning the methodology of transference interpretation. The patient is a professional man who suffered from severe bouts of depression. He had a long pattern of self-induced defeats and a clear masochistic trend which would express itself by the patient leaving his office and going for long walks through dangerous neighborhoods where he risked physical harm. Sometimes he would shoplift a trivial item, risking arrest. Because of certain developmental difficulties, he entertained grievances against his mother and had apparently turned to his father, a successful and engaging person, for the loving relationship he missed with his mother. In this relationship, the fulfillment of his wishes was not possible because of conflicts over the unconscious feminine sexual content of his fantasies.

The patient came several minutes late for the session. He apologized, tried to laugh it off, and explained that he was coming from a meeting with his father. They had been having a wonderful talk. He stated his father becomes a "real windbag" but he finds it difficult to break away from him. (His father is an engaging raconteur.) Also the previous night the patient's young son had been sick with fever and an earache, and the patient had been up most of the night, tending to him, holding him in his arms, keeping him cool and comforting him. At this point the patient stopped talking.

When asked what was concerning him, he responded that he felt that he is not sufficiently productive in the sessions. His wife has been criticizing him for not improving. After another pause, the patient recalled that he saw a natural phenomenon in the heavens (apparently one that had been publicized in the press) and he wondered if the analyst had seen it. The analyst replied that he had and the patient was pleased. The patient feels that the treatment is helping him. He then connects his changing moods with his appointment times. This is followed by a shift in the patient's associations. He begins to think of escaping. He wants to get away from the process, away from his dependency on the analyst. He feels threatened by having a close relationship with him. He thinks that he starts beating himself up because he does not like feeling so disturbed about missing the analyst. Being close is a danger. At this point the analyst says, "I wonder why feeling close to me makes you feel so uncomfortable. What is the danger of wanting to be together?"

The analyst's interventions are cogent and accurate. The rest of the material of the session dealt with the patient's flight from closeness. What was overlooked was the function that the transference served in this particular instance. The analyst never returned to the opening statements the patient made. It was the pleasant experience of being with his father, whose stories he had been enjoying so much, that kept the patient from coming on time. The next association also involved a father-son relationship, but a much closer, more intimate one. The patient had sat up a good deal of the night, cradling his young child in his arms, trying to soothe him in his suffering. This was an experience that must have aroused in him the reality of the strong love that unites father and son, and it was at this point that the patient's thoughts turned to his defensive stance in the treatment, to his wish, as well as to his inability to get close to and enjoy things with the analyst. The analyst didn't have to ask him what the danger was of being close. The patient had already made it clear in his associations to the loving bond between father and son. By focusing exclusively on the transference and tearing it out of the context of the patient's associations, an opportunity was missed to demonstrate to the patient how strong and frightening the loving tie between a father and son was to him. The main issue in the material at this juncture was the defensive function of the transference, the shift from the father to the analyst, and it was this issue that was not dealt with.

Like any other element in the course of free association, transference phenomena have to be understood in terms of their function in the context in which they appear. If one interprets the defensive function of the transference phenomenon, new material emerges in the patient's associations. Insight is deepened and a clearer understanding of the nature of the unconscious wish emerges. I hope to illustrate how one may observe this in actual practice through the next two clinical vignettes.

This material is from the analysis of a professional man, married, with two children. He had had previous treatment, but recent events exacerbated an old problem, namely, depression connected with his inability to control a tendency towards compulsive promiscuity. The background was striking. When the patient was seven or eight years old, he discovered that he was recapitulating his mother's behavior and, by way of his identification with her, trying to bring down upon himself the punishment that he felt she had deserved but had never received. When he was a boy, the patient had a pack of pornographic playing cards. On the back of one was a picture of a woman holding on to the enormous penis of a horse. This image appeared frequently in the patient's masturbation fantasies.

In discussing his anger at his mother for her promiscuity, the patient described how betrayed and humiliated he felt. Also, what was wrong with his father that his mother had to go to other men? Probably he was not adequate. The patient spoke about how inadequate he felt in regard to other people, especially concerning money and professional standing. For example, he had bought a very expensive summer home which he could ill afford and realized that he had done it as an exercise of futile competition with a relative who was extremely wealthy. He was very conscious of being competitive with other men as regards clothes and looks. It was pointed out that the patient had suffered a tremendous loss of self-esteem as a result of feeling inferior and humiliated because of his mother's interest in men who he felt were more interesting and more adequate. He wanted to be recognized as successful to compensate for feelings of inferiority vis-a-vis the mother's lovers.

Up until this point the patient had made no direct references to me in the material. At the beginning of the next session, however, he spoke at considerable length of how he admired me and how he had begun to imitate me when talking to people. He tried to use the same phrases and tone of voice that I use with him. He heard that I was tops in the field, and he would like to be in such a position, but he feels that he doesn't have the background.

The patient then reported that his mistress had come back from her vacation with her husband. He is gratified that she is not sexually interested in her husband. He feels that her husband is not as good a lover as he is, but at the same time he knows that his mistress has had many lovers and wonders how he compares with them. From here the patient began to talk about his feelings about his mother's lovers and his own sense of inferiority. He realizes that his efforts to make a big fortune have hardly been successful. He is bright, but he feels that he could do better with his mind. "The intellect," he says, "is like a club. It's my bat, but it's not up to yours." By this time he was holding his two fists together as if he were holding a baseball bat. Then he put the two fists together near his genitals and said, "It's my phallic powers I'm talking about. I know I'm talking about intellect, but I know I'm talking about penises."

I pointed out to him that for a long time he had been competing in his mind with his mother's lovers. He felt that they had sexual powers that he wanted but could never get, just as now he feels that he would like to have my knowledge but feels that he could never get it. I pointed out the shift from his mother's lovers to me, the analyst.

The patient returned to the theme of curiosity about his mistress' previous lovers. He manages to evoke from her assurances that he is superior to her husband and to her other lovers, but he is not sure whether this includes all the lovers she has had. When he has relations with her, he tries to keep his erection as long as possible. He is very proud of his erection and prizes particularly how his mistress esteems his penis, its looks, its hardness. In this connection, he says, "I feel like a good stud."

"A good stud?" I said.

The patient smiled and said, "Yes, it sounds like a horse." Then his face lit up. "Oh, the horse on the pornographic playing card, the card that I used to use in my masturbation fantasies. That horse," he said, "had the kind of penis my mother would have appreciated."

Interpreting the transference in terms of a defensive shift away from the mother's lovers and onto the analyst facilitated the emergence of a more conflictual wish, namely, to castrate the powerful competitor and to acquire for one's self the kind of penis that the mother would have appreciated.

Finally, I would like to introduce additional clinical material to demonstrate how interpreting the transference as a defensive compromise facilitates the emergence of material that has hitherto been warded off. This material is from the case of a woman who suffered for many years from multiple phobias and anxieties. Her illness began with the death of her mother and was re-exacerbated several years later when the younger of her two brothers died. She was the third child of a poor family. It was obvious that she was quite bright but, "after all, being only a girl," there was no need for her to have any education. Her two older brothers were not successful. As a child, she felt ridiculed and excluded by them. In a previous analysis, issues of competitiveness with men and hostility towards them were touched upon but only lightly. (After her first analysis the patient found employment in a psychiatric facility, where she hoped to engage, if not in actual therapy, then in assisting a therapist.)

In her treatment with me, I observed an interesting form of defense. She assented readily to interpretations, but the insights seemed to have little effect upon her. One of the first things noted in the treatment with me was how she vitiated almost any interpretation. She did so by transposing the insights into interrogative, conditional, negative or subjunctive moods.

The material that follows appeared in the context of the discussion of the patient's competitiveness with men, of her wish to outdo them and how she used "innocent dumbness" in an attempt to defeat me and to undermine the analytic work.

At the session following this discussion, the patient reported that the material had upset her very much, but she is not sure if it could be that or if it was something else, perhaps something physical. She went on to say that she began to feel anxious sometime around midday but had no idea what night have occasioned the anxiety, or perhaps it wasn't even anxiety at all, but maybe something else. "Maybe about my competition with you."

The patient then said, "I had a dream, but I forgot all of it. I only remember that it involved Q."

Q is a young man who used to live across the street. He and his younger brother were friends with the patient's son, T. The two brothers made life very difficult for T. The patient's son would go to play with the boys. Sometimes they would accept him; sometimes they would reject him. Often T came home crying that Q and his brother would not play with him. The patient was at a loss what to do. Q's mother was very relaxed, not the kind of mother who interferes with what her children are doing. Her attitude would be, if they had some kind of misunderstanding, they should straighten it out. Boys will be boys. The patient did not feel that way. She felt certain that she would have intervened.

The patient went on with increasing fury at Q and his brother. The mother should have known better and should have supervised. There were times that the two boys took T with them and locked the door. Who knows what went on behind those doors? Q's mother said she never opened the door, never looked in on what the boys were doing. Who knows what they did to T? The patient went on to describe that she had seen her son the other day. He has so many problems. He has been in treatment for years and doesn't seem to be getting well, can't get his life together. She said, "I wondered to myself, 'What did Q and his brother do to him? Perhaps they damaged him in some way.' It was on the tip of my tongue to ask him what happened, but I felt that

I shouldn't. What good would it do to raise the issue now? But T has been suffering all his life and Q's mother never intervened to see what was going on. It's not fair for two brothers to gang up that way on a younger person. It reminds me of my own brothers and how they used to tease me. There were lots of times they wouldn't let me play with them. Of course, they were four and eight years older, but they would push me aside. That made me feel small and unimportant. <u>When I was thinking of how you said that I was trying to defeat you by competing with you, I didn't like the idea. I think that's what made me anxious this morning</u>."

At this point I intervened by saying, "You switched from talking about your brothers to talking about me and your anger at me in order to avoid facing how angry you were at your brothers."

(Here I was interpreting the transference specifically in terms of defense.)

The patient responded by saying, "Now I remember something about this morning. I had been packing some things away. I had some things I wanted to give away. I had called my niece Kay. She is the daughter of my brother, the younger one— he's dead, you know. I asked Kay to come over and spend the day with me and we would go over some of the things I would give to her. But this morning, as I was thinking about it, the thought came to me: She's now just about ready to leave the house and start on her trip to see me. Perhaps she'll get killed in an automobile accident. Who knows what can happen? Then I was struck by this thought because I never think of people being injured when they are traveling. Why should such a thought come to me? Is it possible I am still trying to get revenge on my brothers?"

I transposed the conditional and the question to a positive statement, namely: "I am still trying to get revenge on my brothers, this time in the person of my niece by having her die."

The patient then continued: "Just like Q and his brother and my son, they used to exclude me from their games. I remember crying and going to my mother, but she would not do anything. She told me to find my own friends or to play with other things. She favored them because they were boys, I'm sure."

Here I pointed out how the patient was transposing the theme from Q's mother to her own mother; that is, mothers who fail in their responsibilities to the younger, girl child.

At this point the patient became very irate and she said, "Why didn't Dr. X (the previous analyst) tell me all these things?" I noted to her that at the moment that she was beginning to get furious at her mother, she turned her attention to Dr. X, just as earlier, when she was angry with her brothers, she turned her anger on me.

It should be noted in the several instances in the material just cited that, at the point of mounting intensity of drive derivatives towards primary objects, transference was defensively interposed. In the particular context of these instances, transference represents a defensive compromise formation. The analyst is substituted for the primary object, but the drive derivative persists unchanged.

Blum (1983) described the consequences of exclusive concentration on the transference as follows: "A 'pure transference' position in analytic work will lead to distortions of analytic process and explanation. Such a position of only valuing transference interpretation will tend to become 'all transference' and mold or artificially force all material into the transference, leading to inappropriate, excessive transference interpretation." (p. 598) The effect of such an approach, as I have tried to demonstrate, will be to overlook the defensive function of the transference and thus deprive the analyst of an important technical tool that he can use as entree to the deeper levels of the patient's problems and to an understanding of their connection to the patient's childhood unconscious conflicts.

Listening to what I have said, I feel I have belabored the obvious but, when I think of the detailed clinical reports that I have heard and read, I feel that this is something that is nonetheless worth repeating. It is not my intention to downplay the importance of transference analysis in treatment. The termination phase, for example, really has to center on the analysis of the transference. What I wish to emphasize is that transference phenomena must not be torn out of their context; they should not be interpreted in isolation but rather as part of the continuum of the record of the patient's associations. If appropriate attention is paid to the pertinent methodological criteria, such as context, contiguity and other significant criteria for proper apprehension of the data, then the precise function that transference serves at a particular juncture in the analysis in the form of a defensive compromise can be better appreciated (Arlow, 1979). Properly interpreted, it may constitute a most effective instrument for deepening the understanding of the patient's problems and for demonstrating dramatically and conclusively how the past is embedded in the present.

References

Arlow, J.A. (1979). The genesis of interpretation. *Journal of the American Psychoanalytic Association,* 27 (Suppl.):193–206.

—————— (1981). Theories of pathogenesis. *Psychoanalytic Quarterly,* 50:488–514.

Blum, H. (1983). The position and value of extra-transference interpretation. *Journal of the American Psychoanalytic Association,* 31:537–617.

Freud.. S. (1912a). The dynamics of transference. *Standard Edition,* Vol. 12, p. 108.

—————— (1912b). Recommendations to physicians practicing psychoanalysis. *Standard Edition,* Vol. 12, pp. 111–120.

—————— (1916-1917). Introductory lectures on psychoanalysis. *Standard Edition,* Vol. 15–16, p. 144.

Nunberg, H. (1925). The will to recovery in practice and theory of psychoanalysis. New York: Nervous and Mental Disease Publishing Co., 1948, pp. 75–88.

Strachey, J. (1934). The nature of the therapeutic action of psychoanalysis. *International Journal of Psychoanalysis,* 15:127–159.

Chapter 6

Countertransference and Psychoanalytic Methodology

Jacob A. Arlow, MD

Commentary: Nancy R. Goodman, PhD

Arlow turns his attention here to what he calls a major issue in current discussions—that is the topic of countertransference and so-called countertransference enactments. Reading this in 2020, this is still a major theme of discussion in our current discourse between analytic communities. All contemporary theoretical schools of psychoanalysis agree on the importance of enactment processes in which the unconscious mind comes into view in the room. Arlow approaches the topic to help clarify technique and therapy. As in many of these papers, he rests his observations on clarifications of the concepts under consideration. He reviews psychoanalytic thinking about transference and countertransference. For him, there is always an unconscious scenario being created by the patient through transference—"a persistent unconscious fantasy" bringing wishes and affects to bear on the analyst. A special aspect of bringing the past into the present is how the unconscious conflict can become known and addressed by analyst and patient. Arlow's insights about the functioning of the countertransference refers to the specific psychic situation in which an unconscious wish in the analyst has been evoked. He recognizes that there is a whole world of feelings and reactions taking place in response to patients but sees this in an informative but different category than countertransference. He honors that…"every thought , every affective experience—represents some commentary on the patient's material, something the patient evoked in him. But this is not necessarily countertransference." (pp. 84–85).

Lively clinical material is used to show how the form of communication can be used when revealing a vivid dream to make the analyst impotent. The validity of this understanding came about because of the analyst's sense of annoyance at the patient and then ability to think how the patient was trying to annoy. Arlow does not view the annoyance as a countertransference but as a mood induced to be noted and worked with—a guide to insight. It is this analytic capacity that shows the empathy of the analyst who does not get caught up in sympathy or over identification; empathy, returns the analyst to understanding. Analysts can be pulled into complementary fantasy enactments of patients' fantasies. Arlow gives examples of how the analyst can become the rescuer, or the beater, or the mothering mother, etc., all responses to unresolved conflicts in patient and analyst—until the analyst recognizes the pattern. This paper uses lively clinical material to illustrate the various points about interplay of transference and countertransference, always centered on the unconscious fantasy. A supervisee coming to recognize a patient's homosexual fellatio fantasy, reports the patient's dream of offering the analysand a cigarette and at that moment offers one to Arlow—who does not smoke. Arlow's writing about these moments in the psychoanalytic discovery process are consistently presented with respect for the way unconscious fantasy becomes known in sessions. Another example of an enactment of a psychoanalyst with a patient applying to graduate school uncovers the essential central fantasy that the patient considers entrance to graduate school equivalent to murder. As in other papers in this series, Arlow emphasizes the movement of the analyst's mind from awareness of sensory impressions in one's own mind, to identification, empathic comprehension, insight, and emerging interpretations.

Countertransference and Psychoanalytic Methodology

Jacob A. Arlow, MD (New York)

It is no exaggeration to say that the major issue in the current discussions of psychoanalytic technique or psychoanalytic psychotherapy these days is countertransference and the so-called countertransference enactments. How we deal with the subject is fundamental not only for questions of technique but also for clarifying issues of psychoanalytic theory. I find it useful, therefore, to begin this discussion by defining the limits of the term in order to make clear what we are talking about. Accordingly, I will attempt to reduce the issues to simple but fundamental and manageable levels.

The term countertransference is juxtaposed to the concept of transference. Transference means "to carry over." Originally Freud intended it to mean the carrying over of the cathexis attached to one object representation to the person or mental representation of the analyst. Later transference came to be understood as the repetition with the analyst of a set of relationships that originated in childhood in connection with the primary objects. Accordingly, transference became a rich source of material for reconstructing the past. In recent years, there has been enormous broadening of the concept, so that any thought or feeling that the patient expresses concerning the analyst is considered to be transference. In a way this is true. Actually transferences are going on all the time, inside and outside of the analysis. But as I understand transference in psychoanalysis, it represents an unconscious attempt on the part of the patient—an unconscious tendency—to impose upon the analyst and the analytic situation an unconscious scenario of the patient's creation, a derivative of a persistent unconscious fantasy.

Transference takes special form in the analytic situation because the analyst does not respond. He does not accept, nor does he vigorously reject the role in the preconceived scenario that the patient unconsciously wishes to foist upon him. As a result of this non-involvement, transference manifestations stand out in bolder relief in the analytic situation than outside the treatment setting. Consequently, it becomes easier to demonstrate to the patient the unusual and contradictory nature of his relationship to the analyst, compared to what he knows to be the true, or what is the real, nature of their relationship. Interpretation of the transference, therefore, makes it possible to demonstrate to the patient how his current experience is distorted in terms of the persistent effects of conflicts from the past. As a result of the analytic work, it is possible to demonstrate the common ground of understanding, where patient and analyst meet, and appreciate the unrealistic, distorted nature of the patient's attitude towards the analyst. This is how we approach the understanding of transference phenomena. This is the kind of material that is the subject of interpretation in the course of analytic work. In other words, it is a special aspect of transference that is the subject of analysis. Since every new perception is experienced in the context of the persistent influence of unconscious fantasying, all interactions bear the quality of transference. The phenomena that are chosen for scrutiny in the course of psychoanalytic treatment are those which bear directly on the nature of the unconscious conflict which the patient has been unable to master adequately.

Countertransference is a concept derived in tandem with the idea of transference. Strictly speaking, something specific in the form of an unconscious fantasy wish has to be a component of the analyst's reaction for it to be considered countertransference. It is related to conflict within the analyst, as well as to the defensive efforts to contain whatever danger is inherent in the derivatives of those conflictual wishes. Something in the patient's approach to the analyst, in the content of his productions, or in his manner of presentation evokes an unconscious wish and conflict within the analyst. Accordingly, not everything the analyst feels, or thinks is necessarily a countertransference reaction of sufficient significance to be a subject for consideration.

These thoughts are what moved Annie Reich to say:

"One of the prevailing misconceptions is the equation of countertransference with the analyst's total response to the patient, using the term to include all conscious reactions, responses and ways of behavior. This is as incorrect as to call transference everything that emerges in the patient in relation to the analyst during analysis, and not to distinguish between the manifestations of unconscious strivings and reality-adaptive, conscious behavior and observations. The analyst is for the patient, and the patient for the analyst also, a reality object and not only a transference object or countertransference object. There has to be in the analyst some aim-inhibited, object libidinal interest in the patient which is a prerequisite for empathy. Conscious responses should be regarded as countertransference only if they reach an inordinate intensity or are strongly tainted with inappropriate sexual or aggressive feelings, thus revealing themselves to be determined by unconscious, infantile strivings." (1960, pp. 389–390)

While one could argue with certain details of Annie Reich's definitions, the basic thrust, I believe, constitutes a useful set of principles to guide the analyst in actual practice.

There are several situations in the psychoanalytic interaction that foster the emergence of reactions in the analyst. As a general rule, it is safe to say that, unless the analyst is suffering from severe physical pain or is intensely and overwhelmingly preoccupied with some realistic problem of his own, everything that occurs to him—every thought, every affective experience—represents some commentary on the patient's material, something the patient has evoked in him. But this is not necessarily countertransference. It is one of the characteristics of all communication. One can demonstrate this in a practically quasi-experimental situation, which I have tried in various seminars, using some striking material presented by a colleague. This is the material of the session. The patient was silent for one minute and then said "I had a dream last night. It's tempting to get all caught up in it and describe it in minute detail because it was a gross sex dream." Here she paused for another minute. "I was almost glad this thing had happened to me so I could tell you about it. I almost feel it was a defense so I could have something to talk about in here. And the reason I feel it was a defense is because I really haven't had any bad sex experiences lately. I've recently had the strength to say no to the people I really don't care about. So I really don't know what would have prompted the dream." Another pause. "I don't know really whether it's just a defense and that's why I don't discuss it, or whether I really am reluctant to discuss it, and that's why I say that. Much as I hate not having safe material to talk about, I really don't want to spend the time discussing the dream as it's pointless. I am beginning to think everything is a defense, and that even debating whether to tell you the dream is a defense." Silent for another minute. "Well, I won't describe the dream in detail, but the most vivid part of it that really may be important." I ask the group what feelings or thoughts occur to them while they listen to the material. All the members of the seminar said that they felt irritated, bored, annoyed, some negative feeling with the idea, "Get on with it, lady!" The material is a beautiful example of how form can be used to express content. The patient's transference wish, as it turned out in the next two sessions when she finally and in piecemeal fashion revealed the dream and her associations to it, concerned her wish to render the analyst impotent. Did he feel annoyed with her? Yes, indeed. Was this countertransference? No. His annoyance was a commentary to himself on the patient's material, a mood created in him that served as a guide to proper insight. "She is trying to annoy me. Why?"

Now let us change the scenario a bit. Suppose, while the analyst was listening patiently, his stomach churned and produced a gurgle, loud enough to reverberate through the room. This would have been a reaction that had gotten out of his control. He had not intended it. How would one handle it? We will leave that for subsequent discussion. Under what rubric would one classify that response?

Here we must turn to the concept of empathy, a concept that has been abused and misused in many ways. It is a basic mode of human interaction and develops out of the common humanity all individuals share from having faced the same problems and dilemmas in the earliest years of life. Empathy is a way of knowing someone else's feelings by way of identifying with a person in the affective situation he is describing. The greater the bond between the individuals, the easier the capacity for such identification. The more confidences a patient shares with the analyst, the easier it is for such identification to eventuate. But identification in itself is not empathy. It leads to sympathy. Identification has to be broken off for the interaction to constitute an empathic understanding of the other individual. Only when the therapist recognizes that the mood, or reaction, or failure to react is something that has been engendered in him by the patient, that in some way it is a reflection of the patient's experience, does the therapist pass from identification and sympathy to empathy and understanding. One form of countertransference, as it is generally understood, represents a miscarriage of the process of empathy. The analyst lingers in his identification with the patient. He identifies with the patient's fears, hatreds, love, self-condemnation, whatever you will, as if they were his own, and he sympathizes. Under such circumstances, the analyst may attempt to institute ways of lessening the pain, discomfort or guilt. Instead of thinking or feeling about the patient, he remains at the stage of thinking and feeling with the patient. Instead of being empathic, he is sympathetic. Instead of interpreting, be consoles or responds.

The following material to illustrate this point is taken from the analysis of a woman in her middle 30's, at a stage in the treatment where her hostility towards men in general, and towards her younger brother in particular, was the subject under discussion. While the therapist, a woman, had been able to point out the inherent hostility in the patient's behavior, she was uncomfortable putting it in the context of penis envy, although the evidence for such an interpretation had been rich and varied. In one session, the patient came in with a dream in which she saw a toilet bowl with a tampax stuck in it. She tried to get the tampax out of the toilet bowl but seems to have had difficulty doing so. When she flushed the water, it turned a bloody red. The patient related the dream and then went on to another subject. The therapist brought her back to the dream. The patient said, "I have nothing to say about it. It's disgusting," and then went on to other subjects for the rest of the session. The therapist never brought the patient back again to the dream, nor did she even suggest that the dream might be related to menstruation. When this was brought to the therapist's attention and it was pointed out how she had neglected to press the patient on the issue, the therapist said, "I didn't get back to the subject because the patient was talking about so many other things that were totally unclear to me, and I was disgusted. It wasn't clear." Obviously it wasn't clear to the therapist because she was disgusted, not only with the patient's behavior, but presumably the patient's material had evoked in her her own identical feelings about menstruation. By way of a lingering identification with her patient, she contrived not to confront something which both of them found displeasing. This is also an example of how countertransference identification can lead the therapist to do nothing when he or she should do something, to feel nothing, or more correctly, to suppress awareness of one's own feelings. Strictly speaking, identification is not an object relation; the analyst has not foisted a wishful fantasy onto the image of the patient. What had happened in this instance was that the analyst and the patient had shared an unconscious fantasy wish and defense in common. A similar example appears in the paper by Beres and myself on "Fantasy and Identification in Empathy." In that instance, while listening to a dream of a patient, I had a visual fantasy—a waking dream—the content of which paralleled the patient's dream. Both the patient's dream and my waking visual fantasy expressed an identical wish, namely, to be reunited with and to give new life to a lost male object (Beres and Arlow, 1974).

The most serious form of countertransference consists of a situation in which the patient's material, derivative of the patient's unconscious conflicts and fantasies, evokes in the analyst conflictual wishes and fantasies of his or her own. Such fantasies may be identical with the patient's, in which case analyst and analysand share similar psychopathology. Or the analyst's fantasy may be complementary, that is, playing out the opposite role assigned to him in the patient's unconscious scenario, e.g., if the patient wants to be rescued, the analyst becomes the rescuer; if the patient wants to be beaten, the analyst becomes the beater; if the patient wants to be mothered, the analyst becomes the mother. All the patient's material may be such as to evoke in one way or another some latent, that is, unresolved conflict within the analyst. In this form of countertransference, the analyst proceeds to behave in a manner unconsciously determined by the conflicts evoked in him by the derivatives of the patient's wishful fantasies. The analyst's countertransference need not always be in the direction of acting out some derivative expression of the unconscious fantasy wish. It can just as well find expression in the analyst's technical maneuvers, in the form of defensive distortions, avoidance, tendencies to divert not only the patient, but more significantly the analyst himself from the impulses and conflicts the patient's material has evoked in him. It is only when some derivatives of the analyst's own conflict present themselves to consciousness in a mode indicating a breakthrough of the analyst's own defenses, in a manner that is clearly inappropriate, that the analyst becomes aware of the fact that he has just experienced a countertransference enactment. In other words, he has lost his analytic stance in circumstances where the analysand cannot fail to be aware of what has happened.

Most of the discussions of such reactions center about unusual or excessive affective response to the patient's productions, usually in the form of strong feelings of anger, sexual arousal, depression, annoyance, boredom, etc. But the less dramatic manifestations of countertransference can be just as articulate and as revealing of the nature of the analyst's unresolved transferences towards the patient. Let me give one such example. This occurred in the analysis of a young man in his early 30's, being treated by a woman analyst many years his senior. The patient had been in analysis several years at the time the following incident occurred, an incident which caused the analyst to seek consultation.

One morning the analyst was waiting for the patient to appear. She waited for the entire hour but he did not show up. She wondered what had happened to him and had a sense of disappointment at his not coming and also at the fact that he had not called. This was unusual for him. When he came for the following session, the patient began by recounting how bad he felt that he had to have missed the previous session, but it was unavoidable. He had arranged with the analyst to cancel that session for business reasons. At that point the analyst realized that indeed that had been the case, and she was struck by the fact that she had completely repressed the cancellation and had been sitting, waiting for her patient to appear. Since she had been somewhat confused about the recent stalemate in the treatment, she decided to seek consultation.

The analyst then began to report on two sessions that she had the previous week. In the first session the patient began by mentioning in passing that he had noticed a ring on her finger and wondered if she were married, and he turned from this immediately to a description of his relationship with current girlfriends. The sum and substance of the associations had to do with the fact that he didn't care for any of them, and this indeed had been one of the reasons why he came into treatment. He found it impossible to get attached for any period of time to any woman or to fall in love. I will skip over the details of the material. Suffice it to say elements about competition with his father was an additional theme in the material that followed.

From a technical point of view, it should be noted that nothing was done about the opening statement the patient made. It was as if there was a conspiracy of silence between analyst and analysand to overlook the patient's interest in whether or not the analyst was married. Nor was the significance of the immediately contiguous element appreciated, namely, the actual pattern of the patient's behavior, that he didn't want any other woman. In the discussion, the analyst recalled how she felt when the patient failed to show up for the Monday appointment. She was aware of a sense of disappointment, as if she had been rejected by a lover. This is a very short presentation for reasons that must be obvious to the members of the audience, but it serves as a good example of a type of countertransference based upon a complementarity of the patient's wishes and the analyst's response, governed by our own complementary fantasies.

When studying our countertransference responses, we must be aware of a certain ofttimes neglected aspect of the analytic situation. Much as we observe and study our patients, they do the same to us. They observe our reactions in order to ascertain what they can do to provoke gratification of their infantile strivings. The repertoire of behavior available to the patient for this purpose is enormous, but one should emphasize the role of silence. By placing the burden of intervention on the therapist, the patient is able to get a good sampling of the spontaneous productions that silence occasions in the analyst. Silence is perhaps one of the most effective instruments for stimulating countertransference responses in the analyst. Moreover, often enough the countertransference reactions and defenses on the part of the analyst are frequently borrowed from the patient with the result that they may share defense in common against those wishes, including the acting out of those wishes. This is something one observes frequently in supervision when the supervisee behaves towards the supervisor very much as the patient behaves towards the analyst. I reported a striking example of this interchange (Arlow, 1963). The supervisee was having some difficulty in recognizing derivative expressions of the patient's unconscious homosexual wishes, centering upon a fellatio fantasy. He reported a dream of the patient's in which the patient, on the couch, turned around and offered the analyst a cigarette. At that moment in the supervisory session, the analyst turned to me and offered me a cigarette, completely disregarding the fact that he knew that I do not smoke.

Becoming aware of the countertransference may stir up in the analyst many different reactions indicating a loss of analytic stance. Affective experiences are perhaps the most common, guilt and confusion being most prominent among these. There are occasions when the analyst ill-advisedly attempts to rationalize the countertransference intrusion to the patient. On other occasions such rationalizations are accepted by the analyst and may even serve as a point of departure for rationalizing one's countertransference to one's self. It is usually the case that the analyst lingers in the identification with the patient, experiencing the patient's fears, hatreds, love, self-condemnation as if they were his or her own. The analyst sympathizes rather than empathizes with the patient. Accordingly, like the patient, the analyst attempts to institute ways of lessening the pain, discomfort and guilt. Instead of thinking and feeling about the patient, the analyst remains at the stage of thinking and feeling with the patient. Instead of being empathic, the analyst is sympathetic. Instead of interpreting, he consoles, responds or rationalizes.

What I believe is an example of such a turn of events may be illustrated in the material that Dr. Schwaber (1990) has presented several times under the heading of "Countertransference—An Analyst's Retreat from the Patient's Vantage Point." The material was from the analysis of a patient with intellectual promise who suffered from severe work inhibitions and neurotic symptoms, among which were indulgence in marijuana and in sexual perversions, practices that he resorted to under conditions of intense anxiety. At this point of the treatment the patient was in conflict over applying for graduate school. He was unable to get himself to do so. The analyst suggested to him that perhaps, if he applied for graduate school, one could learn something about his sexual difficulties. The patient, whom we shall call Mr. K, decided to take the step and shortly afterwards became overwhelmingly fearful. He neglected his appearance, seemed to become disorganized, he began drinking and smoking marijuana, engaging in sexual perversions. "As the deadline approached for enrollment" (these were Dr. Schwaber's words), the patient's anxiety mounted but he felt determined to go ahead despite his intense anxiety. At this point, the analyst asked, "Since you seem to be in such great distress, why do you feel under pressure to apply at this time?"

I would add parenthetically that there are no simple questions in psychoanalysis and every question by patient or analyst implies a declarative statement. What the patient heard was "Do you really have to expose yourself to such agony at this time?" At the next session, the patient announced that he had withdrawn his application for enrollment in graduate school. This was surely not what the analyst had consciously intended, and obviously she was somewhat disappointed by the turn of events. She asked the patient why he reached the decision so abruptly after prolonged agonizing, whereupon the patient responded in a very striking manner. He said, "At least it's no longer a feeling as if I'm going to my hanging," and he remained silent for the rest of the hour, ending up with the statement "I feel damned if I do and damned if I don't." No comment at all was made about this extraordinary statement of "going to my own hanging."

In discussing the countertransference aspects of this situation, Schwaber felt that the source of the difficulty resided in a reluctance to recognize her unwitting participation in her patient's ongoing inner experience. "A demurral against acknowledging that the truth, what I believe even myself in any given moment, is my own psychic truth, no more real than the patient's, whose view may be different and so unsettling. Feeling a lack of concordance with my own sense of myself in this episode with Mr. K, I retreated from listening to his vantage point, remaining instead within my own." True enough, as far as it goes, but what was missed was the analyst's sympathetic reaction to the patient's suffering, not an inability to appreciate the patient's view of his reality, which led her, I believe, to accept naively the statement "At least it's not like going to my own hanging" as an innocent metaphor. The analyst sympathized with the patient rather than empathizing.

There are certain important methodological implications in this exchange and the understanding of the material. What is lost sight of is the fact that psychoanalysis is a form of treatment by discourse, an exchange of information by conversation. In any ordinary conversation, the contiguity and context of the elements is what makes sense of the interchange. In addition, as analysts, we are trained to appreciate figures of speech, especially similes and metaphors. The patient had said something that was totally unreal. He compared enrolling in graduate school with going to his hanging. To question the use of that simile is by no means imposing the analyst's sense of reality on the material. In ordinary conversation, if someone said to his friend, "I got all upset when I started to enroll in graduate school. I began drinking, smoking marijuana, forgot to shave, fell apart. Then, when I decided to withdraw my application from graduate school, all the symptoms disappeared and I felt better," his friend would surely ask "How was that?", to which the individual in this case responds, "At least it's not as if I'm going to my own hanging." One can be certain that the friend would say, "Going to your own hanging? What has that got to do with it?" In the context of the analytic session the patient had said something that was totally unreal. He compared enrolling in graduate school with going to his hanging. In a certain sense, he was correct. His response to applying to graduate school, so extreme and so painful, would be much more appropriate if he were being led to his hanging. But he wasn't being led to his hanging. He was applying to graduate school. Why should he think of being hanged? Who gets hanged? Criminals or murderers. The sequence of events, the context of the situation, the contiguity of the material all indicate that, while the patient was consciously applying to graduate school, he was unconsciously responding as if he were committing the crime of murder. The analyst's countertransference, based on whatever fantasy, which we really do not know, diverted the pursuit of the unconscious source of the patient's anxieties and was consolidated in the analyst's mind in the form of a theory of therapy, a rationalization of the countertransference enactment.

There are certain realities pertaining to the psychoanalytic situation that are often lost because of the exclusive interest in transference per se. I am referring to the fact that there is a reality that brings patient and analyst together. The patient is there for the purpose of being helped; the analyst professes to be able to do so. At some level of the patient's mental functioning, the reality of the experience as an attempt at therapy constantly abides and acts as one of the determining elements in what the patient says. This is particularly true of the first statement the patient makes at the beginning of a session. Similarly, whatever comes to the analyst's mind reflects in some way the stimulus imposed upon him by the patient except for most unusual circumstances in the analyst's experience. Under ordinary circumstances, every thought that occurs to the analyst is a reflection on the patient's material, but not necessarily the correct interpretation, nor is it necessarily a countertransference reaction. In the therapeutic interaction between patient and analyst, mutual understanding derives from the power of human speech to create states of mind in the listener akin to those of the speaker. Rosen (1967) pointed out that "During most conversations, people assume that the reference of the words, phrases and metaphors employed are understood in common. The listener, either implicitly or explicitly, provides the missing links in the verbalized ideas of the speaker. Both speaker and listener often assume that the background information necessary for identifying the subject, object or predicate of the statement is mutually available." (p. 241) As a result of the intimate relationship established in the analytic situation and of the complete candor of the patient's revelations, a bond of mutual identification which facilitates empathy becomes possible.

In an earlier communication (Arlow, 1979), 1 attempted to describe the preliminary stages from which the process of insight and interpretation emerge. While listening passively to the patient, the patient's verbal presentations become the immediate sensory experiences that occupy the analyst's mind, leading to an identification with the analysand. The analyst thinks and feels with the patient, like the patient. Under the circumstances the analyst begins to think or feel how or what the analysand thinks and feels. This is the first step in the process of empathy. As the analyst becomes aware that the mood and thoughts he has been experiencing represent commentaries on the patient's material, he makes the transition from identification to empathic comprehension. If the analyst fails to take that step and remains in a state of identification, he is sympathetic but not empathic. As I have demonstrated, this is a very common source for certain types of countertransference. The thoughts and affects that appear in the analyst's mind occur as free associations. They represent a form of inner communication, the first step in the awareness of the insight which the analyst is about to apprehend. What the analyst has perceived through such introspection is the end result of a process of intuition, which consists of being able to organize silently, effortlessly and outside of the scope of consciousness, the myriad of observations and impressions, facts and experiences, in a word, almost all that he has learned from the patient—to organize them into a meaningful pattern without any sense of the immediate steps involved.

This is the moment in the interaction when countertransference influences are most apt to become manifest. The essential feature, in my mind, is the loss of the analytic stance. Not every thought or response that the analyst has to the patient is necessarily a countertransference in the sense that it is relative to the psychoanalytic enterprise. It is for this reason that the insight that comes from introspection, intuition and empathy must be subjected to certain methodological principles of interpretation. As intriguing and dramatic as the intuitive experience of the analyst may be, it has to give way to a second phase of the interpretive process, one that is based on cognition and the exercise of reasoned judgment. In order to validate his intuitive understanding of what the patient has been saying and of his own response to this material, the analyst must find support and evidence for an interpretation in the data of the analytic situation, that is to say, under precise examination of the text of the patient's productions. The insight and response that appear so intuitively must be put to the test of objective criteria. Most of the time the intuitive work has been so efficient that the sense of conviction is immediate, gratifying and accompanied by recollection of supporting evidence from the patient's productions. Unfortunately, this is not always the case, and this type of experience militates against the use by the analyst of his immediate affective responses as if they were data of observation obtained from the patient. Specifically the concept of projective identification lends itself to an extension of the use of the analyst's affective responses as an instrument for interpretation. With such an approach, verification of interpretation becomes almost impossible. Criteria for interpretation, including the appreciation of the context of the material, contiguity of the elements, the repetitions of the elements, the similarities and the differences that appear in the material, the use of figures of speech, especially metaphor, unusual words and images—all of these serve as criteria to buttress what appears to be an immediate apprehension on the part of the analyst of the patient's communications. When these elements converge into a comprehensible hypothesis, one is in a better position to intervene in the patient's productions. Relying on one's immediate affective, intuitive response can be misleading, but it is a methodological approach that is advocated in many quarters today. If one sees countertransference in the narrow sense of loss of analytic stance that results from lingering at identification with the patient, or using the patient as an object of one's own unconscious fantasy wishes, or sharing an unconscious wish with the patient, it becomes more accurate and reliable.

A countertransference enactment is always disturbing to the analyst, in spite of the fact that we know how common an experience it is. The important thing is to regain one's analytic stance. By that I mean one must become the observer participant once again and focus one's attention on what effect the patient's awareness of the countertransference enactment has upon the flow of his associations, what eventuates from the departure from ordinary, standard, psychoanalytic technique. I am firmly opposed to discussing the analyst's motives and conflicts that produced the enactment with the patient. That is best done within one's self, preferably after the session, perhaps with a colleague or, if necessary, in a consultation. Immediate, on-the-spot self-analysis, with insights communicated to the patient, by and large can only be detrimental. Nor do I believe that instant self-analysis under such circumstances can yield reliable results. Self-analysis is always a problematic undertaking and, under the conditions of countertransference enactment, the countertransference of the analyst to himself represents a particularly overwhelming burden.

My final point concerns the importance of recognizing in ourselves warning signals, indicators of countertransference reactions, psychological experiences that all fall under the heading of potential loss of analytic stance. Although most commonly discussed are the so-called blind spots picked up during supervision, there are other indicators that are important in the everyday practice of the graduate analyst as well—persistent feelings of confusion and frustration when the analyst seems to be unable to grasp the flow of the associations, a sense that he has lost his empathic contact with the patient. We are aware of excessive emotion and loss of control, irritability, sleepiness and boredom, etc., but there are other indicators outside of the analytic situation that one would do well to consider as evidence of possible countertransference involvement. For example, there is preoccupation with a patient outside of working hours, especially when such preoccupation is characterized by changes in mood, such as depression, or a heightened enthusiasm about anticipating the patient's coming. One should be aware of the fact that, when a patient appears in the manifest content of the analyst's dreams or if there are intrusive fantasies concerning the patient, some countertransference evocation is taking place. More subtle but perhaps equally significant is a tendency to recount events in the analysis or to talk to others about the nature of the patient's problems, even when professional confidence is not breached. And finally there are the well known slips of the tongue and parapraxes that appear in connection with the patient, particularly in scheduling, lateness, in forgetting appointments. In general, the range of possible countertransference reactions is almost as wide and as varied as the transference reactions of patients. The difference resides in that much more attention is paid to the latter than to the former.

Chapter 7

BLOWUP

Jacob A. Arlow, MD

Commentary: Nancy R. Goodman, PhD

It is a treat, better than popcorn, to go to the movies with Jacob Arlow. The reader will immediately be drawn into the theater and grateful to have an expert alongside who can decode symbols and interactions into the unconscious fantasy dimensions from which they arise. The domain for which he is known, the world of the unconscious, is shown in his analysis of the film to be exciting, informative, and comprehensible due to his ability to articulate it so well. While Arlow is famous for his metaphor of a stream of unconscious on the reverse side of the movie screen—at all times, he here uses his knowing of the unconscious and the way it becomes known to explain the meaning of the scenes of *Blowup* a 1966 mystery film directed by Antonioni.

We first get into the world of film criticism as Arlow sets up his paper to address the critics' criticisms—it is an illusion, it does not make sense, it is elusive and phony, it is a figment of imagination. As a psychoanalyst, I was immediately intrigued and knew this was the world of psychic reality, a reality ruled by the rules of the unconscious in which one thing can stand for another and time is timeless. I felt breathless in anticipation of reading the paper.

A cameraman who photographs models and acts emotionally removed while wielding the phallic voyeuristic camera thinks he has witnessed a murder—thus blowing up the image to try to discover the truth. Arlow uses all of the elements of this scene and the intent of the total scene—someone is seeing something that seems unreal as their gaze trespasses. This brings Arlow to his central understanding of the primal scene. And it is a man who is the viewer and who once was a child seeing what could not be apprehended in its arousal of so many feelings. The photographer is a man with a particular attitude toward women—seemingly indifferent but actually full of contempt. Once upon a time the mother part of the sexual couple of mother and father made him feel small and inadequate leading him to now, in his repetition of a version of the primal scene, to depict women as pale, skinny, and dead appearing. He seduces with his camera to arouse and lead the women to submission to him and then leave the image as corpse-like. Both the content of a story being told, by patients and on film, leads to metaphor and the metaphor leads to the persistent unconscious fantasies. We are able to see here how the unconscious scene has multiple iterations in which passive and active and doing and being done to alternate but point to one major theme. So there are all kinds of couples in the film and along with threesomes undoing the terrible feelings of exclusion, inadequacy, and mortification of witnessing the twosome one is not allowed into.

The camera gives a potency to conquer the father who was in the scene. Arlow goes through the film highlighting where these turnabouts take place recognizing the talent of Antonioni in so thoroughly represented oedipal unconscious dilemmas. "In *Blowup*, Antonioni has given aesthetic elaboration and symbolic expression to a universal psychological theme the fantasies and effects of the primal scene experience" (p. 102). Vengeance toward the mother can be a way of undoing helplessness and can take many forms. This is true in the film and is true in the consulting room. The topic of memory is of interest to Arlow in many of his writings and he takes it up here in line with Freud who explains how one scene, a screen memory, is made up of unconscious wishes and dreads as well as impressions of the past. What exactly is real? To Arlow the derivatives of unconscious fantasy and their urges and conquests and defeats are the psychic reality of the film. Arlow is clear in his belief that the only way to undo constant repetitions of the disturbances produced by the terrifying primal scene, is to embark on psychoanalytic work so that there is apperception of the memory that can be claimed in all of its powerful presence.

BLOWUP

Jacob A. Arlow, MD (New York)

When "Blowup" was released in 1967, it evoked a storm of discussion and criticism. Opinions concerning the film were highly polarized. Many critics regarded the film as a classic, although, like many members of the audience, they felt they were grasping at something quite elusive. Others, quite frankly, called the film a "phony." One commentator collected examples of negative views of the film. Richard Goldstein of "The Village Voice," for example, called the movie "The Screw-up," attacking it from the point of view of the older generation failing to come to terms with a younger one. Pauline Kael criticized Antonioni for not catching the humor, fervor and astonishing speed in youth's rejection of older values. One critic, Wilfred Sheed, was described as being ruthlessly contemptuous of the film and Judith Crist complained that Antonioni "let a good story get away." A dramatic report came from Arthur Knight. Writing in "Film Heritage," he tells of his first view of "Blowup." It was a special preview offered to members of the industry. He says, "They hated it. It was almost as if Antonioni had insulted them personally by making a picture that departed so radically from conventional story patterns and techniques. Famous directors, writers and producers went from group to group, drink in hand, asking each other what the film was all about and shrugging humorously when an immediate answer was not forthcoming."

Even more favorably inclined critics were baffled by the film. Did it deal with reality versus illusion? Memory as against fantasy? The mod scene of the sixties in London? Had the photographer actually witnessed and recorded a murder? Or was the entire story a figment of his imagination? To others, "Blowup" represented an autobiographical testament by Antonioni of the photographer-film maker as an artist. As one critic, Scott, said, "Antonioni makes a personal statement as an artist. He is at one with Hemmings, who is the photographer. Intelligent, aloof, technically expert, sometimes exploitative, and sometimes even worried by those who get into the viewfinder of his character."

Since we are indeed discussing character and possibly the character of the main protagonist in the film, it may serve as a good point of departure for a psychoanalytic interpretation of the film. We get our first glimpse of the hero in the company of a group of derelicts as he emerges early in a London morning from a flophouse. He had spent the night in a dormitory surreptitiously taking pictures of those men for a book he is preparing on what seems to be primarily the steamy side of London life. We get a different view of his identity as he enters a magnificent Rolls Royce convertible and drives off to his studio, where, in reality, he is a very successful commercial fashion photographer. For all of his success, however, the hero seems detached and alienated, quietly hostile, and seemingly without feeling. The clue to his character is suggested by his attitude toward women. Throughout the film, attractive women keep offering themselves to him but he turns them away with an indifference that borders on contempt. His very photographic technique conveys this. He brings the models, in the opening sequence, into hard focus, revealing all that is callous, callow and stupid in their features. And he makes us share with him contempt for these people. He emphasizes the absence of all genuine eroticism in these women, whose skinniness is akin to the rigidity of dead bodies and the pale makeup contributes to a sense of loss of individuality.

But the photographer himself is by no means anything but a paragon of duplicity. He is a spy acting as a bum. He is a voyeur. He pretends he has a wife and children, then changes every bit of his story. He cheats Vanessa Redgrave out of the film she had come to get. He is a creature of uncertain sexuality, stifled by the beautiful women who are passive and evasive while they offer themselves to him. He is characterized by one critic as "febrile, autocratic, capricious, and, outside of the illusory, professional world of which he is master, he is completely at a loss in the real world."

None of the principal women in the film, it turns out, is trustworthy. Back at his studio, he poses a famous model. As one observer describes it, "as the phallic muzzle of his camera nudges toward the girl, who lies prone before it, Hemmings caresses her with his voice, 'better, easy, good, that's it, more of it, come on now, come on,' as she in turn is shown responding with more warmth to his directions. And, of course, he manifestly eroticizes the situation by kissing her. After the pictures have been taken, he stalks off abruptly, exhausted, leaving the aroused model stretched out on the studio floor. As we learn later, she lied to him about her plans for the weekend.

In the next sequence, he photographs a group of four models with automatic professionalism, commanding them and manipulating them as if they were animals, or inanimate objects. Since we have just seen the film, I will spare a recapitulation of the plot, although in retelling it, certain highlights illuminate the patterns advanced in the film.

What I propose to do is discuss the film by applying familiar psychoanalytic techniques and principles. In a paper on "The Psychoanalytic Process and Creativity," Beres demonstrated that the manner in which a patient organizes and arranges his associations into meaningful configurations, with symbolic and metaphoric implications, resembles the intuitive work of the creative artist. In both case, the patient and the artist have an audience in mind. They bring to the fore the material derived as a result of the dynamic effect of persistent unconscious fantasies. In trying to interpret this film, the criteria employed are those of similarity, repetition, and confluence of theme, as they are organized by coherence and consistency of the data.

The story line of this film is developed through a series of themes explicitly depicting couples making love and being interrupted in the act of making love.

There are several derivative representations of what is known in psychoanalysis as the "primal scene." For example, the photographer observes the couple in the park and his presence breaks up their idyll. He begins to make love to the lady in the park and they are interrupted by the arrival of the propeller. When he becomes aware that he has witnessed a murder and feels he must share his awareness with somebody, the photographer comes upon the artist and his wife having sexual relations. I assume it is his wife; she may be his mistress. The frenzied spectacle of the rock concert, which terminates in the orgiastic dismemberment of the chief musician's instruments, and the intrusion into the pot party where our hero finds his friend wit his model, all are substitute representations of the primal scene, representations familiar in analytic work in the form of screen memories or recurrent dreams. Also included in this list is the scene of the sexual romp between the photographer and two would-be models. This particular variation of the primal scene is arranged so that no one is excluded. The theme of invasion of privacy runs throughout the film. People are walking in and out of everybody's apartments and there is a moment of supreme irony in the park when Vanessa Redgrave says to him, in effect, this is a public park; I'm entitled to my privacy.

We can see then that, accordingly, in "Blowup," Antonioni has transcended the temporal limitations of London, the mod scene and its alienation and vapidity. In "Blowup," Antonioni has given aesthetic elaboration and symbolic expression to a universal psychological theme, the fantasies and effects of the primal scene experience.

Before proceeding, I would like to underscore ever so briefly a number of sequels that have not been sufficiently emphasized in the literature of the primal scene. We are well acquainted with the sadomasochistic concept, the necessity to repeat its relationship with voyeurism, but there are a few others that I would like to emphasize in connection with this film.

The first of these is the deep sense of narcissistic mortification, the wounding of self-esteem which is experienced by the child. It leads to a conviction that he is unloved and unlovable. He feels excluded and betrayed. In both boys and girls this feeling of oedipal defeat is connected with the idea of anatomical inferiority, leading to a persistent sense of disparaging one's own body and attractiveness. It also leads to grandiose exhibitionistic wishes of a compensatory nature and is accompanied usually by fantasies of stealing the paternal phallus and, in the case of little girls, the wish to have a most beautiful body, like the mother's. A further corollary of this response is the narcissistic rage which it engenders. This leads to the second reaction which I would like to stress, namely, the impulse to wreak vengeance on one or both of the betraying parents. The regressive wish for vengeance can take many forms. In addition to fantasies of murder, the most prominent form of vengeance is the tendency to demean and to humiliate the betraying love object. The repetitive enactments of the primal scene which have been alluded to many times in the literature can be seen in two different ways. In many instances in which the individual brings about a repetition of the primal scene, he casts himself in the role of witness. In such situations, there is the actual or implied attempt to break up, to interrupt, to discomfort the couples making love. There are also those vengeful repetitions in which the individual, traumatized by the primal scene, causes others to be witness to his sexual activities. The unconscious import of this behavior is connected with the wish to humiliate and demean. Its purpose is to make the betraying parents experience the sense of humiliation, exclusion and betrayal that the child experienced in the original scene but, in these repetitions, the role of the parent has now been assigned to some other individual, spouse, child, lover, and so forth. This form of revenge takes the form of reversing the roles. A parent, both parents or their representatives are placed in the position of the humiliated and injured observers of the patient's sexual activity. In many dreams, stage performances or spectacles in general are employed to represent a disguised memory or wish connected with the primal scene. It is frequently an important theme in the analysis of photographers, playwrights, movie directors, etc.

With these formulations in mind, let us return to our key insight of Hemmings, the photographer. He is a spy who has lost faith in women. They may pursue him, but he scorns them because he judges them all as betrayers. The model who made overtures to him turns out in the end to be in the company of his friend, caught in a lie about going to Paris. The lady in the park has set up her middle-aged friend to be killed. The teeny boppers are ready to give themselves sexually in order to advance their careers. The wife or mistress of the good friend and neighbor, leaves the bed and offers herself to the photographer. But he will have none of her. He really will have none of all of them. He wreaks vengeance on the mother of the primal scene, in the person of these various surrogates, by his indifference, his betrayal and his disappointing them. He has only contempt for all of them.

In each primal scene sequence, one can detect derivatives of typical wishes connected with the primal scene, wishes which are gratified symbolically or directly. In the scene in the park with the middle-aged lover, who would correspond to the father of the primal scene, the old man is killed. The artist's wife leaves her husband and comes to the photographer, so that the artist is the victim in this respect. At the rock concert, Hemmings ends up holding the choice trophy, the musician's instrument—the stiff, elongated guitar bridge. When Hemmings comes back from seeing the corpse in the park, he touches the great big propeller in the same way as he has touched the corpse in the park under the trees. In the sequence with the two would-be models, far from being excluded from a twosome, Hemmings is the center of a threesome, a not uncommon representation of a wish of the primal scene trauma, in which the child hopes to be included in the sexual activity.

In certain respects, "Blowup" may be described as an atypical detective story, an ambiguous whodunit which miscarries and is never solved. Pederson-Krag wrote about individuals addicted to the reading of mystery stories. The plot of the typical detective tale, she points out, is usually a thinly disguised version of oedipal fantasies. The victim is almost never a sympathetic character.

He makes a brief dramatic appearance as a corpse, holds the center of the stage all too briefly, and is then removed. He represents the father of the Oedipus phase. The work of the detective corresponds to the insatiable curiosity of the child regarding the sexual act. "The clues in the story," Pederson-Krag writes, "disconnected, inexplicable, and trifling, represents the child's growing awareness of details never understood, such as the family sleeping arrangements, nocturnal sounds, stains, incomprehensible adult jokes and remarks. The criminal of the detective drama is innocuous until the final page." She concludes that, in real life fantasies, the criminal is the parent towards whom the child's positive feelings had been directed, the one whom the child wishes least of all to imagine participating in this secret crime.

From my own data and clinical experience, this would seem to be only half the tale. Basically, the criminal is the detective himself. This would correspond to the unraveling of the first detective story in history, Oedipus Rex. Oedipus undertakes an inquiry to discover the murderer of Laius only to reach the conclusion that he himself is the culprit. Pedeson-Krag concludes that, becoming the detective, the reader of the mystery stories gratifies his infantile curiosity with impunity, redressing completely the helpless inadequacy and unconscious guilt remembered from childhood. However, we could also say, and use "Blowup" as an example, the curious onlooker registering all in his mind, or in this instance, in his camera, has murder in his heart. The camera, far from the passive indifferent recorder of external events, is in this instance, as in many others, an active, aggressive, intrusive instrument. Hemmings, the photographer, stalks the couple in the park. He hides behind a tree and then he hides behind the fence and the bushes, just like the murderer did, and he shoots with his camera as the murderer was shortly to do with his gun. The phallic quality of the camera has already been noted earlier in this discussion, and of course its powerful force endows the photographer with the narcissistic supplies he needs to replace the mortification of the primal scene comparison with the father. To quote from one of the authors, "the talismanic authority of the camera is nowhere more evident than when it is used as a sexual instrument as in the sequence where Hemmings is first photographing the model. More than an isolated extravagance, the episode establishes a pattern running through all the scenes in which he exhibits strength. His camera, its threats and its promises, confer upon him a mastery over all of his associates. (You know the time that he goes without the camera are the times when he really is weakest.)" The power and the symbol of the phallic instrument represented by the camera is repeated several times in the film in various fantasy elaborations of the primal scene, i.e., the acquisition of the propeller, the anterior appendage of a plane where all the power and thrust reside, and in the acquisition of the bridge of the guitar, the prize trophy from the frenzied spectacle (another primal scene representation) of the rock n roll band. A striking and somewhat enigmatic element is added when Hemmings returns to the park to reaffirm his sense of reality, the authenticity of the murder, by viewing the corpse once again. As he does so, he is frightened by a clicking sound, which most viewers of the film interpret as reminiscent of the sound of a camera. This is a dramatic example of retaliation in kind. The instrument that he has used against others has now been turned against him and he flees in terror.

This leads us to the unique feature of the elaboration of the primal scene conflict in the film "Blowup." The film is a parable on the function of memory, of repression of the traumatic primal scene. This theme is first introduced in the sequence in the park where he says, "We've just met" and she says, "Forget you ever met me; we've never met." Then it is introduced in the antique shop with the photographer and the young owner. An antique shop, after all, is a repository of mementos of the past. The owner wants to get away from antiques. She thinks of going to Nepal but the photographer says, "Nepal is full of antiques." In effect, he is telling her she cannot liberate herself from the memories of the past no matter bow far away she goes, In the same vein, photographs represent recorded impressions of past events. They are the analogue of memory. The lady in the park asking the photographer for the roll of film, the records of the events he witnessed, is like the mother of the primal scene soothing the shocked child, trying to cajole him into forgetfulness. But so long as he has the film, the living memory is the reproach to the mother for the primal scene.

A further representation of the same trend is expressed in the scene at the pot party. Here the photographer's collaborator or editor or good friend fills the role of the father of the primal scene. He cannot understand what he takes to be the incoherent babbling of the photographer, He urges him to forget about the body in the park, that is, the nightmare which shook the little boy up, and he tells him instead to take some pot and go to sleep. When the photographer wakes from sleep, he goes back to the park, but the evidence is gone. The corpus delecti is not there. This is the final representation of the act of definitive repression which reproduces, of course, the theft of the pictures and of the negatives. It represents the loss of memory, memory which, above all, validates for each of us the reality of the present in terms of the consistent memory of the past, the continuity of the individual. This is, perhaps, the most poignant and original aspect of "Blowup"—the search for the memory which cannot be recovered, of which only fragments and hints remain, fragments disconnected and out of context, blown up out of all proportion and rendered meaningless and unreal by their enormity.

It is this groping search for the meaning of the past that unites the artist in the film with the photographer. The artist says that his abstract paintings are like clues in a detective story and his wife, when she examines the last remaining fragments of the blown up photograph of the murder in the park, casually resembles very much some of our husband-lover's abstract paintings.

This, perhaps, will enable us to understand somewhat the final enigmatic scene with which the film closes. Failing to find the corpse in the park, the photographer has lost the last concrete bit of evidence that can validate his memory and his very reality. The photographer comes upon the clowns in the park. These are unreal, deceiving figures who try to palm off illusion for reality, fantasy for memory, like the comforting, deceiving mother in the primal scene. By having him fall into their make-believe (by the way, the picture makes it very clear at their invitation) and ultimately disappearing, the film attests to a gnawing doubt of the traumatized witness to the primal scene, a doubt that grows out of being unable to recapture the essence of his own motivations, a doubt that leads to his alienation and to depersonalization.

Thus, the hero of "Blowup" becomes a kind of 20th Century Everyman. The photographer-hero has witnessed and recorded a traumatic event; his life has been altered thereby but, unfortunately, out of the vast storehouse of his memory, that is, out of all the pictures, he cannot retrieve the one that contains the record of the trauma. Accordingly, he has lost his connection with the past, and has in his hands only a fragment of the experience. Without analysis, his life becomes an endless neurotic quest for a memory he cannot retrieve but one which he also cannot forget. The memory of the event is lost but, in disguised form, it is constantly repeated in the unconsciously determined patterns of his life, his love and his art.

Chapter 8

How Does the Analyst Listen, What does the Analyst Hear?

Jacob A Arlow, M,D.

Commentary: Nancy R Goodman, PhD

In this article, we are able to hear Arlow's thinking about psychoanalytic listening. In this paper he is providing us with a pathway to finding the unconscious fantasies of patients. The contours of listening appear with a clear vision of how he himself understands what he is listening to in order to hear the patient. Building on Freud's and Ana O's early definition of the talking cure and chimney sweeping, he defines a dynamic interaction of analyst and patient who are affecting each other in their enlarging of understanding and insight. A "very special conversation" takes place with the analyst being quiet or intervening, being affected by the theoretical and technical concepts including ideas about pathogenesis. Arlow is clear that he sees adult's difficulties arising from unresolved unconscious conflicts from childhood such that the compromise formations have taken the form of unconscious fantasies or related groupings of unconscious fantasies. It is the derivatives of these unconscious fantasies that appear, and that the analyst listens to.

Here, as in other articles, free association is seen as the means by which the unconscious fantasy derivatives can become heard and known through listening.

Very importantly, Arlow considers this to be the most respectful way to truly hear the patient without making pre-formed assumptions—that is to conduct a special kind of listening. There are many types of material that are identified: context, contiguity, repetitions, contradictions, discontinuities, and particular words. This list is in line with Freud listening to slips of the tongue and dream images. Arlow highlights the centrality of figurative speech and metaphor as he understands a royal road to the unconscious fantasy. It was particularly interesting to me that Arlow depicts the analyst-patient interchange as an intersubjective event. The intersubjective relationship of analyst and patient bring about the transference, the metaphors held there, and often transference as defense. He gives an example of a patient hating a relative in order to not bring the full brunt of hatred to the figure of the analyst. "Metaphor is the principal element of figurative speech. It serves to extend language and meaning when words are not quite adequate nor sufficient." A patient's exclamation that he will be incarcerated brings forth his longstanding terror of being left out of the primal scene and being castigated for his curiosity. Or, a patient stating he is going into a lion's den is seen by Arlow as finding the meaning of his fear of going into the woman's vagina. His examples demonstrate his respect for the meanings in patients' minds. At the end of this paper, Arlow entices with the statement that in other papers, he will say more about how he listens to himself.

How Does the Analyst Listen, What does the Analyst Hear?

Jacob A. Arlow, MD (New York)

Listening is so fundamental to the psychoanalytic enterprise that one is tempted almost to deal with the subject aphoristically, that is, to list a series of well-contained, indisputable summaries of the analyst's experience as he listens to his patients. But the experience is far too complicated to permit so simple a reduction.

There are several classical epitomizations of analysis that come to mind when one approaches the subject. One is the statement that psychoanalysis is a talking cure. True enough, but that is only half the story. The other, more dramatic and poetic, refers to psychoanalysis as a form of chimney sweeping. These characterizations we have inherited from the early days of analysis. The implication was that the patient could talk himself out, either to the point where he ultimately recalled the traumatic incident at the core of the neurosis or, as in the latter characterization, the noxious, disturbing material finally was drained out of his mental apparatus. It should be noted that, in both of these characterizations, the role of the analyst as listener is hardly taken into account.

Nowadays our approach is quite different. We have come to appreciate how therapy is a dynamic interaction, through which two individuals affect each other for the purpose of modifying the characteristic mental responses of the patient and thereby alleviating his suffering. This interaction, which we call the therapeutic process, takes the form of discourse, of communication by way of conversation, whose purpose is to enlarge understanding and insight. But if, indeed, analytic therapy takes the form of conversation, it has to be noted that it is a very special form of conversation and it is to these specific features that we must now turn our attention.

Every conversation has its own specific features, depending upon the general and specific context. Above and beyond all other considerations, the nature of the verbal encounter derives its specific quality from the context in which the two individuals have come together. Are they strangers? Do they speak the same language? Are they friends, one of whom is appealing to the other for understanding and assistance? Is this a session devoted merely to gossip? And so forth. Depending upon the quality of the relationship and its specific context, many things can be left unsaid, many things can be mutually understood, many statements can be understood in a very special way. They reverberate with the nature of the individuals' relationship to each other and what experiences or purposes they have shared in the past or are undertaking in the present. As we can see, ordinary conversation, even of the most casual type, is no simple matter. It is governed by unspoken but usually mutually understood rules that both participants have tacitly accepted.

Now let us turn to the psychotherapeutic interaction. In addition to all the factors governing communication and conversation listed above, there are several essential, fundamental qualities that impose a distinctive meaning to the psychotherapeutic interaction. To begin with, the situation is tilted. one of the participants in this ongoing conversation is in need of help, dependent upon the other to supply insight or other factors which the patient himself has not been able to muster. By seeking out a therapist, someone who has been analytically trained, the patient acknowledges that there are forces within him which he cannot understand or control, forces of which he is unaware, whose functioning has brought about pain, suffering, inhibition, misfortune, etc. His hope is that he may be helped by having someone listen to him, learn how his mind works and make those crucial connections in his thoughts that the patient himself could hardly fathom.

The therapist, on the other hand, is in quite a different position. He is a professional who, by virtue of training and special experience, in effect asserts that, by listening to the patient, by recognizing significant connections that have eluded the former and bringing then to his attention, he can help the patient in his predicament. In the course of the evolution of the treatment, the patient may come to regard the therapist in many different ways and imagine him as exercising all sorts of roles or functions. The fundamental fact remains—and this must never be overlooked—namely, that what has brought these two individuals together in the treatment situation is that the patient is there to be helped. No matter how far removed from the immediacy of the patient's thoughts, this fact is an abiding reality that forms the background of every verbal and other interchange between patient and therapist. No matter how obscure or distant, the fact is that the patient at some level is always aware that what he says and does in the treatment situation is somehow connected with his wish to get well. All is determined by this overriding concern.

So while psychoanalytic therapy takes the form of a conversation, it is indeed a very special kind of conversation. There are two distinctive features to the interaction which separate therapy from the ordinary forms of conversation. The most unusual requirement, and the most difficult one to carry through, is for the patient to speak with complete candor, reporting as honestly as possible the thoughts that come to his mind. No criterion may be employed to justify withholding a mental presentation. Actually, it is impossible for the patient to honor this requirement to the fullest, but the breaches in the patient's adhering to the fundamental rule furnish important clues to unconscious conflicts whose derivatives the patient continually seeks to disregard.

The second factor that differentiates the analytic interchange from ordinary conversation concerns the role of the analyst. Unlike the expectations that pertain to the interchange during an ordinary conversation, in the therapeutic discourse the analyst is free to intervene or not to intervene, to respond or not to respond at those junctures in the patient's free associations which, in an ordinary conversation, would have required some response on the part of the opposite member. This freedom of activity helps demarcate the analyst as a professional with a specific therapeutic task as opposed to a sympathetic or responsive listener in an ordinary conversation.

To understand what the analyst listens for, what he listens to, and what he hears, we must have some appreciation of the analyst's theoretical and technical concepts. Up to this point in this presentation I have been speaking about "the analyst," but basically I am speaking about myself. Analysts differ widely in their theoretical and technical approaches, and this determines how they listen and what they listen to and, in turn, what they actually hear. Over the years, from reading, clinical conferences, and from various symposia, I have been impressed with how the analyst's theory of pathogenesis seems to play a major role in what the particular analyst hears and responds to in the material that he gets from his patients. It seems logical enough that how one understands how the patient got ill originally should have some connection with the techniques to be used to get him well. In that spirit, I would state in briefest terms my understanding of the process of pathogenesis and how it has influenced what I listen to, what I hear and what I do in the treatment situation. Simplistically stated, I see adult neurotic difficulties as the outcome of unresolved unconscious conflicts from childhood. At some level of mental functioning various compromise formations are affected in order to mitigate the untoward results of these conflicts. When the compromise formations prove inadequate to the task, then various unwelcome sequelae supervene. Usually these compromise formations take the form of an unconscious fantasy or of a series of related unconscious fantasies whose derivative manifestations may appear in conscious life in the form of symptoms, inhibitions, perversions, etc. They represent a persistent pressure upon the mind for actualization in some kind of act or fantasy. The process of defense against the unpleasant affects that would result if the derivatives of the conflictual wishes were not modified leads to compromise expressions which intrude into the course of the patient's free associations, betraying their presence to the listening analyst through countless manifestations.

This is where the technique of free association becomes overwhelmingly essential in the therapeutic process because it lays bare for observation the interplay of the specific elements in the patient's mind that he connects with each other. It makes it possible to observe how the patient's mind actually works rather than how you think it should work. There may be missing links in the sequence of the patient's thoughts and these are the crucial junctures for which the analyst's listening may supply the appropriate connections.

Over the years I have directed, or perhaps I might say more accurately, skewed my listening in keeping with certain criteria that may be used to process the patient's productions and which enable me to hear in what the patient has been saying evidence of unconscious wishes, tendencies, guilt, fantasies, etc. Depending upon these criteria, I can feel comfortably assured that I am hearing a message that the patient is transmitting in spite of himself.

Let me list the criteria that guide me in listening to the patient and in validating the interpretations that I make of the patient's unconscious mental processes. Foremost among these is the context in which the material appears. Next is the contiguity and sequence of items as they appear in the patient's associations. Then I listen to repetitions, to similarities and contradictions, to discontinuities in the patient's productions, to alterations from the declarative mode of expression, to the use of figurative language, especially metaphor, and to the appearance of material that doesn't seem to fit into the continuity of the patient's thoughts, i.e., a break in content. What I will try to do now is to illustrate and explain these principles of listening.

In any continuing relationship the context during communication makes it possible to understand the flow of thoughts, even when one or another may have been omitted or not heard in the course of the conversation (Rosen, 1967).

119

The missing elements are inferred by the opposite member. Accordingly, at any moment in the psychoanalytic discourse, there are a number of contextual dimensions that impart information beyond the literal meaning of the spoken word. First and foremost, as cited earlier, is the overriding consideration that the two individuals have come together for the purpose of helping the patient. In addition, I listen to what the patient is saying in the context of the events of his life. As analysts, we recognize that in the record of current experience we discern the influence of the past or, to put it another way, the past is embedded in the present. A further element that shapes my listening is the specific state of the transference at the time because it reflects how the treatment is going in keeping with the nature of the current intersubjective relationship. Meaning grows out of context. Each statement by the patient bears a contextual relationship to the antecedent and to the following mental presentation, as is the case with the position of a word in a sentence, the position of a sentence in a paragraph, etc. Any particular mental product—a thought, a parapraxis, a dream or a fantasy—taken out of context and not examined as part of the dynamic flow of the associations in the analytic situation may be interpreted in many ways. It becomes really comprehensible only when seen in the context of the specific dynamic configuration in which the material appears.

It is against this background of context that I pay special attention to the first thing that the patient says, even if it may be a casual remark about the weather or some practical concern about the schedule. Most of the time, the first thing the patient says at the beginning of the session serves as the leitmotif for the rest of the session. Whether he returns to the opening statement or not, I am predisposed to view the subsequent material, especially if it concerns the analyst, in the context of the opening statement.

During treatment, as in any form of conversation or communication, understanding is advanced and deepened by the sequence in which the contributions of the individual participants appear. In a certain sense, while the patient is associating freely, he is carrying on a conversation with himself.

While for a while we may hear only one or another side of the exchange, we are nonetheless privy to the outcroppings of an internal debate. The order in which elements appear in the course of the patient's associations endows meaning and sends a message. Contiguity implies relatedness and it is a principle that governs all communication. In that respect, the principles that we apply when listening to our patients differ not one whit from our reactions in everyday life. This is a principle we take for granted inside and outside of the analytic situation without paying attention to it. For example, 1 approach the secretary of a clinic and ask her if she is busy. She says no, what can she do? I ask if she will type a 16-page single spaced memorandum for me. She replies, "Oh, that reminds me, Dr. Arlow. I'm making up the summer schedule. When are you going on vacation?" Whether the secretary was aware of it or not, the sequence of the material, the contiguity of the elements indicate some displeasure at the request I made of her. An even more remarkable and amusing example of this mechanism, ratified by consensual validation, occurred to me many years ago during the Second World War. One of my friends had been inducted into service and was about to leave. We were having a farewell dinner. My wife did not attend because we had a newborn baby at home. One of our friends had been staying at our home while his wife was in hospital, having delivered her child. They had moved to the suburbs but had kept the same obstetrician, and therefore had been guests at our home during this period. At the dinner party, one of our friends told a joke which centered on the theme of a houseguest discussing with his host his having had sexual intercourse with the host's wife. It was a pretty good joke and, after the laughter subsided, my friend B, who was sitting next to me, turned to me and asked, "Is Ben still at your house?" Everyone in the party broke into laughter. They had made an interpretation as to what was on B's mind, who for the rest of her life nevertheless steadfastly refused to acknowledge that she had any such thought involving my wife and my household guest.

In the course of treatment there are many circumstances in which the contiguity and sequence of elements in the course of communication leave no doubt of the presence of some intention of which the patient was not at all aware. We follow this principle all the time but often fail to recognize its full import. The meaning of the more obvious examples rarely escapes us; the more subtle ones often do unless we are especially tuned to appreciating the significance of contiguity and sequence. One patient, for example, was bemoaning her unhappy lot in life as a consequence of having been raised in an extremely dysfunctional family. She was lamenting the fact that it would be most difficult for her to get married. "Just imagine, " she said, "my wedding announcement in the *New York Times*. Miss So-and-so, the daughter of Mr. and Mrs. X, is about to be married. Her father is a chronic paranoid schizophrenic and her mother is a borderline psychotic personality." In the midst of this bitter irony, she was overcome by a surge of violent impulses. Her next thoughts concerned the wish to destroy everything in the therapist's consultation room. That she is angry at her parents and would wish to destroy them is clear enough; that follows from the contiguity of the elements. However, it should be noted that her thoughts are not about her parents but about her therapist. This constitutes a safe displacement of the impulse onto someone whom the patient knows she would not injure. This form of displacement onto a relatively innocuous object is an example of transference used as a defense, and accordingly what one hears in this displacement is a defensive shift of the aggression onto neutral territory in an effort to spare her parents. This patient may be clearly aware of her violent wishes against her parents. Her wish to spare them and protect then is at that moment outside the scope of consciousness.

While, in listening to the patient's material, I attend specially to context, contiguity and sequence of elements, I also appreciate the simultaneous role played by repetitions of the same theme or variations and repetitions of similar themes. How these elements combine with the other criteria that I have been discussing may be observed in the following clinical vignette. The patient is a man in his middle 30's who works at a menial job as a taxi dispatcher, in spite of the fact that he is clearly a person of high intelligence, as attested to by his keen observations, precise language and wide reading. He had attended college for a year but dropped out. The patient lived at home and, except for occasional visits to prostitutes, had no sexual life. During this period in the treatment, there appeared recurrently in his associations reference to a memory of an angry confrontation with his father at the threshold of his parents' bedroom in the middle of the night. Mostly the patient remembered the overwhelming fear engendered by his father's anger. As the story keeps recurring repetitively in the course of his associations, the patient responds somewhat jocularly, "I know what you will say about this. It has to do with the primal scene. I read about it in the books, but I have no recollection that anything of this kind ever happened." Instead what followed in the associations were two sets of repetitive memories. One set had to do with women who had disappointed him, who had betrayed him, lied to him or mistreated him. The other repetitive theme was that of being excluded from various activities, particularly not being permitted access to the conversations and plans of his two older brothers. He complained that he was always being kept in the dark. In this context, he had the following memory. His two older brothers shared a room in the attic. They were always laughing and whispering and would not permit the patient to participate, or even to enter their room. The room was situated at the very end of a steep staircase that led into the attic. One day the patient heard his brothers whispering and laughing in their room. As silently as he could, he crept up the stairs and leaned against the door to hear what was going on inside. Apparently the brothers became aware that he was listening. What they did was to open the door slightly so that the patient's balance was disturbed and he fell forward, and then they shut the door vigorously, sending the patient tumbling down the staircase. "They could have killed me," the patient noted, "all because I was trying to listen in to what they were talking about." At this point the patient referred once again to a professor he had had in his first year of college before he had dropped out. This man had recognized the patient's potential and arranged for him to be in a very special course for people who showed academic promise. When this opportunity was offered to the patient, he left school.

So many of the principles that I use in listening and understanding patients are illustrated in this account. The memory of the confrontation with his father at the bedroom door keeps recurring and becomes intertwined with two themes; grave disappointment and anger at faithless, betraying women, and danger from acquiring knowledge that is being denied to him. Instead of a recollection of the primal scene, we are offered a substitute but similar representation in the story of attempting to listen in on his brothers. As in the recollection of the confrontation with his father, the element of dire punishment is central. He could have been killed for wanting to learn what he was not supposed to know. The next contiguous element in his associations, which comes in sequence, is an account of his learning inhibition. When offered an opportunity to increase his knowledge, he withdrew. In this context what I hear is an unconscious, unspoken thought of the patient's, namely, "acquiring knowledge of sex is dangerous. I may be killed for it." Apparently this specific inhibition extended to involve many other areas of knowledge and learning. In listening to this material, I realize how I had been attuned most acutely to the consequences of the context, contiguity and repetition in the material presented.

Patients have particular styles of expressing themselves verbally and analysts correspondingly have their own predispositions to how they listen and what they hear. These considerations apply particularly to the characteristic forms of language that the patient employs and that the analyst selectively attends to. Of these I find the most influential to be the figures of speech the patients employ. Listening carefully to figures of speech is a most valuable adjuvant to understanding the patient's associations. Figurative language is evocative and multi-layered in meaning and is particularly suited to play on the analyst's sensibilities. Metaphor is the principal element of figurative speech. It serves to extend language and meaning when words are not quite adequate or sufficient. The words of a metaphor do not literally mean what they say and, if attended to and listened to carefully in context, they will reveal a wealth of unconscious communication. Let me cite most briefly two examples. A sexually inhibited patient, who was also competitively timid, kept refusing invitations for dinner at a woman's home. It was clear that the occasion was to serve as the prelude to sexual intercourse. When I inquired as to why he was persistently refusing her invitation, the patient replied, "Do you want me to go into that lion's den? And besides, she has a picture of her boyfriend over the bed." What I heard was the following: for the patient to have dinner was tantamount to an invitation to have intercourse. By taking the metaphor seriously, i.e., literally, he equated the woman's genital with the lion's den. Inside the den lurks a dangerous beast—the woman's boyfriend who would destroy, if not the patient, then the penis that entered the den. I give special attention in my listening to the patient's language and particularly to the figures of speech and the metaphors that the patient employs. They constitute valuable conduits to unconscious fantasy thinking.

Closely allied to the significance of the use of metaphor is the way I attend to the words the patient uses, specifically if they are unusual words or do not fit precisely the situation in which they appear. For example, one patient had the misfortune of having a mother who was chronically actively psychotic, behaving sexually and aggressively in ways that were both humiliating and frightening to the patient and his siblings. The central theme of the patient's problems was his unconscious identification with this psychotic mother. At one point in the treatment he was reviewing the severely damaging effects of things that he had done. He had destroyed his marriage, alienated his children and threatened his financial situation. He complained, "Why didn't somebody warn me? Why didn't they explain the consequences? Why didn't they stop me?" Then he reflected and he realized that the issues had been explored, the possible consequences were known to him, not only from the treatment but from friends in whom he had confided. Several of them had urged him to stop his course of action in terms that were clear and unequivocal. The patient reflected on this and said, "Nothing could have stopped me, nothing short of restraint and incarceration." Those two words I heard with special emphasis. They were inappropriate; they did not belong. I asked the patient, "Restraint, meaning physical restraint?" and he said "Yes." "And incarceration?" I asked. These two terms, he stated, were appropriate to a psychotic individual. He had been behaving like a lunatic and could only be stopped by physical restraint or incarceration. The identification with his mother was clear enough. A segment of his history was being recapitulated. He was repeating the long discussions that he had had with his older sister when they were much younger and throughout the later years. Why didn't their father physically restrain the mother? Why didn't he put her away?

In listening to patients I also pay particular attention to the contradiction between the explicit language used in comparison to the actual situation. This is a basic theme that Freud alluded to in his paper on "Negation" ( ), when he noted that certain ideas cannot be admitted into consciousness unless they are stated in the negative. Here again this is something that recurs in everyday speech. We may be aware of it but we do not pay attention. For example, in the *New York Times* last week, a young Chinese woman standing on the corner, waiting for someone to come along to employ her, had a conversation with a newspaper reporter. He discussed with her the fact that many women in her situation were presumably being hired, only to find themselves raped and sold into slavery. The woman replied, "It is very dangerous. It is unavoidable. I don't think it's going to happen to me." To any objective listener, these statements are self-contradictory. The woman has clearly admitted into consciousness the notion that this could happen to her and, for whatever reason, she is willing to take the risk. Thus, in listening to patients, when there occurs a statement in the negative, I hear it as a potential positive. It is a way of permitting a thought to enter consciousness in a flimsy negative disguise. But I apply the same principle to statements made in the interrogatory, in the subjunctive and any other mood the patient may employ. I hear in each one of these statements the possibility of a direct expression of a repudiated thought or impulse. To me these various forms of expression represent attempts to snuggle into consciousness thoughts and impulses that one is trying to repudiate.

One final example. I listen very carefully to the manner in which the patient replies to some observation I may have made about a hitherto repressed impulse or thought. Whether the patient says "yea or nay" is less important than the manner in which the patient reacts to what I have said. I listen particularly to how the patient responds because I have come to recognize such moments as recapitulations of a portion of the patient's psychological history. What I mean by this is the following. When being made aware of some thought or impulse by my intervention, the patient responds to me in the same way as he or she responded in childhood to the same impulse when it arose spontaneously from within the patient. The patient relives the original confrontation with an unacceptable thought recognized as one's own.

These are only a few examples of the principles that guide me as I listen to my patients. Time does not permit further elaboration of this theme, nor does it permit another aspect of the analyst's listening, namely, how I listen to myself, but that is a matter for another symposium.

Chapter 9

From Communication to Insight

Jacob A. Arlow, MD

Commentary: Nancy R. Goodman, PhD

This article presents a rich understanding of what is involved in listening to patients psychoanalytically. Arlow describes the process that evolves between analyst and patient which he sees as a particular kind of conversation. Throughout the article there is awareness of underlying unconscious dimensions, in both the patient and the analyst, written about with respect for the depth and intimacy of what transpires in the analytic office. Subjectivity and intersubjectivity elements of the special psychoanalytic conversation are revealed through theoretical perspectives and through very personal examples. The concepts of transference and countertransference are defined in very modern conceptualizations and as the centerpieces for the movement from empathy to intervention. In this article, Arlow suggests that the word interpretation may carry too much authority and distance and should be replaced by the term intervention. The intervening invites reflection and destabilizes the existing equilibrium between impulse, defense, and punishment. There are many novel ideas in this paper which are inviting to consider and arouse curiosity and interest. As he centers in on the importance of empathy he uses the terms empathic understanding, empathic comprehension, and empathic insight.

There is an important distinction between identification with the patient which can bring about misguided countertransference that when recognized returns the analyst to true empathy and understanding. Essential subjectivity of the analytic dyad is literally felt by the analyst leading to insight that can be spoken. There is constant movement from Id to empathy to insight. Arlow is generous with his own clinical experiences especially what we today would call a reverie during sessions. He shows the powerful type of attention used in listening requiring listening to one's subjectivity. His example involves his own daydreaming in response to a patient's dream. They both involve reunions with a dead father. As Arlow is thinking his mind has been in a twilight zone between life and death and the wish to reunite, his patient reports watching an episode of "Twilight Zone". In the paper, this brings him to the topic of metaphor in psychoanalysis. "Psychoanalysis is essentially a metaphorical enterprise. The patient addresses the analyst metaphorically. The analyst listens and understands in a corresponding manner (p.25)." This is what leads to the finding of the unconscious fantasy. Throughout this paper, the way the analyst and patient are with each other is put into evocative and meaningful language.

From Communication to Insight

Jacob A. Arlow, MD

The present era is one of great change in psychoanalysis, change in both theory and technique. Psychoanalysis has never really been a completely unified science in regard to either theory or practice—we know, for instance, too well the history of schisms and conflicts and we recall Ferenczi's very early experiments in technique. Nonetheless, the fact is that for a long tine certain paradigms of technique stemming from Freud's early papers on the subject dominated the way technique was taught and, consequently, the technical role the analyst pursued in his practice. Freud, it will be recalled, was a gifted writer as well as a skillful teacher. In his papers on technique, Freud summarized his approach through a number of compelling metaphors, for example, the image of the analyst as a mirror, reflecting only what was presented to him, and the analyst as a surgeon, putting aside all personal feelings for the essential goal of helping the patient. In this connection, almost as an aside, Freud stated that these principles would also serve to protect the doctor. (From what we know about the early history of psychoanalysis, this comment of Freud's was more than a theoretical reflection.)

For both the candidate in training and the neophyte analyst, overwhelmed by the responsibility of treating a patient and struggling with the transferences imposed upon him, such precepts offered a safe refuge and were therefore readily consolidated into the traditional role of the therapist as a rigid, detached, objective commentator on the stream of the patient's associations.

In time, and with increasing experience on the part of many analysts, these precepts have been challenged. A deeper understanding of what makes people fall ill, the analysis of the phenomena of countertransference and, above all, an acute awareness of the fundamental subjectivity of the analyst were the significant considerations that led to altered views of the therapeutic interaction.

As I attempted to demonstrate in a previous communication (Arlow, 1986), how an analyst conceptualizes the goals of therapy and the specific technical procedures he employs depend in large measure on the precise theory of pathogenesis to which he subscribes. It is not difficult to understand how proponents of different theories of pathogenesis would organize their therapeutic efforts according to their notion of how the patient became ill in the first place. For the self -psychologist, who views the patient's difficulties as the outcome of thwarted self-esteem and injured narcissism during the early years of life, an effort to restore self-esteem through the therapeutic interaction with the analyst follows quite logically. For those who stress the vicissitudes of early development, specifically the significance of impaired or inadequate mother/child relationships, the psychoanalytic situation serves as a setting for the readjustment and the repair of the developmental process damaged by deficits.

It is, as Friedman (1973) indicated, a form of replacement therapy. For others, the psychoanalytic situation constitutes an experience of contact with a new object, a kind of corrective therapeutic interaction, endowed with special transference qualities, activating a developmental potential. For the Kleinians, who regard the introjection of a destructive parental imago as the essential factor in neurosogenesis, the therapeutic effect of psychoanalysis results from the benefits derived from contact with a benign superego representative in the person of the analyst, who may be substitutively introjected into the patient's ego (Strachey, 1934). These are just a few of the competing schools of thought concerning pathogenesis and therapy, each viewing the necessary interaction between analyst and analysand in a somewhat different way.

132

From the analysis of the Dora case down to the present time, the main thrust in psychoanalytic technique has been directed towards the analysis of the transference. In seminars evaluating the analyzability of potential patients, the essential criterion is often expressed in the following terms: Is this patient capable of developing a transference neurosis? Candidates are urged to foster or, at least, not to interfere with the development of the transference and, as far as possible, to "bring everything into the transference." As a result, it often happens that bizarre thoughts, feelings and bits of behavior are overlooked and not investigated because they did not seem to have an immediate bearing upon the transference. Some people make a sharp distinction between transference phenomena and the issues of so-called current reality, as if these latter issues were of secondary importance.

In the past two decades, the role of the countertransference has risen in importance in considerations of therapeutic technique. There is, however, no essential agreement on precisely what to include under the heading of countertransference. At one extreme are those who maintain that any reaction to or interaction with the patient constitutes a form of countertransference. Others have a more circumscribed, parsimonious view of the subject. They would reserve the notion of countertransference only for those instances where the patient serves as the object of one of the analyst's unconscious fantasy wishes. To be sure, the relationship of any individual to others in his experience is at some level influenced by some interaction with the important early objects of his past. In the psychoanalytic situation, however, the transference that we deal with concerns situations in which the analyst, by a process of displacement, serves as a substitute object for a conflictual wish embodied in some unconscious fantasy directed towards an original childhood object. In keeping with this stricter view of the transference, I would delimit the concept of countertransference to those instances in which the analyst is involved with a derivative of an unconscious fantasy of his and displaces onto the patient conflictual wishes originally associated with a primary object. As we know, the range of responses, affective and otherwise, to the analysand is wide indeed, but, according to the terms I have just described, not every response can be regarded as a manifestation of countertransference. The importance of this distinction will become apparent shortly.

At the present moment, however, what is clearly in the forefront of discussions of technique is the issue of the essential subjectivity of the analyst. The therapeutic enterprise is seen as consisting of two related intersubjectivities, that of the patient and of the therapist, and clearly major interest has fallen on that rather neglected aspect of the therapeutic dyad, namely, the therapist's subjective experience. As Kris (1951) noted, the analyst in the treatment situation is both a participant and an observer. Until now the role of observer has been emphasized. Just how does one conceptualize that the analyst is at the same time also an active participant, one who is constantly monitoring the stream of his own thoughts, fantasies and feelings, even as he observes the same presentations of his patient? How does the analyst process what he observes going on in his own mind, and how does it influence what he says and does in relation to the patient? Clearly the responses of the analyst constitute in part a record of his/her interaction with the patient. If so, what should be said about it? How much self-revelation is acceptable? And, most important of all, how does one judge? It is inevitable that such considerations must determine how the analyst listens and how he reaches conclusions concerning the patient's psychology. There are judgments that have to be rendered and decisions that have to be made. How does he/she know if his/her understanding of the material is correct or incorrect, and, if the patient refuses to accept the interpretation, is it always necessarily defense or resistance? The analyst could be wrong. There are those who maintain that, if the analyst pursues his or her line of interpretation in the face of the patient's objections, the analyst is merely engaging in a pattern of benign authoritarian forbearance. On the other hand, if the patient accepts the analyst's line of interpretation, is he/she merely being compliant, acceding to his/her vision of the analyst as being superior because of his/her knowledge and training? It may have been for such considerations that Freud suggested that important interpretations should be made during periods of positive transference, that is, when the patient feels attached and loving towards the analyst and would therefore accept the interpretations rather than subject them to critical investigation.

In a certain sense, it seems to me that the issue of authority is deeply embedded in psychoanalytic theory and practice because the analyst's interventions are described as interpretations. When we interpret something to someone, we explain to them the meaning of something which they themselves could not fathom. In this spirit, the analyst is effectively saying, "I know something about you that you don't know and that by yourself you could not understand." Personally I think that the term interpretation, derived originally from the analysis of dreams and symptoms, is an unfortunate one. I believe a more appropriate term would be intervention since, in my view, what the analyst does when transmitting his understanding to the patient is to destabilize the dynamic equilibrium the patient has established between impulse, defense and self-punishment. In any event, in reaction to the potential intrusion of an authoritarian stance into the analyst/analysand relationship, many analysts have given a politically correct twist to their critique of the analytic situation. They maintain that there are two interacting subjectivities, that of the analyst and that of the patient, and that they are equal in significance. The analyst is just as subjective as the patient. There are times, they maintain, that the patient may be aware of the analyst's motivations more clearly than the analyst himself.

Inevitably these considerations lead to the question of the anonymous stance of the analyst. In reality, the concept of an anonymous, inscrutable analyst is an illusion, as Greenson (1967) pointed out many years ago. Much as we observe our patients, they observe us. Many of the conclusions they reach about the analyst are incontrovertibly accurate, others are clearly mistaken, and there are observations which may or may not be correct, observations concerning which the analyst cannot pose a definite judgment. As a result, the question arises repeatedly as to how much self-revelation is warranted or whether such self-revelation helps or hinders the psychoanalytic process.

All of these issues compel us to take a new look at the nature of the psychoanalytic enterprise. Fundamentally, psychoanalysis is a talking cure. It is treatment by means of conversation, a very special kind of conversation, it is true, but a conversation, nevertheless. It is an exercise in discourse, that is, advancing understanding through communication. There is an implacable reality that brings the patient to treatment and binds him to the therapeutic relationship, namely, he understands that there is something wrong with the way his mind works, something is out of control, and that this state is due to factors operating within him and of which he is not aware. Otherwise he would not consult a psychoanalyst. But the roles of analyst and analysand are not equal. Neither are they symmetrical. Whatever authority the analyst may be said to have over the patient, it derives from the analyst's superior knowledge of psychopathology and psychotherapy, from his training as a professional. Even in a typical conversation between two individuals, outside of any treatment situation whatsoever, there is a comparable asymmetry when one of the participants unburdens his or her problems to a sympathetic friend who has been enlisted for the purpose of supplying understanding, comfort, reassurance or support. They may be friends of long standing but, at that specific juncture in their relationship, they are not equals in relationship to the problem. Their functions are different. on either side the expectations and functions are most dissimilar. It would ill behoove the recipient of such confidences to shift attention away from sympathetic identification by interjecting a recital of his or her personal tribulations. In any conversation, the role that the listener plays depends upon the context which brought speaker and listener together. In the analytic relationship it is a cry for help.

What happens in the psychoanalytic situation as the analyst exercises his role as helper? As the analyst listens passively, the patient's verbal presentations become the immediate sensory experiences that occupy the analyst's mind. The patient's spoken presentations become the analyst's auditory presentations, and in this process identification of analyst with analysand takes place. The analyst thinks and feels with the patient and, over the passage of time, sharing the feelings, the hopes, the disappointments and the secrets of the patient, the process of identification is enhanced. In general, sharing confidences establishes an emotional bond between two people and fosters a process of mutual identification. This makes it possible for the analyst to begin to think and feel how and what the analysand thinks and feels. A certain degree of identification is common in all human contact. It is what makes sympathy possible, but the process goes a step further during analytic treatment. Identifying with the patient makes it possible for the analyst to feel sympathetic but, when he becomes aware that the mood or thoughts he has been experiencing represent commentaries on the patient's material, he has made the transition from sympathetic identification to empathic comprehension. If the analyst fails to take that step and remains in a state of identification with the patient, he is sympathetic but not empathic. This is one of the most common factors underlying certain types of countertransference. Thinking with the patient is quite different from thinking about the patient. I would now like to offer two clinical vignettes illustrating the differences, subtle though they may be, between identification and countertransference on one hand and empathic understanding on the other.

We are indebted to Dr. Renik who, in a recent publication (1993), presented a detailed and candid account of his subjective experience and self-analysis in the course of a session. Because of time considerations, I will present a compressed version of his account, which he correctly identifies as an everyday clinical sequence in the practice of almost any analyst.

The patient is describing her joyless marriage and, as he listens, the analyst is aware of a sense of discomfort, a feeling of immobility. His limbs feel heavy. Different possible interventions come to mind but he decides against using them, feeling that they would not eventuate in anything useful. He states,

"I note that the remarks I keep thinking of making all aim at a rather active investigation of my patient's situations—questions about her attitudes towards her husband and the future of their relationship... I have an urge to rescue her from her marriage and end her distress. The feeling is a familiar one to me, reminiscent of, among other things, my childhood wish to be my mother's savior." Renik adds, "We could summarize this vignette by saying that a piece of self-analysis led me to become aware of an omnipotent rescue fantasy generated by my own psychology, a fantasy that was not appropriate to my actual task as an analyst and my responsibilities towards my patient. The insight I gained was quite useful. Keeping it in mind allowed me to avoid embarking on a mission of my own I might otherwise have pursued at my patient's expense." Renik states further, "Once I became more fully aware of my state of mind and some of its personal, historical determinants, I allowed myself to facilitate more actively my patient's exploration of how she was dealing with her husband. The outcome of this line of investigation was analytically quite fruitful too. Eventually, as you might expect, we even cane to look into my patient's need to elicit rescue by me and her difficulties in initiating her own efforts to extricate herself from her marital problems." (p. 557)

This is an apt and honest description of how countertransference interferes with the pursuit of the analytic purpose and how a bit of self-analysis helps to keep the process on track. What happened here was that the analyst had remained fixed at the stage of identification with the patient. His countertransference made him sympathize with the patient. He was not being empathic. Empathic understanding is the first step towards insight. It consists of becoming aware of the fact that one's reaction to the patient represents some commentary on the patient's wishes, that the mood, thoughts, fantasies, whatever, stimulated in us by the patient's productions represent beginning understanding of the patient's conflicts. "Eventually," Dr. Renik adds, "as you might expect, we even cane to look into my patient's need to elicit rescue by me and her difficulties initiating her own efforts to extricate herself from her marital problems." We do not know how big a period of time is covered by the word "eventually," but in fact that insight had been available if the analyst had empathically realized that his own countertransference represented his commentary, his beginning understanding of the patient's unconscious wishes.

I will now cite an experience of my own, previously reported in the literature, to demonstrate the quick transition from identification to empathy and insight. This was an experience reported in a paper with Dr. Beres, entitled "Fantasy and identification in Empathy" (1974).

The patient was a middle-aged professional man born in Europe. When he was two, his father left for the United States but did not call for the family until he was 10. During those eight years a maternal uncle played the role of father surrogate for the patient. He and the patient shared the same bed. The patient idolized him. When it came time to leave Europe, the uncle refused to come along with the family. He must have disappeared during the Holocaust, but the patient would not accept this until, many years later, he received confirmation that his uncle was executed by the Germans the day they entered their little town. Much of the analysis concerned the patient's longing for the uncle and the wish to be reunited with him.

At the beginning of one session, the patient reported the following dream. "I see myself in a house with some cousin of mine in the country. It was not yet dark but it was no longer light. I seemed to be alone in the house. My cousin was elsewhere. I could not see him. I called out 'Peter' and somebody, in a joking way, called back 'Joey.'"

I heard no more of this from the patient when suddenly I found myself having a vivid visual dream. I was in a European airport standing in the terminal. It was the kind of airport typical of many European cities. The passengers debark from the plane at some distance from the terminal and are brought in by bus. As the bus approached the terminal, among the passengers I recognized my father, who had been dead for a number of years. Many thoughts about my father came to my mind during this dream. As a matter of fact, the last time I had seen him alive had been at an airport, except the circumstances had been reversed. He was waiting for me in New York upon my return from a visit to Europe, which had included a sentimental side trip to the city in which he grew up. It suddenly came to me that I was in a twilight zone between life and death, in that in-between land where it is possible for the living and the dead to be reunited.

At that moment I thought about the patient's dream. The patient had been in a house in the country. It was not yet dark but it was no longer light. The patient too was in the twilight zone and, at that moment, I realized that the names Peter and Joey, which occurred in the dream, were actually Anglicized forms of the names the patient and his uncle used to call each other. At this point I began to emerge from the intrusive visual fantasy and I heard the patient saying, "Last night I was watching television. The show was *The Twilight Zone.*"

Strictly speaking, this was not a countertransference reaction on my part. The patient was not the object of any wish of mine. I had a dream or fantasy conveying a wish identical with that of the patient's. However, at the moment that I recognized how my thought of the twilight zone coincided with the element of "no longer light but not yet dark" in the patient's dream, I passed from identification with the patient, thinking like him, to thinking about him. This was the moment of empathic insight. It is this transition from identification with the patient to understanding about the patient that marks the difference between sympathy and empathy. It is a safe rule in therapeutic technique that, unless the analyst is involved in severe physical pain or preoccupied with overwhelming personal difficulties, whatever occurs to his mind in the course of listening to his patient is some commentary upon the patient's material and should be regarded as such. It is the beginning of insight.

The thought or affect that appears in the analyst's mind occurs as a free association and represents a form of inner communication. It is the first step in the awareness of the insight which the analyst is about to apprehend. What the analyst perceives through introspection is the end result of a process of intuition. Intuition consists of being able to organize silently, effortlessly and outside the scope of consciousness the myriad observations, impressions, facts, experiences, in a word, almost all that one learns from the patient, to organize all of these elements into a meaningful pattern without any sense of the intermediate steps involved.

When we examine closely the full range of communication between analyst and analysand, such phenomena no longer suggest anything bizarre or supernatural. In ways other than verbal ones, the patient and the analyst are constantly communicating with each other. This is a two-way street but for the moment we are concentrating on the effect of the patient's communications on the subjective experience of the analyst. The patient's behavior, facial expressions, body posture, etc., transmit meaning which augments, elaborates and sometimes even contradicts what the patient articulates verbally. The timbre of the voice, the rate of speech, the metaphoric expressions and the configurations of the material transmit meaning beyond what is contained in verbal speech alone. All of these are perceived, sometimes subliminally, and are elaborated unconsciously. This mode of communication may be compared to the various means the artist employs in affecting his audience. There is something aesthetic and creative about the mode of communication in the psychoanalytic situation (Beres, 1957). Accordingly, I like to think of this aspect of the analyst's experience as the aesthetic phase of the therapeutic interaction. What comes to the analyst's mind, however, is not necessarily an immediate apprehension of the patient's unconscious processes. It is usually only a clue, a signpost pointing in the direction of approximate insight.

The insight that comes from introspection, empathy and intuition constitutes only the first part of the interpretive work. There is both an art and science in psychoanalysis and art alone, i.e., the subjective factors just discussed, cannot in themselves serve as the basis on which scientific discourse is founded. As intriguing and dramatic as this aesthetic experience on the part of the analyst may be, it has to give way to a second, or additional, phase of the interpretive process, one that is based on cognition and the exercise of critical judgment.

In order to validate his intuitive understanding of what the patient has been saying, the analyst must find supportive evidence in the data of the analytic situation, that is to say, in a precise examination of the text of the patient's productions. The insight that seemed to appear so intuitively must be put to the test of objective criteria in conformity with the data at hand. Most of the time the intuitive work has been so efficient that a sense of conviction is immediate, gratifying and even accompanied by recollections of supporting evidence from the patient's productions. However, this is not always the case.

Since I have suggested that we consider the psychoanalytic interchange as a special form of conversation, it is important to bear in mind that precision of comprehension evolves from the principles that underlie communication in general. Foremost among these are the context, the sequence and the contiguity in which the ideas are presented. In a continuing relationship, context during communication makes it possible to understand the flow of thoughts even when one or another element nay have been omitted or not heard in the course of the conversation (Rosen, 1967). They are inferred by the opposite party. Also, at any moment in the psychoanalytic discourse there are a number of contextual dimensions that impart information beyond the literal meaning of the spoken words. To begin with, there is always the important element, often forgotten or overlooked, that what brought analyst and analysand together to engage in this verbal exchange is the fact that the patient is there in order to get well. Whether the patient is aware of it or not, whatever he or she selects to say is determined by the notion, "In order for me to get well, my therapist has to know this." This is the abiding reality that is often overlooked.

The next contextual element consists of the events of the individual's daily life. In the record of current experience we discern the influence of the past. To state it aphoristically, the past is embedded in the present. A further element, and always an important one, is the specific state of the transference, because it reflects how the treatment is going and what the current intersubjective relationship consists of. And finally, there is the all-important context in which specific elements appear in the course of the therapeutic interchange. Meaning grows out of context. Each statement by the patient bears a contextual relationship to the antecedent and to the following mental presentation, just as is the case with the position of a word in a sentence, the position of a sentence in a paragraph, the position of a paragraph in the total text. Any particular mental product, a thought, a parapraxis, a dream or a fantasy, taken out of context and not examined as part of the dynamic flow of associations in the analytic situation, may be interpreted in many ways. It becomes really comprehensible only when seen in the context of their dynamic configuration.

The boundaries of context change in the course of treatment. They change with the events of everyday life and, above all, in response to the evolution of the transference. Accordingly, the same words or referents in a changed situation or context may signify something quite different from how they appeared in an earlier, different context. Think, for example, of the many different ways in which one can understand and use the words "to love." By interpreting data isolated from their appropriate context, one can prove anything. On the other hand, being sensitive to the significance of context, the analyst can appreciate the import of the first thing that the patient says or does in the session. These productions establish the context for the subsequent material. They adumbrate the theme for the session, particularly if the opening statement concerns the analyst. Even if the opening statement as such is not interpreted, it nevertheless constitutes an especially significant communication.

In analysis, as in any form of conversation or communication, understanding is advanced and deepened by the sequence in which the contributions of the individual participants appear. While associating freely, the patient is actually carrying on a conversation with himself. While for a while we may hear only one or another side of the exchange, we are nonetheless privy to the outcroppings of an internal debate. The order in which elements appear in the course of the patient's associations endows meaning and sends a message. Contiguity implies relatedness and it is a principle that governs all communication. As a result, not everything that is communicated has to be expressed. The connecting links may be inferred or may he mutually understood or meant to be understood. In the treatment situation, the analysand may not be aware of the link that establishes meaning when two seemingly disparate elements are juxtaposed. The essential task that the analyst fulfills during treatment is to supply the connecting links that bind one thought to another.

In a certain sense, the evolution of the patient's productions during a session may be compared to a certain type of musical composition. There is an opening statement or theme, which is then repeated in several variations, often in a contrapuntal mode, and then there is the closing coda. The similarities and opposites that characterize the patient's productions indicate the persistent effect of the conflictual unconscious fantasy and the derivatives it presents to consciousness. Sometimes the manifest presentations are all of a kind, centered on a common theme or object, but at the same time any specific mental representation may be balanced off immediately by a countervailing negative or denial. A negative has the effect of indicating, "I said it but I would like to take it back." Accordingly, in interpreting the record of the patient's associations, not only are the positive representations available for understanding, but also the conditional, the subjunctive and the interrogatory modes. Every negative implies a positive. Every subjunctive implies an affirmation. Every question implies a declarative statement.

Patients have particular styles of expressing themselves verbally and analysts, correspondingly, have their own predispositions to attending selectively to different aspects of the patient's productions. These considerations apply particularly to the characteristic forms of language the patient employs and the analyst selectively attends to. Of these, one of the most influential ones are the figures of speech the patients employ. Analyzing figures of speech is a most useful adjuvant in the process of interpretation. Figurative language is evocative, multi-layered in meaning and particularly suited to play on the analyst's sensibilities. Metaphor is the principal element of figurative speech. It serves to expand language and meaning when words are not quite adequate or sufficient. The words of a metaphor do not literally mean what they say. A torrent, for example, cannot roar, but Shakespeare made it do so and thus enriched and expanded the image of a man struggling against a turbulent river. In many instances, valuable insight may be realized by treating figures of speech, especially metaphors, literally.

Psychoanalysis is essentially a metaphorical enterprise. The patient addresses the analyst metaphorically. The analyst listens and understands in a corresponding manner. Under the influence of his or her unconscious conflicts, the patient apprehends and perceives the world in a metaphoric way and reacts correspondingly. Transference is, in a large measure, a metaphorical conceptualization of a relationship. Significantly the words "metaphor" and "transfer" have the same meaning, to carry over from one situation to another, in words, actions or thought. The patient feels and thinks one thing about a specific person, the analyst, while unconsciously meaning and thinking about another person, an object from childhood. Transference in the analytic situation is a particularly intense, lived out metaphor of the patient's neurosis. By and large, metaphors represent outcroppings of unconscious fantasy and, as such, they constitute expressions of the patient's basic conflicts. There are circumstances in an analysis where some large segments of the work center around the understanding of one or two basic metaphors. This is so because the manifold variations of metaphoric expression of the basic themes regularly lead to the uncovering of an unconscious fantasy. In fact, the unconscious fantasy itself represents a metaphorical apprehension of the distillate of childhood experiences and fears that have remained dynamically active into adult life. The same considerations apply to other figurative expressions, symbolism in particular. It makes a difference in what context and by what specific form something is symbolized. Figurative language and unusual expressions take advantage of the weak spots in the patient's defenses. Thus, for example, a patient who experienced relief when he decided not to undertake a certain competitive enterprise said, "It is at least as if I am no longer going to my own hanging." The same ideas could have occurred to the patient as a fantasy or as a dream instead of in the form of a so-called ordinary figure of speech, a simile (Schwaber, 1992; Arlow, 1995).

The subjectivity of the analyst is complemented by the cognitive dimensions of his/her training and experience. He/she cannot rely on immediate intuitive apprehension alone. What he/she does is more than interpret the nature and content of the patient's unconscious conflicts and the techniques by which the patient fends off derivatives of these conflicts. What the analyst really does is to demonstrate to the patient how his/her mind works. He/she explains the causal links that exist among the various component forces in conflict within the patient's mind as they appear in context. For this reason, it is more important to observe how the patient responds to a particular intervention than to struggle with the accuracy of the details of the interpretation. It is not an absolute truth that the analyst tries to impart, but rather the best understanding of the experience that the observations permit us to formulate (Brenner, 1995). A corollary of this principle is the need to check on the significance of what the analyst does by observing the dynamic effect that his/her interventions have produced in the nature and the flow of the material that the patient subsequently produces. In fact, in the evolution of the analytic process, how the patient responds to the analyst's interventions mirrors or replicates how the patient originally responded to those same forbidden impulses when as a child he or she became aware of them. Those responses constitute the form of defense instituted by the ego during the process of pathogenesis.

An appropriate balancing of the elements of the analyst's subjectivity, namely, intuitive apprehension, on one hand, and disciplined, cognitive processing, on the other hand, should diminish the need for the analyst to reveal too many aspects of his/her subjectivity. Many of the dilemmas posed by the interaction of the two intersubjectivities, analyst and analysand, I would suggest, could be resolved or mitigated by a more rigorous application of consistent psychoanalytic methodology. The benefits would accrue to both patient and analyst.

References

Arlow, J.A. (1986). The relation of theories of pathogenesis to therapy. In: *Psychoanalysis: The Science of Mental Conflict: Essays in Honor of Charles Brenner,* ed. by A. Richards and M. Willick. Hillsdale, NJ: The Analytic Press, pp. 49–63.

——————— (1995). Stilted listening: psychoanalysis as discourse. *Psychoanalytic Quarterly,* 64:215–233.

Beres, D. (1957). Communication in psychoanalysis and in the creative process. *Journal of the American Psychoanalytic Association,* 5:408–423.

——————— and Arlow, J.A. (1974). Fantasy and identification in empathy. *Psychoanalytic Quarterly,* 3:26–50.

Brenner, C. (1995). Unpublished paper on "Authority in Psychoanalysis."

Friedman, L. (1978). Trends in the psychoanalytic theory of treatment. *Psychoanalytic Quarterly,* 47:524–567.

Greenson, R.R. (1967). *The Technique and Practice of Psychoanalysis.* New York: International Universities Press.

Kris, E. (1951). Ego psychology and interpretation in psychoanalysis. *Psychoanalytic Quarterly,* 20:15–30.

Renik, O.(1993). Analytic interaction conceptualizing technique in the light of the analyst's irreducible subjectivity. *Psychoanalytic Quarterly,* 62:553–571.

Rosen, V.H. (1967). Disorders of communication in psychoanalysis. *Journal of the American Psychoanalytic Association,* 15:467–490.

Schwaber, E.A. (1992). Countertransference: the analyst's retreat from the patient's vantage point. *International Journal of Psychoanalysis,* 73:349–362.

Strachey, J. (1934). The nature of the therapeutic action of psychoanalysis. *International Journal of Psychoanalysis,* 15:127–159.

Chapter 10

The Relationship of Models of the Mind to Clinical Work

Jacob A. Arlow, MD

Commentary: Nancy R. Goodman

The premise of this paper is that analysts have a model of the mind in their minds which influences and guides what they say and what they do in sessions. Arlow considers the structural hypothesis to be an "organic development", the best model of the mind, and as the article shows, his basic model of the mind includes the influence of unconscious fantasy throughout.

There is an interplay of forces within mental conflict referring to representations of the ego, id, and superego. The analyst and patient can see resistance, defenses, fantasies, impulses, thoughts, affects, motives, and wishes and their denials in the ongoing development of material in sessions. In the internal conversation different developmental organization with their concomitant forces come to the fore. As the process unfolds, he sees the analyst interventions as disturbing compromise elements making it more likely to better identify the features of his model, the structural model. Dreams provide entrees to the different voices of the patient including through the past development as well as the present disequilibrium. Compromise formations are central and discovery of their dynamics bring about discovery of the mind. "From our clinical work we learn to appreciate that what appears in consciousness is a derivative of an unconscious conflict—which is organized in the form of an unconscious fantasy."

Again here, we hear Arlow's belief in free association and its flow that allows discovery of derivatives of unconscious fantasy. His clinical examples demonstrate fully his line of thinking about the structural model, free association, and presence of derivatives indicating the compromise formations. A male patient plays "mascot" to men in business as he did to his older brother whom he idealized. As an awareness of masculine inferiority, originally to his brother, became revealed in a new repetition of this pattern, he has a dream about a watch someone was trying to get away from him. Dr. Arlow points out how in the dream he does have possession of the watch. There are series of "yes I have it" and "no I do not have it" throughout the session. At the time, his brother was dying from a serious illness and a vacation break was coming up. The pattern of having and not having and the underlying confluence of forces appeared vividly in the session showing the psychic history being activated with the analyst. There are further clinical examples, all presented with the layers related to Dr. Arlow's believing in the model of the structural theory and its components.

The Relationship of Models of the Mind to Clinical Work

Jacob A. Arlow, MD (New York)

In the course of his clinical work, the analyst is profoundly influenced by the model of the mind to which he subscribes. While he may not be aware of this at all times, his theory of mental functioning constantly guides what he says and what he does. It influences how he attends to what the patient is saying, what he perceives in the patient's productions, and how he organizes his observations.

The structural hypothesis represents an organic development from the fundamental postulates of psychoanalysis. The concepts that make up the foundations of psychoanalysis are psychic determinism, dynamic conflict (the interplay of opposing trends or impulses) and unconscious mental processes. For me, the idea that intrapsychic conflict is the basic dimension of mental functioning in general and of psychopathology in particular is inexorable and unequivocal. The cumulative observations of almost 100 years of psychoanalytic experience confirm this. The nature of our investigative instrument, the psychoanalytic situation, articulates it. In fact, as Freud described in his "Autobiographical Study" (1925), the psychoanalytic situation and its quintessential component, free association, were designed to facilitate the emergence into consciousness of derivatives of persistent unconscious conflicts. In describing his turn to free associations, Freud said, "Hypnosis had screened from view an interplay of forces which now came in sight and the

151

understanding of which gave a solid foundation to my theory." (p. 27, author's emphasis) The dynamic principle in psychoanalysis is a parallel expression of this interplay of forces, the concept of mental conflict. In the vicissitudes of human experience and development, conflict is an unfailing attribute.

Structural theory was devised precisely for the purpose of organizing and clarifying the phenomenology of mental life as consequences of conflict. The decisive criterion by which each mental element is assigned its place in mental structure is the role that it plays in conflict. The more intense the conflict, the clearer the delineation among the various structures .of the mind (Anna Freud, 1936). When the ego acts as the executant, harmonizing and integrating the demands of the id and the superego, it is difficult indeed to delineate the boundaries of psychic structure. In any event, considerations of conflict were what led Freud to reformulate his theory of mental functioning in terms of the structural hypothesis and, to my way of thinking, this theory remains the best model, the most effective and comprehensive theory by which one may conceptualize the phenomenology of mental activity.

Within the psychoanalytic situation, free associations offer a living record of the moment to moment functioning of the patient's mind. It is not a placid, continuous scroll of recollections. It is a dynamic record, reflecting a relatively unstable equilibrium of forces in conflict. The phenomenology of this instability is rich and varied, and its dynamism and significance can be grasped in their fullness during the psychoanalytic situation, as one observes and studies the moment to moment variations in the patient's communications. The patient's productions reflect the changing contribution emanating from the several psychic agencies, and they encompass the well-recognized phenomena ordinarily described under the heading of resistance and defense, as well as intrusive fantasies, impulses, thoughts, affective states, parapraxes and so forth.

The interplay of the forces in conflict determines the form and sequence in which the elements of communication appear in the course of free association. Accordingly, from the patterns that the elements communicated assume, meanings beyond those conveyed in the literal, expository prose can be inferred. Such inferences articulate motives and wishes quite unknown to the analysand, as well as the methods and reasons for disowning and denying such wishes and impulses.

As in any conversation, precision of comprehension depends upon the context, sequence and contiguity of the ideas presented. Context makes it possible to understand the flow of thoughts, even when one or another element may have been omitted or not heard in the course of the conversation (Rosen, 1967). The contiguity or the juxtaposition of ideas usually means that somehow the elements are semantically related, very much in the way that one word following another gives meaning to a sentence and one sentence following another gives meaning to a paragraph. In fact, one of the ways of dramatizing our understanding of the nature of the psychoanalytic process is to view it as corresponding to the record of an internal conversation. Although the phrase "internal dialog" has often been used, it is not sufficiently precise, because the inner argument advances through several protagonists. Many voices are involved and each expresses a different representative of the conflicting forces at work, e.g., the pressure of the impulses, warnings, prohibitions and threats, judgments drawn from experience, et cetera. All of these so-called inner voices represent contributions from the events of various periods in the individual's past, interactions with important persons who helped mold character and ideals, as well as the effects of the vicissitudes of individual experience and learning. Under different circumstances and in different situations, regrouping of these voices, or forces, takes place. The participants in the conversation ally themselves at different times and for differing reasons with one or another of the protagonists of the inner conflict.

We know from clinical experience how exquisitely this state of affairs may be reproduced in dreams. In some dreams it is possible to demonstrate how each character represents a thought or attitude that is part of the ongoing argument in the psyche. In the psychoanalytic situation, the analyst is privy to this internal argument, to its rich details and to its historical development. Technique consists of intervening from time to time to make sure that each voice is heard, that each one of the protagonists in the inner debate has his say in turn and does not overwhelm and totally obscure the other participants. By avoiding the role of being a pleader or defender of any of the participants in the argument, the analyst fulfills Anna Freud's (1936) advice that the technical position of the analyst should be equidistant to all of the psychic agencies—the id, ego, superego.

The purpose of this quasi-parable is to illustrate the principle that the structures of the mind, as organized around the concept of the role each one plays in intrapsychic conflict, do indeed reflect and specify some aspect of the functioning of the psyche of a person, the analysand. As a set of hypotheses, the agencies of the mind in structural theory summarize and bring into meaningful relationship, in the most parsimonious way, the clinical observations concerning the vicissitudes of the patient's conflicts, as revealed in the psychoanalytic setting. What the psychoanalytic situation does is to make it possible for the analyst to observe how the dynamic equilibrium in the mind shifts and changes under the influence of current experience, the transference and, above all, as a result of the analyst's interventions and interpretations. In order to bring the nature of the conflict into consciousness, the analyst intervenes in such a way as to shift the dynamic equilibrium in favor of one or another of the forces in conflict. How the patient attempts to reestablish the equilibrium during the course of treatment, i.e., in response to the analyst's interventions, often replicates the vicissitudes of the process of pathogenesis. Thus, any interpretation on the part of the analyst should be regarded as an intervention that tends to destabilize the dynamic equilibrium which the ego struggles to maintain. From the vantage point of psychoanalytic technique, this means that the analyst should concentrate on the dynamic effect his intervention produces, rather than on whether the patient accepts or rejects the interpretation. This is a subject that should receive full treatment in connection with the analysis of defense.

Because of the effect of the interplay of opposing forces in the mind, what finally appears in consciousness represents a compromise formation. Towards this compromise formation each of the various agencies of the mind—the ego, the superego and the id—has made its specific contribution. From our clinical work we learn to appreciate that what appears in consciousness is a derivative of an unconscious conflict. In several publications (Arlow, 1969a, 1969b), I have called attention to the fact that, at a certain level, the ego's attempt to resolve fundamental, recurrent intrapsychic conflicts is organized in the form of an unconscious fantasy. Essentially the interpretive work during psychoanalysis consists of reconstructing the nature of the unconscious fantasy from the derivatives which it produces in consciousness and analyzing and resolving the consequences of the specific component contributions of the forces in conflict. Sometimes the question is raised by those apparently influenced by the topographic model, "Where is the unconscious fantasy located? To what system does it belong? Is it part of the ego, the id or the superego?" Actually the situation is the other way round. The id, the ego and the superego, or, to be more precise, representatives of their influence are to be found in the unconscious fantasy.

What has been presented thus far is a brief and perhaps skimpy description of the relationship of the structural hypothesis to clinical work. The rich implications of the relationship between this theory of mind and our therapeutic efforts emerge most clearly from a detailed critical examination of the psychoanalytic process over a period of time. With due regard for considerations of time and confidentiality, the best one can do under these circumstances is to present a relatively small segment of analytic work to portray how effectively the structural model helps to integrate and clarify the meaning of the data of psychoanalytic observation.

This material is from the analysis of a businessman in his 40's, who entered treatment for overeating and inability to control his drinking and smoking. Outstanding among the presenting symptoms were feelings of depression and inferiority. The material to be presented centers about the patient's relationship with his older brother, his only sibling, who is nine years his senior. Prom childhood on, the patient idealized his brother, as well as his brother's friends. Throughout his life the patient would attach himself to older, powerful male figures whom he admired. His relationship to them was that of a mascot. As a mascot he was privy to the activities of the older men and by watching carefully and taking in what he observed, he was able to acquire much of their knowledge and skills. The patient has always been short of stature and quite insecure about his masculinity. In the period that antedates the material to be described, he had become acutely aware of his feelings of phallic inferiority.

The material to be described represents the events of two sessions just before the summer vacation. At the time the patient had reason to be concerned about his brother's health.

The patient began the session by discussing one of his employees, whom he was about to fire. She is not keen about the job either, because she wants to go into another business. She is not a reliable person. She has been in psychiatric treatment for a long time, and at the present time is involved in a dispute with her therapist. Because of this dispute she feels that she has a right not to pay the bill. She had left a previous psychiatrist without paying his bill also.

The patient then reported that his brother seemed to be doing better and went on to describe how anxious he had been and how reassuring the doctors were when he spoke to them.

The patient's next association was a dream, which follows. "I dreamt I was holding an old style pocket watch in my hand. It had a chain. I was dressed in an old-fashioned suit with a vest, and I was trying to put the watch into my pocket. I was having a great deal of difficulty doing so. There were two intertwined padlocks on the chain, and this made it difficult for me to get the watch into my pocket. Finally it seemed like someone or some force unseen by me was pulling the chain and watch away from me, but I kept holding on to it, determined to keep possession of it. Then I woke up."

The patient said he never had such a watch. He then recalled that his father had such a watch and, in fact, his father did wear the kind of clothes that he had been wearing in the dream. Actually he does not have any suits with vests. His father was a dandy. He used to spend a great deal of money on clothes and bought himself that onion-type watch. The patient then said that he did not know where the watch was. Almost immediately he corrected himself. "Of course I know where the watch is. My brother has it. What happened was that at the time of my father's death six years ago, my mother divided his personal belongings. She asked my older brother if there was anything in particular that he wanted and he said all that he wanted was the watch." The patient said, "I never wanted the watch." "Oh," he said, "that wasn't true. I did want the watch, but not for myself. When my older daughter turned 21, I thought it would be a proper gift to give her now that she had attained her status as an adult. It occurred to me that I would like to get that watch as a gift for her. I thought about it for a while and then decided that I would not ask my brother for it. There was a wrist watch that belonged to my father and I thought I would take it, but before I could say anything, my mother said that she would take the wrist watch."

I pointed out to the patient that in the dream he finally did get possession of the watch. He protested, "No, I never wanted that watch for myself, but I did have it in the dream and I wanted to put it in my pocket. but I couldn't. But I had the watch. My brother got the watch when my father died. How did I get the watch in the dream?" After a pause, he looked up and said, "Is it possible that I inherited the watch from my brother? But that would be ridiculous. One of his children would have gotten it." I observed to him that he had had the dream at a time when he felt his brother was safely out of danger.

He then added that he was puzzled by the interlocking of the padlocks that made it impossible for him to get the watch into his own pocket. Padlocks were something you put on the door to prevent the house from being burglarized. A small boat of his had been stolen recently and since that time he had put such padlocks on his new boat. In any event, the patient went on to add, in the dream he could not enjoy possession of the watch because someone or something was taking it away from him and he could not get it into his pocket. "In the end," he said, "I didn't have the watch, but I didn't let go of it either." He added that his father had been especially proud of that watch. He recognized that the watch is a symbol of authority, the kind of heirloom that is passed down through the generations.

At the following session, the patient reported that his brother was not doing as well as previously. He elaborated his concern in some detail. He hoped that in time there would be improvement, but he expressed some doubts.

The patient then reported that he had mentioned the dream of the watch to his wife, as if it were an amusing experience. "Of course," he said, "I omitted any reference to the fact that one of my associations was that I had inherited the watch as a result of my brother's death." His wife pointed out to him that he must have had some need to have the watch for himself, because she knew the watch he was referring to and it would have been a most inappropriate gift for their daughter. It was much too bulky to hang around a girl's neck. The patient responded by saying that this was exactly what he had learned in the session. It was so obvious now that he had used the occasion of his daughter's birthday as an opportunity to express the wish to get the watch for himself. He must have wanted it all the time.

Without transition, the patient said that this reminded him of his father's clothes. "My mother gave me my father's shirts and some other items of apparel after my father died. I have the shirts at home, as well as in my summer place. I have had them now for six years and I have never worn them. I give all sorts of reasons why I don't wear them, but they are not very good reasons. For example, even if they didn't fit well, I could wear them up in my summer place. It wouldn't make any difference there. Everybody dresses informally. I could also wear them around the garden. The same is true of those shirts of my father's that I'm keeping at home. It's also true about the suits that I have of my father's. I can neither wear them nor can I discard them. On several occasions I thought of getting rid of them, of giving them away, but somehow or other, I can't seem to do this."

The observation was made that both the watch and clothes are items that one wears and one is seen wearing. To this, the patient responded, "Oh, but I never connected the watch with the shirts." When I pointed out to the patient that this was exactly what he had just done, he thought for a second and began to laugh. It was all so obvious. He had been talking about the watch and then, without transition, ideas of the shirts had come to his mind. He seemed a bit sheepish about having contradicted the association that he himself had made. He acknowledged that it must represent part of the trend we had discussed in the previous session, of wishing to be in his father's place and have his father's authority.

In this minute segment of an analysis, we can perceive the manifold ramifications of the patient's conflicts. Let us examine only one set of phenomena pertaining to the conflict over the wish to acquire his father's prized possessions. When derivatives of this impulse begin to attain the quality of consciousness, the patient's response is an immediate denial followed by an affirmation. He does not know where the watch is—yes, he does, his brother has it. He never wanted it—yes, he did, not for himself but for his daughter. He did not get the watch, but in the dream it ends up in his possession. However, he cannot put it into his pocket. In the dream, however, he is wearing his father's clothes. In reality, he cannot wear them nor can he get rid of them. The all-pervasive conflict is clearly manifest in the dream, in his associations and in his inhibition about wearing his father's clothes. His conscious concern about the brother's health is counterposed by a fantasy of inheriting the watch through his brother's death. The wish to steal is balanced off by the fear of being stolen from. The contributions of each one of the psychic agencies—ego, id and superego—is apparent in the material, and the forms and methods of their combinations and compromise lay down distinct guidelines for the future course of therapy.

To return to the clinical material. Further attempts to probe the dream proved unsuccessful. He could make no associations to putting the watch in his pocket. He protested only that he was unable to do so, and that in the end the watch seemed to be in the process of being taken away from him. In an attempt to bring the dream and the material back into the context of the transference, I pointed out that this was a striking dream to have just before the vacation. The patient seemed surprised and said, "Is that right? I wonder why you think so." Then after a pause he said, "I'm supposed to come back on the Tuesday after Labor Day, but I won't be able to do it. I won't be back until the following Thursday."

Thus, on the next to the last working day before the vacation, the patient brought in a dream about the imminent departure of his secretary and the threatened departure of his brother. His secretary left her psychiatrist with his money in her possession, and in the dream the patient was left with his brother's, formerly his father's, watch in his possession, after the brother's apparent demise. To oppose his acquisitive and hostile wishes, the patient enlisted a wide array of defensive maneuvers—reaction formation, denial, projection, displacement and repression. The behavior of the patient towards the watch in the dream is duplicated exactly in his behavior towards the items of apparel that he had inherited from his father. He could not enjoy their use nor could he give them up. (Parenthetically, as a general rule in a dream, the behavior of the person depicted as the dreamer reflects the ego's attitude concerning the intrapsychic conflict it is the attitude with which the dreamer readily identifies himself and which is most acceptable to him.) Inhibition, renunciation and self-punishment are all apparent in the material. To repeat, the dynamic interplay of forces representative of ego, id and superego functioning explicates the material most effectively and serves as a guide to the technical approach to the material.

The next, very brief example will illustrate how analyzing the clinical data within the framework of the structural hypothesis may afford precise criteria for the making of a very specific interpretation. This material is taken from the analysis of a patient being treated through a clinic. He is a brilliant man who had the misfortune of being born with a physical deformity that is clearly visible. Understandably, he is deeply enraged at his cruel fate.

At the beginning of the session, the patient began to elaborate, half in jest, half in earnest, various plans to put the leaders of the world in an embarrassing situation. Progressively the aggressive component of his fantasy became more open and clearer, eventuating in the thought of unleashing an atom bomb on the city of New York. After describing this fantasy with some relish, the patient added jocularly, "But of course I would give you some warning so you could get out of town." After a momentary pause, he asked the analyst, "Say, what about the confidentiality of the material that goes on here?"

The analyst responded with a question, "Why do you ask?"

The patient's response was logical and precise. He said, "I have worked in clinics and I know the routines. Files are kept very loosely. Many people have access to the files. In your clinic I know that the patients are not identified by name but by number. However, with my defect, I would be readily recognizable to anybody who reads the chart or to the secretaries who do the typing." The analyst did not respond to this statement, and the patient continued with his associations, the significance of which do not concern us at the present time.

The reality of the patient's concern is not the issue here. He could have posed the same question the first day he entered treatment and any time thereafter. The true significance of the question is established by its context in the material and its contiguity to a very specific thought, a thought that appeared in consciousness in a spirit of spoofing and was cloaked in reaction formation. The thought concerned the wish to destroy not only the city of New York but the analyst as well. What was the nature of the patient's conflict at this moment? In part, he was opposed to his own hostility towards the analyst; it made him feel ashamed and guilty. Part of the inner dialog had been omitted. The full text, if we could restore it, might have read something along these lines: "I'd like to kill everyone in the city, even my analyst. But that's not right. He's trying to help. It's a terrible thought. I'm ashamed of it. I don't like myself for thinking such thoughts. What would people think if they found out? I hope they never do." The contribution of each of the component parts of the psychic apparatus—ego, superego and id—is clear enough and does not have to be elaborated.

Referring to the concern about confidentiality of the records, a more appropriate response on the part of the analyst might have been, "Why do you think this thought came to you just now?" The reality of the patient's concern is unquestionable, but the immediate significance of the concern is established by its context in the session and its contiguity to the specific reference to the analyst. The aggressiveness of the id and the jocular defense of the ego are easy enough to discern, but the contribution of the superego can be clearly inferred by an examination of the dynamically determined sequence of elements in the patient's associations. Such an occasion could be an opportunity to open the exploration and discussion of the patient's guilt and of his need and concern for other individuals, elements in his psychology till now overshadowed by his bitterness against fate.

SUMMARY

As far as clinical work is concerned, the structural hypothesis seems to be the most useful and effective set of concepts to apply to the data of observation obtained within the psychoanalytic situation. More than any other model of the mind, it clarifies the vicissitudes of intrapsychic conflict and accordingly helps establish criteria for the validation of interpretations and reconstructions, as well as guidelines for the future course of therapy.

References

Arlow, J.A. (1969a). "Unconscious Fantasy and Disturbances of Conscious Experience." *Psychoanalytic Quarterly,* Vol. 38, pp. 1–27.

———— (1969b). "Fantasy, Memory and Reality Testing." *Psychoanalytic Quarterly,* Vol. 38, pp. 28–51.

Freud, A. (1936). *The Ego and the Mechanisms of Defense.* New York: International Universities Press, Inc., 1948.

Freud, S. (1925). "An Autobiographical Study." *Standard Edition,* Vol. 20, pp. 3–74.

Rosen, V. (1967). "Disorders of Communication in Psychoanalysis." *Journal of the American Psychoanalytic Association,* Vol. 50, pp. 467–490.

Chapter 11

Some Reflections on the Structure of Memory

Jacob A. Arlow, MD

Commentary: Nancy R. Goodman, PhD

As in many papers, Arlow puts in tales of his own personal experience to illustrate his ideas. Here is a story of his waking up with a remembering of a name, the name of a teacher he had 70 years before. He wonders how that name appeared because if asked he would never have remembered it. Thus begins the adventure of reflecting about the structure of memory in which Arlow recalls he wanted to find a clinical example of forgetting and remembering the primal scene. The story of what took place in P.S. 173 so long ago and a love story. The way to the primal scene was discovered through the path of associations which take the reader from yellow notes (like Freud's yellow flowers in Screen Memories?) to red hair to voyeurism, to wanting to forget and wanting to remember, an argument between his mother and father over the milkman, and a ride from the milkman in the horse-drawn wagon and a rescue fantasy of his. The stream of memories ends with seeing a horse drawn hearse indicating death as the punishment for such thrilling wishes. This beginning to the paper also opens the door, in such an inviting way, to Arlow's thinking about memory as a psychoanalyst who believes in the constant presence of unconscious fantasies in all functions of the mind and does so with respect, curiosity, and excitement.

Many basic Freudian and Arlowian concepts are visited in this paper about the way the mind defends against knowing what is painful and forbidden.

A review of the way Freud developed thoughts about childhood trauma and memory is presented reminding us of Studies on Hysteria and the statement that hysterical patients suffer from "reminiscences". Free association carries the key to remembering as does the idea of constructions made by the analyst as listening to fragments. Arlow appreciates Freud's writing about his own forgetting of the name Signorelli and association to an unfortunate suicide of his own patient. Arlow is a proponent of the idea of compromise formation and suggest that Freud's forgetting was a failure at such a compromise leading him to write: "Every bit of forgetting is a form of remembering".

Arlow demonstrates more about forgetting and remembering as related to the primal scene with clinical material from a patient who actually witnessed the aftermath of a fire and the excitement of the fire engines and that deaths had occurred. Nothing of the primal scene between parents was remembered but was always present in the patient's need to organize events with elements arising from the traumatic experiences his childhood. As in dreams which lead to memory traces, the visual carries the sensations to a feeling of truth about recollections. Arlow reminds the reader that dreams and the visual are themselves metaphors. The patient is gathering images in dreams and the analyst is gathering images as he or she works. The analyst is re-visualizing the dreaming of the patient. Here Arlow reviews his thinking about empathic identification in the work of listening. Arlow writes in a contemporary way of the place of action in defending against recollections of painful memories using an example of a patient who repeats being left out and angry with no memory of the original leaving out, the primal scene, he keeps providing evidence of through repetitive actions. And, most notably, repetitions of feelings enter the transference. He tells of a patient whose childhood feelings of envy, rage, and fear of punishment, awaken in the transference with Arlow and are uncovered through dreams and associations. An example of a patient with somatic symptoms is used to show how recollections of an exciting sexual encounter became a symptom, a headache.

[Handwritten designation: B19]

Some Reflections on the Structure of Memory

Jacob A. Arlow, MD

Originally I titled this paper "The Structure of Memory" but, on further reflection, I realized that a more modest title was in order.

In the middle of the night some year or so ago–was I awake or asleep?–there floated across my mind the name Ms. Bunzelman, a name I recognized immediately. She had been the assistant to the principal of P.S. 173, which I had attended some 70 years earlier. I had long since forgotten her name and if, during the intervening years, anyone had asked me to recall it, I an sure I never could have done so. In the predawn darkness I pondered the question "What was Ms. Bunzelman to me and I to Ms. Bunzelman that she should enter my consciousness after a 70-year hiatus?" I had had almost no dealings with her. The only thing I could recall was going to her office to get a supply of yellow notepaper, the 2-1/2 by 6 inch scraps on which short memos or notes were usually written. I soon put the matter out of my mind.

Months later, as I was beginning to prepare to write a paper on the structure of memory, a connection cane to my mind, one which had not occurred to me during the nighttime recollection of her name. But now there was a specific context. I had been thinking of introducing the talk with a clinical illustration of forgetting and remembering in the so-called primal scene situation. In this new context, I recalled an incident that took place when I was in the 8th grade at P.S. 173. Our teacher was Mr. G, a creative, dynamic, inspiring man. He had brought his young son to school on one or two of the holidays, so we knew that he was married. One day Mr. G gave me a folded yellow slip of paper, the kind that I remembered getting from Ms. Bunzelman, and asked me to bring the note to Miss T, a woman teacher in the school. Somehow I felt that this was no ordinary educational missive so, contrary to my principles and practice and certainly contrary to what Mr. G expected of me, I unfolded the yellow slip to read a cryptic message that went "A book of verses underneath the bough, a loaf of bread, a jug of wine…" Although I had not yet come upon Mr. Khayyam's *Rubaiyat,* it seemed clear enough to me what the message was intended to convey.

In the context of thinking about the primal scene, I could begin to see the connection to the name of the principal's assistant. Poor Ms. Bunzelman, the unimportant outsider! She entered the picture merely as the purveyor of yellow slips, one of which was the centerpiece of my curiosity-inspired, voyeuristic transgression. She represented a loop in a most complicated web of threads that in my mind led from yellow slips of paper, to a particular slip, to a significant message, to a relationship that I must have surmised much earlier. The name Ms. Bunzelman was a nodal point, an organizer of a complex, dynamic structure of interrelated memories. But I was also aware at this juncture of a distinct disinclination to pursue further the enigmatic intrusion of Ms. Bunzelman's name into the functioning of my memory.

In spite of the clearcut wish not to remember, a certain image of Ms. Bunzelman's hair, reddish brown in color, kept returning to my mind. I am not even sure if this was indeed the color of her hair, but it was definitely the color of the hair of the mother of one of my friends, a woman who always seemed depressed and somewhat distracted, as if constantly ruminating over the pain of lost love. I never knew if this was really the case, but I immediately connected her image with the mother of another friend, who was depressed as well. In this case, however, I was definitely aware of the cause, her husband's blatant infidelity.

169

At this point four memories came to my mind as if in a row. Throughout my life I had had no difficulty recalling them on separate and isolated occasions. Of the four, the first one had been a recurrent memory. I am four and a half years old, seated at the dinner table, staring at a soup plate, from the rim of which there is missing a triangular piece, about one inch across. I an crying because my parents are quarreling. My father is angry and threatens to smash a dish. I had had no further insight into this memory until shortly before my sister died, when I asked her about the incident. She corrected one detail. It was not my father who threatened to smash the dish. It was my mother. But she added another important point. My father had accused my mother of being too friendly with the milkman. I mention the detail of his occupation because now a memory of a seemingly totally innocuous nature that I had recalled many times seemed to fall into context. In this memory I am on my way to school and a milkman gives me a hitch in his horse-drawn wagon. I had reason, therefore, to remember and to forget the milkman.

In both of the next two memories I am standing in the sane place, right in front of the entrance to my public school. Our principal, Miss Quinn, a very old, gray-haired lady used to come to school in a cabriolet drawn by two white horses. This, incidentally, is not a fantasy. It was customary for whatever student was passing by at that precise moment to open the door and to assist the principal out of the carriage. Now, in the context of the string of these memories, I could readily recognize a rescue fantasy, obviously consonant with the fairy tale of Cinderella.

In the next memory that came to my mind, I am standing in the same spot, observing across the street a small white hearse drawn by two horses, typical of the kind that was used in those days for the funerals of children. Its placement in this sequence of memory hardly needs any explication. The punishment for arrogant usurpation is deadly.

These four memories are structurally related to each other, taking off from their source, the color of Ms. Bunzelman's hair. They seem to branch away

170

and yet at the same time thematically reconnect with another branch of the same theme, developing out of the original nocturnal recollection of a name. It is as if the memories are all part of a gigantic, interconnecting network, reestablishing contact even in the most circuitous fashion. What may seem like a far-fetched, irrelevant and isolated detail may serve as a joining point for streams of memories that demonstrate a certain underlying coherence.

From the beginning to the end of his career, from the "Studies in Hysteria" (1895) to "Constructions in Analysis" (1937), Freud considered the goal of psychoanalytic technique to be to get the patient to recall the forgotten past, to overcome the so-called childhood amnesia. From his early observations he had reached the conclusion that the repressed memories of traumatic events of childhood functioned like noxious foreign bodies in the psychic apparatus. In various guises the memory of the traumatic events intruded on the functioning of the mind in the form of distorted versions of the unrecollectable memory. It was this that led Freud to say that hysterical patients "suffer mainly from reminiscences" and that symptoms represent the forgotten events of childhood. To help the patient get well, one must get him to recall the forgotten traumata and to integrate the memories and their associated affects in their proper place in the individual's memory system. At first Freud tried many different ways of attaining this goal, with only partial success. When hypnosis failed, he tried other measures to overcome resistance to recollection. In his memoir, "An Autobiographical Study" (1925), Freud described how he found a solution to the problem. "While I was in this perplexity, there came to my help the recollection of an experiment which I had often witnessed while I was with Bernheim. When the subject awoke from the state of somnambulism, he seemed to have lost all memory of what had happened while he was in that state, but Bernheim maintained that the memory was present all the same; and if he insisted on the subject remembering, if he asseverated that the subject knew it all and had only to say it and if, at the same time, he laid his hand on the subject's forehead, then the forgotten memories used in fact to return, hesitatingly at first but eventually in a flood and with complete clarity." (pp. 27–28) It was thus that Freud came upon the method of free association which forms the core of psychoanalytic technique. It is the experimental and therapeutic technique which is the source of our special knowledge of the workings of the human mind. Under standard conditions which minimize external influences, it is the best method yet devised to observe how the human mind works.

How effective has this new technique been in facilitating the emergence into memory of the forgotten past? It was assumed that, if one waited long enough and patiently enough, the repressed memory would emerge into consciousness. As we know, and as Freud knew, this is by no means always the case. Freud confronted the issue in his paper, "Constructions in Analysis" (1937). The patient's symptoms and inhibitions, he said, are the consequences of certain forgotten experiences and the affective impulses called up by them. If these lost memories cannot be recovered, they must be constructed from the fragments of the memories, even as they occur in distorted forms in dreams, or by allusions to the repressed material and by "bits of repetitions of the affects belonging to the repressed material, to be found in actions performed by the patient." (p. 258) Freud continued, noting "the path that starts from the analyst's construction ought to end in the patient's recollection, but it does not always lead so far." (p. 265) Freud adds that, if the analysis has been carried out correctly, the patient experiences an assured conviction of the truth of the construction, and in many cases this eventuates in a satisfactory result.

Although it is rarely commented upon, when Freud abandoned hypnosis and began to use the technique of free association, he applied this new approach to the psychology of forgetting. The example he gave was the analysis of his inability to recall the name Signorelli. Without saying so, Freud used free association to overcome his having repressed the memory of an unfortunate turn of events in his practice, i.e., the suicide of a patient. The record of the intermediate thoughts that came to his mind before he actually recalled the forgotten name is, in actuality, the record of his free associations. Examined from this point of view, one can see how that record sheds light on the manner in which the elements in the free associations are related to each other. The various elements that came to his mind were in one way or another related to the forgotten element he was seeking to recover. They were related by sound, by theme, by any of a number of connecting links. Freud also indicated that the processes of forgetting and remembering are dynamic ones. He stated, "I forgot the one thing against my will when I wanted to forget the other thing intentionally. The disinclination to remember was aimed against one content; the inability to remember emerged in another. By a sort of compromise (emphasis added) that reminded me just as much of what I wanted to forget as of what I wanted to remember and that showed me that my intention to forget something was neither a complete success nor a complete failure." (1905, p. 4) Continuing in the same spirit, he said, "It is probable indeed that a suppressed element always strives to assert itself elsewhere, but is successful in this only when suitable conditions meet it halfway." (p. 6) In effect, he was referring to what we now recognize as the principle of consonance, the mutual interaction and stimulation of conscious and repressed elements, affected by a certain third factor common to both. In the sequence of thoughts that come to one's mind, one should be able to detect some manifest or implied connection of content.

In modern terms we would say that Freud's inability to remember the name Signorelli constituted a failed compromise formation. The wish to block the memory of the patient's suicide out of his mind failed, but the impulse was displaced onto the name Signorelli, the forgetting of which was no great help to Freud's state of mind. The memory of Signorelli, it would seen, was an innocent victim of Freud's conflict—really some unconscious conflict evoked in him, of which the memory of the suicide of the dead patient was an unpleasant reminder. In effect, what I am saying is that something else— we know not what—was the primary object of repression. Without further associations, of course, we cannot deepen our understanding of the situation. It is sufficient that Freud demonstrated in this example the dynamics of forgetting and remembering. My thesis is that, in a paradoxical way, we might say that every bit of forgetting is a form of remembering. In the analytic situation the presentations of recollections to consciousness during the process of free association take on in their structure the nature of screen memories. They are evidence of the fact that we cannot forget what we are unable to recall. In the treatment situation and in a good part of our experience outside of the analytic situation, we keep remembering what we have forgotten. We are the stuff of memories.

This structural organization of memory is constantly being recast and refurbished in keeping with both the persistent unconscious conflicts and with the challenges that new experiences present. To illustrate the determinants of the structure of memory, permit me to cite in a most selective way some of the clinical data that I presented in a previous communication for an entirely different purpose, namely, my paper on "The Revenge Motive in the Primal Scene." (Arlow, 1980).

The evocation of a dream and the reconstruction of a primal scene trauma resulted from the stimulus to memory from a gratuitous combination of current events. After hearing that several fire fighters had died in a fire downtown, the patient felt very sad. He went to the opera that evening and saw what he considered a silly spectacle. At a dinner party he knew that he was privy to a secret affair that two of the people there were having and, while the plot of the opera seemed silly, the music was particularly appealing. These actual events formed the day residue of a dream with a typical primal scene reversal theme, i.e., he was embracing a woman in a bathroom when his wife came in and found them. From several details he was able to identify the particular bathroom as one in his uncle's house, which he and his family visited when he was age four. There had indeed been a fire in a factory across the street from his uncle's home and the firemen were still searching through the rubble for the remains of some of their comrades who had died in the conflagration. The patient could recall in great detail many of the perceptions that excited him during the visit; certain new musical instruments of his uncle's, some antique precursors of the victrola. In addition, there were detailed memories of exciting sounds, smells and visual experiences. Yet in spite of the detailed recollections, the overwhelmingly convincing evidence of the primal scene experience and the patient's sense of conviction, there was no recollection of actually being in the parents' bedroom and witnessing them having intercourse, and that he felt hurt, angry, humiliated, murderously vengeful and fearful of retaliation. Instead, what we observe is how, in his subsequent history, the events of life were selectively ordered and organized into a set of memory structures, ultimately clustered around the elements of the traumatic experience, but obscuring and preventing recollection of the actual event.

As noted, in the early history of psychoanalysis, getting the patient to recollect the forgotten traumatic events of childhood was the fundamental direction of therapeutic efforts. Following the mishaps associated with the failure of the seduction hypothesis, fewer and fewer cases of actual recollection of traumatic experiences have been reported. Hardly any appear in the current literature, with the exception of the claims made by those specializing in multiple personality disorders. To be sure, there are, there must be, many instances of discrete traumatic events but the precise recollection of such experiences seems difficult indeed to evoke.

Memory systems seem to be structured according to sensory, affective and thematic approximations and associations of the individual's important conflicts. They are not necessarily linked by identity, although a fortuitous set of identical or related perceptions may serve as a most powerful stimulus to recollection. In the example of the night at the opera, the knowledge of the forbidden liaison and the news of the catastrophic fire served to intertwine so many separate memory strands as to foster, i.e., facilitate, the process of recollection, at least as it was exemplified in the dream.

In examining the structure of memory, one observes how a set of coherent memories become organized about specific sensory modalities. Like Ms. Bunzelman's name, a sight, sound, smell or taste may serve as the nodal point in a complex web of associated threads of memory. In the case cited above, various sounds, musical and otherwise, revealed an underlying structure of memories connected with the specific event. The same may be said of the visual image of fire and its multiple connecting strands, and no one in this audience needs to be reminded of how the taste of a madeleine stimulated Proust in his incredible examination of memory. Reiser (1991) summarized this principle as follows: "Memories are stored and arranged in the mind according to (and coded by) sensory percepts registered during the remembered experience." (p 91) In fact, however, as has been demonstrated earlier, the situation is not that simple. There is a defensive dynamic that operates to encompass even the most obscure, seemingly completely unrelated element into the nexus of memory. The situation resembles what Freud (1900) said about day residues in dream formation. They are selected precisely because they seem to be remote and unimportant.

Not surprisingly, the function of memory is most often expressed and perhaps even conceptualized in terms of recollection of visual experiences. Seeing is believing and the ability to recall images of past events before the mind's eye endows it with a sense of verisimilitude. Since memory is so often enlisted in the service of defense, concentration on the visual element of a particular experience may further an inner demand, either not to remember or not to forget. Into the latter category falls the common experience of fixing important events in one's life by attaching to them the recollection of the precise setting or activity in which the individual was engaged at the time. On the other hand, there are those instances in which one concentrates on a specific visual detail in order to repress a larger, more painful experience. To give an example of this mechanism, I cite a patient in whose associations appeared the design of the wrought iron decoration on the landing of the fire escape of his father's factory. This image recurred frequently in the course of his associations until finally it appeared in its appropriate larger context. The patient had been standing on the fire escape landing, overhearing a bitter quarrel between his parents over the father's interest in his secretary, a splendid example of the inability to forget and the unwillingness to remember.

This indeed constitutes both the substance and the function of screen memories. They represent, as Freud (1899) indicated, a substitute presentation to consciousness for something that must remain repressed. The screening function of memory may take many forms. In some instances, the manifest expression of the substitute memory may contain elements of the repressed, traumatic event. in other instances, a substitute memory appears, related thematically to the repressed event but without any manifest element of the forgotten trauma. I have seen instances in which a number of screen memories appeared in a series, stereotypically repeated each time the material of the analysis began to approach a particular painful event. The screen memories served as a bulwark in depth, protecting the individual against the emergence of painful affects. In this connection, one may observe a similarity to the reorganization and realignment of memories that takes place in the case of the personal myth as described by Kris (1956). From this point of view, the personal myth represents a restructuring of the memory system for purposes of defense. I have cited a similar case of a false memory of an injury which never took place, a supposed injury which served as the organizer of a structure of memory to rationalize the defensive derivatives of a feminine identification in a male patient (Arlow, 1991).

There are three items that concern visual function and memory that can only be touched upon in passing. First is the reminder that dreams are really metaphorically distorted visual memories. In fact, Freud began the "Interpretation of Dreams" (1900) with a consideration of hypermnesis of dreams, the fact that in dreams one is able to recall events and memories long since forgotten. It would appear that, in the absence of external stimulation of the visual apparatus, the internal contribution from the visual cortex during sleep tends to objectify in a quasi-realistic, i.e., hallucinatory, way previous patterns of registration.

The second point I would like to make relates to visualization and memory in the mind of the analyst as he conducts his work. It was Lewin (1955) who pointed out how, in a certain sense, the analyst dreams along with the patient, to wit, as the patient recollects and reports his dream, the analyst revisualizes it, as it were, in his terms with his own images. Slowly the picture, as it would seem to appear in the patient's mind, is replaced by the parallel, if not identical, picture in the analyst's mind. On one occasion I had the experience in which, while the analysand was reporting to me his dream of the previous night, I went into a dreamlike state and had a dream of my own which was parallel, practically identical, with the manifest elements of the patient's dream. This is in support of Lewin's thesis that the analyst becomes identified with the patient, and this identification makes it possible for him to store in his own mind the memories that the patient has been presenting to him. Empathic identification makes it possible for the analyst to store and to retrieve the patient's memories which have now become his own (Beres and Arlow, 1974).

Only a passing comment can be made on the relationship between the consistency of memory and one's personal identity. A continuing store of reliable memories supports and maintains one's sense of identity (Jacobson, 1954; Arlow, 1969).

We are all accustomed to thinking of repetition as an exercise to aid memory but, on reflection and from analytic experience, we come to realize how repetition in action is in itself a form of memory. Perhaps the most fascinating and intriguing examples of this principle consist of the so-called "anniversary reactions" or the "secret calendar." On certain days of the year or after the passage of a definite amount of time, some individuals perform certain acts or experience persistent, inexplicable changes of mood whose origin they are unable to understand without psychoanalytic investigation. It is as if a fragment of memory had been translated into action or into a mood while the specific event from which these behavioral and affective responses originated escapes awareness.

As already indicated, certain forms of repetitive behavior may constitute an acted-out form of memory and at the same time a defense against the recollection of the painful memory. For example, for several weeks this patient had been talking about a number of related themes—the feeling of being excluded, the punishment for being curious, interest in activities going on behind closed doors, anger at women who betrayed him, etc. Finally at one point the patient said, "I know what this sounds like. I've read about it in books. It's that primal scene idea but I have no memory of any such event in my life. Nothing like that ever happened." With this he became strongly assertive and argumentative although the analyst at no time had mentioned the primal scene. The patient then continued, "I do remember something that happened when I was about six or seven years old. My two older brothers had a room in the attic at the top of the stairs. One day I heard them whispering and giggling. I was curious to know what was going on so I leaned against their door and listened in. They must have become aware of that. They opened the door slightly and, as I fell forward, they banged the door shut so strongly that I tumbled all the way down the stairs. I could have been hurt but they were only laughing." Paraphrasing Santayana, what this patient could not remember he repeated. Viewed another way, it is clear that the memory of listening in on his brothers' conversation was offered up as a substitute for discussing the possibility of a primal scene experience. Here once again we can observe how what memory serves up as recollection can be enlisted in the service of keeping something forgotten. Technically this patient's behavior of listening in on his brothers may be considered a form of acting-out, namely, what he could not articulate as a thought or memory he expressed in action. It is very common in the analysis of patients such as these, who have been traumatized by a primal scene experience, for them to arrange a reenactment of that experience. Either

179

they continue to intrude on other couples' private activities or arrange for others to intrude upon their own private functioning. Such behavior is at once both wish fulfillment and a form of memory.

In analysis, of course, the most striking and intriguing example of repetition in action as a form of recollection is the experience of the transference. It would be possible to use any number of examples to illustrate this principle. However, I have chosen the specific example which follows because I wish to emphasize the defensive role of memory, its function as a compromise formation between really remembering and really forgetting. What follows is a very condensed account of a few weeks of analytic work.[2]

The patient, a young married man in professional training, of late has felt that the analyst approves of him and looks upon him favorably. As the patient was ascending the stairway in the hall leading to the analyst's office, he encountered a young boy. As he passed him he felt an impulse to attack the young boy. This surprised him. On the couch, while he was relating this incident, the analyst moved. The patient felt that the analyst was going to slap him or perhaps even shoot him. He had a passing thought that perhaps the young boy was the analyst's son.

The next bit of material concerned the patient's conflict with his wife about having a child. She wants one but he is opposed to it. If she gets pregnant, he says he will insist that she have an abortion. Having a child at this time, before he completes his professional training, would interfere with two things that he loves doing best of all, skiing and eating at first class restaurants.

Shortly after this, as a result of certain economic reverses, the patient's mother-in-law informed the young couple that the financial subsidy that she had been giving them, a generous one, would have to be curtailed sharply. The patient was disappointed and angry with his mother-in-law. The patient then told about a seminar that he had been attending. The instructor favors

---

2 I am indebted to several of my students who made some of the material available to me.

him above all others. On this occasion, when she left the meeting for a short time, the members of the group made disparaging remarks about her. These remarks disturbed the patient. That evening he had the following dream. He is in the basement of the old house that he lived in during his childhood. He is seated at an elegant table and the basement has been transformed into a most attractive dining room. Instead of the rough-hewn walls of stone, the walls are now covered with plush red velvet material. The woman teacher who favors him comes into the room and they begin to be intimate. Among the associations to this dream, the patient mentioned that the plush red velvet walls reminded him of the lining the uterus. From this and other material the fantasy of being safely nourished and loved in the confines of the mother's body became evident.

In this context of rivalry for a mother figure's love and food, the patient recalled the following incident. When he was four years old, in the backyard of his house a bird's nest had fallen out of a tree and one of the fledglings had fallen out of the nest. The patient approached the little bird, intending to put it back into the nest. At that moment, however, the mother bird flew towards the patient's face, frightening him. In his confusion he stepped on the fledgling and killed it. When the patient finished recalling the account of this event, he added, "This was about the time that my younger brother was born."

Thus, the original event of the encounter on the staircase leading to the analyst's office and the fear of being punished led to a train of events and memories which ultimately eventuated in the recall of an incident, or perhaps even only a fantasy, which corresponded precisely to the elements of the analyst's original interpretation of the patient's associations, namely, his aggressive wishes towards sibling figures and his fear of being punished. Thus, thrusting the fledgling from the nest and destroying it would correspond to a wish to injure and/or dislodge the younger brother from his mother's abdomen and the fear of being punished. These thoughts or memories, however, the patient did not recall. Had he perhaps at one time violently bumped his mother's abdomen when she was pregnant with his younger brother and been slapped for it? Or had he only wished that he should have done it and was afraid that he would have been punished for it? The memory or fantasy of dislodging the fledgling bird and killing it in this instance served a screening function, helping to keep in repression the recollection of an impulse or an event concerning assaulting his mother's pregnant body. Clearly in this instance the transference episode led to a memory of a derivative, substitute representation of an actual wish or experience. It was offered up as a screening substitute for the recollection of the actual event or fantasy.

Looking back at Freud's dictum that hysterical symptoms replace the memory of actual traumatic events, it would be perhaps more accurate to say that they displace such memories, that they help serve the function of keeping such painful recollections out of consciousness. This may be a tiny semantic change, but it serves to underscore the thesis that I have been presenting. To illustrate my thesis, I will cite some material from the analysis of a conversion symptom. This material is taken from modified analytic work with a woman well on in years. She had two periods of rather prolonged analysis, which proved helpful in many ways but did not bring her relief of certain phobias, e.g., anxiety about eating in restaurants, and conversion symptoms, chief among which were very distressing headaches. The stumbling block in her previous treatment seemed to concern an event which took place when she was about eight years old. She was living in a tenement. There had been a fire in one of the apartments on an upper story. After the fire had been extinguished, a fireman was designated to stay in the apartment to prevent it from being vandalized. At first the patient and some of her girlfriends, out of curiosity, went to see the apartment and the fireman, who seemed to be a genial enough person. After a while, the patient began to come to the apartment by herself. Then something happened. The patient did not know what but she recalled being very upset and running from the apartment. Shortly after that her family moved from that tenement and the patient wondered if something about what happened between her and the fireman had become public knowledge and therefore forced her parents to move.

In the course of our work, the amnesia surrounding the experience with the fireman lifted slowly and in stages. First she recalled just sitting and talking with the fireman. Then she remembered his going to the bathroom and leaving the door of the bathroom open. Later she was able to remember that she had gone to the entrance of the bathroom and had watched the fireman urinate. A good time later she remembered how they sat at the little bridge table that was set up in the kitchen of the burned out apartment and played cards. She then remembered that he also played with her, putting his hand underneath the table and fondling her genitals. The door to the apartment was open so that the patient and the fireman could be observed by someone passing by in the hall. Now the patient recalled that, on the day that she fled in panic from that apartment, she and the fireman had gone into a back room, out of view of the hallway. What happened there she could not recall.

At a session somewhat later, the patient began to extol my intellectual capacity—how well I remembered things, how cleverly I put various bits of information together so that they began to build up into a pattern, what a good head I had on my shoulders, how admirable, how she enjoyed seeing the way my mind works.

I said, "It sounds like the way you felt about the fireman." At this the patient said, "I have a terrible headache now." I asked her to describe it to me.

This was her description. "It begins at the base of my neck. Everything feels engorged and hot and swollen. Then I feel a throbbing in my neck which goes up to my head and my head begins to swell, and the throbbing keeps getting worse until I feel I may have a stroke and die."

The patient recognized immediately the similarity of the description of this symptom to the tumescence of a penis. I noted that, if she was feeling swelling and experiencing throbbing, it meant that she must have held the fireman's penis. Perhaps she felt him ejaculating. She did not recall any of this, but she did remember that he took a handkerchief out of his pocket. Thereafter she fled and never went back to the apartment again. It is clear from this material that the patient identified herself, or at least that part of the anatomy from her neck up, with the fireman's penis and the symptom took the place of the actual memory of feeling the penis engorge and ejaculate. The latter she did not recall. Whether further work would have resulted in a completion of her memory of the event we cannot say, but we can observe that throughout the years the recollection of the details of the experience had been warded off by the appearance of her conversion symptom, which recapitulated or, perhaps more precisely, was a memory of what she had seen and felt.

In a certain sense repetition in action as a substitute for remembering is a constant feature of the psychoanalytic therapeutic experience, although it may not be recognized as such. In fact, however, how the patient responds to the analyst's intervention or interpretation, especially to the elucidation of the drive derivative, tends to recapitulate the psychological history of the patient. The patient responds to the analyst's intervention as earlier in his or her life he or she responded to the same impulse derivative when it rose from within the individual.

The variations of the patterning in the structure of the memory system are so rich and varied that one could expand on illustrations almost without end. The seemingly far-fetched connections by which the web of memory is held together resemble very much the process of dream creation and representation. I have tried to emphasize in this presentation how memory constitutes a compromise formation, structured in keeping with a defensive function, namely, to avoid the unpleasure or pain connected with the recollection of certain experiences or fantasies. Freud (1914) approached the subject when he said, "In some cases I had an impression that the familiar childhood amnesia which is theoretically so important to us is completely counterbalanced by screen memories. Not only some but all of what is essential from childhood has been retained in these memories." (p. 148, emphasis in the original) Of course, this was written in the context of certain specific theoretical formulations concerning technique, particularly the importance of getting the patient to recollect forgotten incidents. The concept of defense, as it was later developed in the structural theory, is not yet fully appreciated in these statements. Nevertheless, the screening function of memories falls very well under the rubric of what we now recognize as compromise formations in the service of protecting the individual against painful affects (Brenner, 1974).

If one overlooks the defensive needs that underlie the structuring of memory, it is easy to fall into the impression that analyst and analysand together may create a fitting narrative to comply with what is compatible with their mutual needs and interests. What emerges from the considerations that I have been reporting is the fact that, while the derivative representations of the memory are subject to almost infinite variation and connection because of considerations of defense, nonetheless the underlying dynamic originates from a forgotten experience, an actual event and/or a fantasy that was once real and painful. As I have indicated in a previous communication (Arlow, 1969), the original painful experience of childhood is from the very beginning an amalgam of externally confirmable, i.e., "real," experience, together with the wishful, magical fantasy thinking characteristic of the early years of the child's mind.

Clinical observation leads us to the conclusion that the important memory systems of the individual are structurally organized to serve as a bulwark against the recollection of painful events. It seems as if we remember in order to forget and that we succeed at neither.

References

Arlow, J.A. (1969). Fantasy, memory and reality testing. *Psychoanalytic Quarterly,* 38:28–51.

——— (1980). The revenge motive in the primal scene. *Journal of the American Psychoanalytic Association,* 28:519–541.

——— (1991). The personal myth. In: *The Personal Myth in Psychoanalytic Theory,* ed. by Hartocollis. Madison, CT: International Universities Press, pp. 21–36.

Beres, D. & Arlow, J,A. (1974). Fantasy and identification in empathy. *Psychoanalytic Quarterly,* 43:26–50.

Brenner, C. (1974). On the nature and development of affects *Psychoanalytic Quarterly,* 43:534–566.

Breuer, J. and Freud, S. (1895). Studies in hysteria, *Standard Edition,* Vol 2, pp. 1–17.

Freud, S. (1899). Screen memories. *Standard Edition,* Vol. 3, pp. 303–322.

——— (1900). The interpretation of dreams. *Standard Edition,* Vols. 4 and 5.

——— (1905). Psychopathology of everyday life. *Standard Edition, Vol. 6, pp. vii–296.*

——— (1914). Remembering, repeating and working through. *Standard Edition.* Vol. 2, pp. 147–156.

——— (1925). An autobiographical study. *Standard Edition,* Vol. 20, pp. 3–74.

——— (1937). Constructions in analysis. *Standard Edition,* Vol. 23, pp. 255–269.

Jacobson, E. (1954). The self and the object world. *Psychoanalytic Study of the Child,* 9:75–127.

Kris, E. (1956). The personal myth. *Journal of the American Psychoanalytic Association,* 4:653-681.

Lewin, B. (1955). Dream psychology and the analytic situation. In: *Selected Writings.* New York: *Psychoanalytic Quarterly,* 1973, pp. 264–290.

Reiser, M. (1991). *Memory in Mind and Brain.* New Haven, CT: Yale University Press.

EDUCATIONAL OBJECTIVE

The purpose of this communication is to demonstrate how memories are organized in a systematic way, serving at once both a function of assembling the significant events of the past into a meaningful pattern, and at the same time acting as a bulwark against the recollection of painful, traumatic events. As a mental function, memories are systematically arranged in keeping with the general psychological tendency towards compromise formation.

Chapter 12

Time and Mind: A Psychoanalytic Perspective

Jacob A. Arlow, MD

Commentary: Nancy R. Goodman, PhD

This paper brings together philosophers, historians, and psychoanalytic thinkers about the topic of time—how to conceive of it and times clinical significance. Arlow is presenting this paper in a lecture series on Psychoanalysis and the Humanities giving the audience a psychoanalytic perspective. He gives an overview of the way the subject matter has been written about in Western cultural history. He then switches to address questions most relevant for psychoanalysts concerning the feel and connections of present, past, and future; the development thrust from infancy on, the way psychoanalysts listen to associations (of their patients and of themselves) and the essential nature of the unconscious and memory. It is enriching to observe how he weaves this all together. Elements he defines as essential for understanding time in general, duration and succession, take on particular meaning when considering the development of a sense of self, the flow of associations during psychoanalytic sessions, the psychic productions of dreams, and the here and now of sessions. For Arlow, the self is a timebound concept indicating that inner experience of past, present, and future are held together to form the self. He quotes

189

Harticollis, a psychoanalytic writer about time, in stating that the self is the container of consciousness. Arlow has written much about the distortions of time presented by patients such as *déjà vu*, derealization, and depersonalization; and emphasizes that unconscious desires, the wishes of childhood, are the basis for the eeriness of such experiences. Following from earlier writing, he here reiterates the importance of listening to such states of mind to identify them and to also hear the derivatives of drive configurations throughout development.

Addressing how the child comes to have a time sense he returns to understanding about the infant, the infant who subjectively knows movement between need and gratification. He is thorough in tracing ideas from Freud such as the way the wish and the fantasy arise from unpleasure and distress. It is very moving to read his weaving together the infant feeling of satiety or frustration and the growing sense of remembering the body of the mother and the face of the mother. These impressions appear and function in time and space. One can feel the infant developing internal objects in his descriptions. The free association process and dreaming bring attention to sequencing and propinquity where Arlow sees the unconscious wishes to appear. The reordering of what comes first and last found in many dreams he sees as expressive of the "heart's desire". Death is what Arlow calls the inevitable confrontation often greeted by the mind's creation of fantasies pertaining to a time warp, meant to undo the rules incest taboo separating the generations. In this paper, we find a page missing and wonder what he would say about the wish to conquer death. Thus some patients living in sense of suspended time are keeping their oedipal wishes ready to be fulfilled. This is brought to the transference so that the now is what was in the past and is still in conflict. As if addressing our present-day crisis of COVID 19, Arlow expresses the powerful intersect of reality and unconscious fantasy in stating that current events activate derivatives of unconscious fantasies and unconscious fantasies influence perceptions of current events.

Time and Mind: A Psychoanalytic Perspective

Jacob A. Arlow, MD (New York)

It is an honor indeed to participate in this lecture series on "Psychoanalysis and the Humanities," sponsored by the Kanzer Foundation. The subject I have chosen for this evening's presentation, "Time and Mind: A Psychoanalytic Perspective," is intended to continue in the spirit of previous presentations in this series.

Time is a subject that is central to our human experience, for time is essentially a question of man. It is inseparable from his humanity. "Time has no reality apart from the medium of human thought and experience. While a great variety of temporal phenomena have a reality independent of man, man is nevertheless the only being on earth with an awareness of time, a being for whom the problem of time is not merely one of theory, but one which is supremely and intimately related to the conduct of his life" (Kummel, 1966, page 32). An element of poignancy is added when we consider that man is probably the only creature conscious of his limited sojourn within the bounds of time.

Accordingly, it is my intention to discuss how considerations of time enter into psychoanalytic concepts of the mind and, in turn, how such concepts contribute some understanding to how we experience time. This is a vast subject. No one volume, let alone a single lecture, could deal with the issues in a comprehensive fashion. Nevertheless, it may prove fruitful to concentrate

191

on some aspects of time that seem central to the psychoanalytic theory of the mind.

Fundamentally, psychoanalysis is a time-related discipline; that is to say, as a mode of treatment, it is an historical discipline. It began as an effort to understand how disturbances of the present are determined by experiences of the past. Genetic propositions of etiology are fundamental to psychoanalysis. In part, it may be said that psychoanalysis attempts to free the individual of the baleful influence of the past by reordering the patient's view of the etiological, temporal sequences of his experience and by filling in the gaps in the memory of those sequences. The goal of treatment is to free the patient of the consequences of unresolved conflicts of the past, in order to enable him to effect a more adaptive resolution of these conflicts for the sake of his future.

Although it has engaged man's imagination since the beginnings of recorded history, time has remained an elusive subject. As we know, time is not sensed by direct awareness. There are no receptive structures for time comparable to the retina and the cochlear apparatus. Most students of the subject agree that we do not have any truly primitive experience of time as such. "Our direct experience is always of the present and our idea of time comes from reflecting on that experience" (Whitrow, 1980, page 61). Thus, Whitrow, says, "our sense of time is neither a necessary condition of our experience, as Kant thought, nor a central sensation, as Mach believed, but an intellectual construction. It depends on processes of mental organization uniting thought and action. It is a late product of human evolution, in all probability closely related to the development of language" (page 64).

Far from being a simple matter of direct sensation, even our psychological present must be regarded as the product of an elaborate construction. It is intimately related to our past, since it depends upon our immediate memory, but it also determines our attitude to the immediate future. The vagueness which seems to characterize its temporal extension is inherent in its nature. The construction of the present, wrote Janet (1928), prevents a precise determination of its duration, for, in the words of Whitehead (1920), "the temporal breadths of the immediate duration of sense awareness are very indeterminant and dependent on the individual percipient. What we perceive as present is the vivid fringe of memory, tinged with anticipation" (pages 72–73).

What unites thought and action is the concept of change. Without change, Aristotle noted, time does not exist. But what changes—the changes in our sensations or the changes in our thoughts? The empirical philosophers, Locke, Berkeley and Hume, agreed that the notion of time originated in an awareness of succession of ideas in the mind. According to Hume (1874), without a succession of <u>perceptions</u>, we have no notion of time. Time "is always discovered by some perceivable succession of changeable objects" (page 342). Locke placed greater emphasis on the awareness of the succession of one's own <u>thoughts</u>. According to him, a person at rest, without perceiving any motion at all, is aware of his own thoughts as they appear one after the other. In such a case, the individual would be observing succession without motion of physical objects. Thus, while Hume underscored awareness of changes in physical objects, Locke (1894) emphasized awareness of the experience of the self. The manifold implications of these thoughts will become apparent presently.

In this connection Kummel (1966) posed the problem: If the notion of time is understood as deriving from a succession of present moments, the question inevitably arises as to the possibility of <u>duration</u> in time. On the other hand, if characterizing time as a simple before and after relationship is not adequate, what is the specific nature of the relationship between past, present and future? Simply put, "We conceive of time either as flowing or as enduring. The problem is how to reconcile these concepts. Duration without succession would lose all its temporal characteristics and would have to be conceived as an unchanging present. Pure succession without duration is equally inconceivable. The theory of time, therefore, cannot impose an either/or alternative between these two characteristics, but must instead seek to understand them in their necessary correlation" (pages 34–35). Fraser (1975) attempted to resolve the problem as follows. In its broadest sense, he wrote, time could he considered as a construct that refers to the perception or imputation of change against some background that is taken to be relatively permanent. For a change to be perceived or imputed, there has to be both succession and duration; that is, when two successive events are separated by an interval, the interval between them is called duration. Hence, duration is defined by succession. The reverse also holds true. For two events to be successive, there must be a time gap, a duration between them.

If time may be considered as a construct that refers to the perception or imputation of change against some background that is taken to be relatively permanent, the question arises: What is that background? What is it that changes and yet endures? A suggestion to the solution of this problem, it seems, was made by Locke (1894) when he said, "For whilst we are thinking or whilst we receive successively several ideas in our mind, we know that we do exist, and so we call the existence or the continuation of the existence of ourselves, or anything commensurate with the succession of any ideas in our mind, the duration of <u>ourselves,</u> or any other such thing coexistent with our thinking" (page 239). These considerations would lead me to suggest that the relatively permanent background against which change is perceived is, from its very inception, the self. In our awareness, it is the self which is enduring and yet continuously changing. It is the self that has a history, a succession of events that have been endured. It is the self that has a past, present and future.

The self concept is a difficult one. It is a unique and curious symbol. There is nothing in the external world which corresponds to it. It represents an object, the "I," which is assumed to function totally in the external world, as do all other objects, yet it cannot ever be totally apprehended by our senses, as one can do in the case of other objects, to some of whom we impute selves as well. We think of ourselves as residing in our bodies and to a certain extent we incorporate the body image partly into our concept of ourselves. It may be in part an imaginary construction; yet it is one of which we have a sense of more or less immediate apprehension. As in the case of other objects, we do not always understand it, nor do we always like it, but we feel secure in the knowledge of its history, which we can conjure up in the form of re-presentations, which constitute the memory of an organized past, of a continuity of identity. What can be re-presented to the mind, as a record of past experience in the case of the self, is not only the record of past perceptions, but representations of inner experience, memories, thoughts, theories, concepts, a good portion or which constitute the exclusive property of the self.

The self is a timebound concept. The sense of continuity and permanence of the self concept is stoutly maintained. There is an inwardly acknowledged conviction of self identity and continuity that parallels but remains forever stronger than the sense of continuity and permanence pertaining to an object. Identity implies that a self or an object is the same entity at different points in time, no matter what changes or transformations may have taken place in the intervening years. Earlier representations of the self may have been repudiated or disavowed; hut the sense of connection is hardly ever sundered in an absolute way. The disruptions and dissolutions of the sense of self in the psychoses, of course, represent a notable exception.

No sense of time would be possible without the consciousness of self, for there is no meaningful concept of the self without consciousness and there is no consciousness without the self—the self is the container of consciousness (Hartocollis, 1983, page 45). Thus, Schilder (1936) stated that any disturbance or the sense of self inevitably must result in a distortion of the sense of time. He did not document this statement with clinical examples, but appropriate illustrations are not difficult to find. I have noted several examples in previous communications (Arlow, 1959, 1966, 1984), e.g., depersonalization, derealization, déjà vu.

As a consequence of empathic or intuitive processes, a sense of self is projected or recognized in others. A sense of selfhood may even be projected onto institutions and nations. These are endowed with a sense of a continuing, collective identity, with the illusion of permanence. But all illusions of permanence and grandeur, whether of the self, of others, of institutions or nations, fade into nothingness as the individual becomes aware of the reality of death. For the individual, death means the extinction of self, of consciousness and, accordingly, of time. The self can no longer serve as the unchanging background for the construct of time. By way of compensation and illusory wish fulfillment, the shattered sense of a persistent, unchanging self is projected outward onto objects we hope or assume will persist forever. Thus, the poet endows nature with a consciousness, so that it may serve as the permanent witness to his passing life and love. The astrophysicist imagines an enduring consciousness, observing the cosmic changes, and the religionist posits an all-knowing eternal deity, with a self-consciousness not very different from that of his own creations. Nothingness is as inconceivable as death is unacceptable.

Analytic, as well as non-analytic observers, agree that the beginning of time sense is intermingled with the impression of physiological duration connected with the intervals between need and gratification. In his paper on "The Primal Cavity," Spitz (1955) conjectures the state of mind of the very young infant as a set of impressions without time or space relationship. There is a simultaneity of impressions independent of any recollections of the past. When there is no separation between self and the external world, experience is without a time dimension. It is truly timeless.

But, as Freud (1900) put it, the exigencies of life in the form of somatic needs alter the infant's primordial bliss. Feelings of unpleasure, which are of undoubted survival value from the evolutionary point of view, give rise to distress.

"A change can come about in some way or other (in the case of the baby through outside help). An experience of 'satisfaction' can be achieved which puts an end to the internal stimulus. An essential component of this experience of satisfaction is a particular perception (that of nourishment, for example), the mnemic image of which remains then associated thenceforward with the memory trace of the excitation produced by the need. As a result of the link that has thus been established, the next time this need arises, a psychical impulse will at once emerge, which will seek... to re-evoke the perception itself, that is to say, to reestablish the situation of the original satisfaction. An impulse of this kind is what we call a wish; the reappearance of the perception is the fulfillment of the wish; ... thus the aim of this first psychical activity was to produce a 'secondary' perceptual identity—a repetition of the perception which was linked with the satisfaction of the need" (p. 565).

Freud developed these ideas in connection with the psychology of dreams. He expanded the implication of these concepts when he turned to more general principles of mental functioning. While hallucinatory wish fulfillment could achieve an identity of perception, it did not bring about the essential diminution or disappearance of the feelings of unpleasure. Thus, need tension directed the mental apparatus to the significance of the external world, for in the real world lay the promise of experiencing a set of perceptions that could abolish the unpleasure occasioned by physiological needs. Thus, the psychic apparatus had to form a conception of the real circumstances in the external world and to endeavor to make a real alteration in them.

Thus, we see that, at its inception, Freud saw the mind as passing judgment or, as we would say today, processing the data of perception according to the criteria of familiar or unfamiliar, pleasurable or unpleasurable, internal or external, thought or image, real or unreal. Categorization of mental presentations according to the criterion of familiarity perforce introduces some precursor of the notion of the past and of memory. A meaningful concept of the past is only achieved later in the course of development. "For memory to acquire the quality of 'pastness' it is necessary to perceive the fact that the recalled experience can no longer be altered, either by the subject's own action or passively by some intervention from the outside." (Hartocollis, 1983, page 39). Also, since no new experience can, in fact, achieve a complete perceptual identity with a memory of previous gratification, it may safely be assumed that the grouping together of mental presentations according to pleasure involves a set of approximations rather than identity. Accordingly, various memory systems or schema may be established, in which experiences are associatively linked according to the criterion of similarity. Thus, from early on, there is a very human tendency to assimilate experience metaphorically, a tendency that paves the way for symbolism and makes possible the later development of art and poetry. Precisely how the brain stores the organized patterns of perception and memory has proved to be an elusive problem, but clinical experience, using the technique of free association, furnishes convincing evidence of how concepts and memories are related and connected according to similarity.

If feelings of frustration in the interval between need and satisfaction give rise to a sense of duration, it is the experience of gratification of those needs that articulates the crucial significance of succession of impressions, of the sequence of events. Out of repeated experiences of need gratification, events begin to fall into a pattern of sign and satisfaction, to an ordering of events in sequence that becomes meaningful in terms of need gratification. The succession of events that begins with an awareness of need accompanied by sensations of unpleasure, and which then culminates in need gratification and alleviation of discomfort, falls into a linear pattern of contingent meanings. The contiguity of events in a linear time sequence brings each element in the series into a relationship of meaning or causality with the other. Contiguity of elements in time becomes the basic underpinning of our primitive concepts of causality. We never quite give up the idea of post hoc, ergo propter hoc. As a result of the ability to interpret each element in the linear sequence as one in a series of signals leading to gratification, a more distal signal, i.e., the appearance of the mother's face, may serve as a reassuring, symbolic substitute for the actual experience of gratification the child has begun to anticipate. This is the dawn of the future. It is also, as Kris (1950) pointed out, one of the first steps in the development of object constancy. The ability of the child to anticipate quietly that the mother will return to alleviate his discomfort signalizes that she exists as a separate entity, independent of his immediate feelings of distress. In terms of object relations, the point is that the development of object constancy really means the evolution of an organized concept of a sense of sensory impressions that functions independently in time and space.

The temporal ordering of signals has its obvious counterpart in the temporal ordering of symbols. The most significant example is to be found, of course, in the specific human capacity for speech and language. To be meaningful, communication by speech and language must conform to certain temporal orderings of words. Changing the context or contiguity of elements inevitably changes meanings. If the rules of linear succession of the elements in the sentence are violated, communication becomes either obscure, ambiguous or totally disrupted. This holds true not only for meaning conveyed in sentences, but also in the relationship of one sentence to another. Certain elements in the sequential order of meaning may be omitted in conversation or writing, but they are usually unconsciously substituted in consequence of established modes of communication. However, if the necessary information or words linking utterances or sentences in appropriate temporal and communicative significance are omitted, meaning is impaired and communication becomes impossible. Defensive distortion of time relationships is one of the factors which renders dreams unintelligible. "Quite a common technique of dream distortion consists in representing the outcome of an event or a conclusion of a train of thought at the beginning of the dream and of placing at its end the premises on which the conclusion was based or the causes which led to the event" (Freud, 1900, page 328). In secondary process thinking, causes precede effects in time.

Appreciating the significance of the succession of thoughts and actions in the psychoanalytic situation is of paramount importance. The context and contiguity in which associations appear are among the best means of understanding the unconscious processes in a patient's mind. Succession of elements, similar or opposites, creates the framework within which meaning is extracted. This principle was enunciated by Freud in "The Interpretation of Dreams" (1900), in which he said, "In a psychoanalysis, one learns to interpret propinquity in time as representing connection in subject matter. Two thoughts which occur in immediate sequence without any apparent connection are part of a single unity, which has to be discovered. In just the same way, if I write an 'a' and a 'b' in succession, they have to be pronounced as a single syllable. The same is true of dreams." (p. 247), and "Dreams reproduce logical connection by simultaneity in time and the element of causality is represented in the dream by a temporal sequence. Either one image is transformed into another, or one sentence is followed by another." (p. 314).

This principle, it seems to me, has not been honored sufficiently in clinical practice. During the actual conduct of psychoanalytic therapy, the analyst for the most part responds intuitively to the temporal patterning of the patient's associations. By this I mean that the significant connections are effected in the analyst's mind outside of the scope of consciousness. This is appropriate, but there is a great yield of insight to be achieved by enhanced sensitivity to the moment-to-moment unfolding of the patient's associations, to the cognitive processing of the successive ordering of the patient's thoughts as they appear in consciousness. Examined in this light, the stream of the patient's associations is a sample in time, not only of the dynamic effect of unconscious wishes, but also of the contributions of each of the component parts of the psychic apparatus.

The link between the linear concept of time to causality and then to science is an obvious one. To test a prediction, the tenses—past, present and future—must be kept distinct, and there must be precision about succession and duration. The scientific concept of objective time as opposed to human time is a triumph of man's ability to express relationships, movement and change in spatial terms. By conceiving of time in units that are equal in size, unlimited in extension and infinitely divisible, science has been able to extend control over the physical world. Against this background, some authors have proposed generalizations that relate the level of technological and scientific attainment to the presence or absence of a linear concept of time. Thus, Melges (1982) states that Western time is linear and Oriental time is circular. Certain cultures, it is claimed, have a nonlinear concept of time because their language has no words for past, present or future. Instead of speaking of the future, for example, they have "present anticipations." The author concludes that "cultures that have no concept of linear time appear to be vulnerable to the influence of myths and magic, perhaps because they have no ready method for distinguishing fact from fantasy" (page 8).

There are dangers in generalizations, especially those based on extrapolations from one culture to another. To begin with, the ordering of thoughts and events in sequence is inescapable. Furthermore, the concept of recurrent cycles of large segments of time does not rule out the linear sequential arrangements of events in any

[Page 19 of the paper ends with the above text. Pages 20 and 21 are missing; page 22 begins with what follows.]

results. A remembered sequence of events, elements of the past and anticipation of reappearance of the perception in a certain setting in the future, help create what is considered real, as distinguished from what is thought in the mind. Thus, the nature of reality is fashioned by the notion of a predictable sequence of events. When the experienced and inevitable order of events is violated, the experience is interpreted as unreal. In dreams, the total disregard of the accustomed order of events is one element which brings about the quality of unreality or absurdity. In the same way, when we observe a motion picture film being played backwards, we interpret the experience as unreal, because time reversal is not part of our experience.

In dreams, it is possible to re-order time relationships "nearer to the heart's desire." In reality, it is not possible. The past cannot be undone. The inexorable advance of time is the great frustrater of infantile omnipotence and wishful thinking. It resonates earlier experiences of wishes inhibited or denied by the parents. Thus, time and reality become identified with the frustrations imposed by authority figures and caretakers. Time becomes one of the chief instrumentalities of the reality principle in subduing pleasure and, on that account, to a certain degree it is forever after resented (Gifford, 1960; Yates, 1935). In the iconography of Western civilization, time, in the guise of the omnipotent father, comes to symbolize the ultimate frustrater.

For the gravest insult to the self is, of course, the inevitable confrontation with death. That is a dimension of one's experience in time that cannot be avoided. Accordingly, there is a rich literature in our culture based on fantasies of eliminating, mastering, controlling or suspending time indefinitely. Particularly striking are those fantasies of time warp, which have their source in the oedipal conflicts. These are fantasies in which the time experience is altered so as to make possible the loving union of two people from different generations, temporarily becoming roughly the same age in a world of suspended time.

The most definitive retreat from time perhaps takes the form of lapsing into a state of timelessness, of attaining a feeling of eternity. The most popular avenue of entree to that domain of bliss appears to be by way of drugs or meditation. Discussions of timelessness usually convey a sense of mystical transcendence. Timelessness has been identified with the so-called "oceanic" feeling, with a sense of merging with the universe that is supposed to characterize certain experiences of religious ecstasy. Most psychoanalysts, following Freud's lead (1930), regard the attainment of a sense of timelessness as a regressive recapitulation of the experience of blissful satiety which the infant enjoyed while falling asleep in his mother's arms.. This is a difficult proposition to substantiate. Clinical evidence to support the hypothesis has not been forthcoming.

From my own investigations (Arlow, 1959, 1966, 1982, 1984, 1986), I have come to interpret experiences of timelessness as representing the intrusion into conscious mental life of derivatives of unconscious conflict. For a variety of motives, the wish for endless duration, for nothing ever to change, is experienced consciously as already fulfilled, much as occurs in the manifest content of a dream. One patient, for example, experienced timelessness while in a state of exultation over a success which she felt she owed to her father. He was ill and she wished to be able to endow him with health and life so the two of them could live happily ever after. Another patient, whose castration anxiety was experienced in terms of fear of death, never wanted to grow older. In a situation evocative of severe castration anxiety, he would defensively experience a sense of timelessness as a form of victory over death. Other distortions of the sense of time, as observed in déjà vu, depersonalization, derealization, expansion or contraction of time, and in premonition (Stein, 1953), demonstrate the effects of the same mechanism, namely, the intrusion of elements of wish, defense or punishment into the conscious experience of time.

When Freud spoke of the timelessness of the unconscious, what he wished to emphasize was that the wishes of childhood remain persistently active in the mind. They do not change with time. (Loewenstein reported this from his correspondence with Freud on the subject, 1958, p. 151.) These wishes become part of the persistent unconscious fantasies that continue to exert their influence on mental activity. They create a mental set against which the data of sensation are selectively perceived, registered, interpreted and responded to (Arlow, 1969a, 1969b). For example, in connection with remembering, Bartlett (1932) maintained that memory is not a set of static engrams, but is influenced dynamically by the changing framework of associations determined by the evolution of our interest and our powers of reason and imagination. In other words, recall is a constructive process and never literally repeats our past experience or activity. Memory, in particular, is affected by the persistent influence on the present of the dynamic unconscious fantasies from the past.

This leads us directly to the all-important question of the flux of time. In common with many authors, Jaques (1982) raises this question as his point of departure. "All the difficulties of understanding the meaning of time are contained in the riddle of past, present and future. Are they coterminous? Does one flow into the other? Does the future become the present and then the past?" (p. 4) But the flux of time is precisely the concern of psychoanalysis. As already noted, our direct experience is always of the present. Perhaps more than any other discipline, psychoanalysis sheds light on the coexistence of past, present and future. In a most penetrating contribution to the subject, Loewald (1962) points out that psychic structures must be regarded as temporal in nature. They exist in time and they develop in time. The time concept involved is psychological time, which implies an active relation between the temporal modes past, present and future. From the point of view of objective time, what we call the past, as in transference, is not <u>in</u> the past but in the present. It is active in the "now." Furthermore, as I have indicated, there is a reciprocal interplay between unconscious fantasy and external stimuli. Current events activate the appearance of derivatives of unconscious fantasies and unconscious fantasy wishes influence how the present experience is apprehended. As regards the future, Loewald states, "In terms of psychic time, the relation between ego and superego can be seen as a mutual relation between psychic present and psychic future. In the structure of the superego, the ego confronts itself in the light of its own future. The establishment of the superego completes the constitution of an inner world, whose dimension may be said to be the temporal modes past, present and future" (page 264).

Let me give a few examples to demonstrate how the psychoanalytic approach integrates the three dimensions of time—past, present and future. Nowhere is this better illustrated perhaps than in the phenomenology of transference. In transference, the experience and the fantasy wishes of the past are foisted upon objects in the present and are felt as anticipations of gratification in the future. In the analysis of premonition, for example, a repudiated (death) wish of the past, dynamically active in the present, is experienced as an inevitable but a dreaded anticipation of the future (Stein,1953). In déjà vu, a perception of the present, which portends danger in the future, is reassuringly endowed with the quality of an experience in the past, an experience of a danger that has already been successfully mastered. Psychoanalysis thus represents the method that supplies the depth and detail to Whitehead's (1920) beautiful summary of the flux of time previously quoted: "What we perceive as the present is the vivid fringe of memory tinged with anticipation" (pages 72–73).

Because our session here is not timeless, I must find a point to conclude. In "Beyond the Pleasure Principle," Freud (1920) appears to have anticipated much of tonight's discussion when he wrote, "Our abstract idea of time seems to be wholly derived from the method of working of the system PCP-Cs and to correspond to a perception on its own part of that method of working" (page 28). If we translate the terminology of the topographic theory into structural language, Freud seems to be saying that our abstract idea of time seems to derive from the interaction between perception and self observation. In previous communications, I have suggested that variations in the relationship between these two fundamental factors of experience are among the fundamental determinants of alterations of the experience of time. The further pursuit of that subject must be left for some other time, for the subject is as vast as time is boundless.

References

Arlow, J.A. (1959). The structure of the déjà vu experience. *Journal of the American Psychoanalytic Association,* 7:611–631.

———— (1966). Depersonalization and derealization. In: *Psychoanalysis—A General Psychology. Essays in Honor of Heinz Hartmann,* ed. by R.M. Loewenstein et al. New York: International Universities Press, pp. 456–478.

———— (1969a). Fantasy, memory and reality testing. *Psychoanalytic Quarterly,* 38:28–51.

———— (1969b). Unconscious fantasy and disturbances of conscious experience. *Psychoanalytic Quarterly,* 38:1–27.

———— (1982). Scientific cosmogony, mythology and immortality. *Psychoanalytic Quarterly,* 51:177–195.

———— (1984). Disturbances of the sense of time. *Psychoanalytic Quarterly,* 53:13–37.

———— (1986). Psychoanalysis and time. *Journal of the American Psychoanalytic Association* 34:507-528.

Bartlett, F.C. (1932). *Remembering.* Cambridge: Cambridge University Press.

Fraser, J.T. (1975). *Of Time, Passion and Knowledge.* New York: George Braziller.

Freud, S. (1900). The interpretation of dreams. *Standard Edition,* Vols. 4 and 5.

———— (1911). Formulations on the two principles of mental functioning. *Standard Edition,* Vol. 12, pp. 218–226.

———— (1920). Beyond the pleasure principle. *Standard Edition,* Vol. 18, pp. 3–64.

———— (1925). On negation. *Standard Edition,* Vol. 19, pp. 235–239.

———— (1930). Civilization and its discontents. *Standard Edition,* Vol. 21, pp. 64–143.

Gifford, S. (1960). Sleep, time and the early ego. Comments on the development of the 24-hour sleep-wakefulness pattern as a precursor of ego function.

Journal of the American Psychoanalytic Association, 8:5–42.

Hartocollis, P. (1983) Time and Timelessness. New York: International Universities Press.

Hoffer, W. (1949). Mouth, hand and ego integration. *Psychoanalytic Study of the Child,* 3–4:49–56.

Hume, D. (1874). *A Treatise on Human Nature,* edited by T.H. Green and T.H. Grose.

London: Longmans, Green & Co. (quoted by P. Fraisse in The Psychology of Time, 1963.)

Jacobson, E. (1964). *The Self and the Object World.* New York: International Universities Press.

Janet, P. (1928). *Revolution de la Memoire et de la Notion du Temps.* Paris: Chahine.

Jaques, E. (1982). *The Form of Time.* New York: Crane Russak.

Kris, E. (1950). Notes on the development of some current problems of child psychology. *Psychoanalytic Study of the Child,* 25:24–46.

Kummel, F. (1966). Time as succession and the problem of duration. In: *Voices of Time,* edited by J.T. Fraser. New York: George Braziller, pp. 31–55.

Locke, J. (1894). *Essay Concerning Human Understanding;* edited by Alexander Campbell Fraser. Oxford: Oxford Clarendon Press.

Loewald, H. (1962). Superego and time. *International Journal of Psycho-Analysis,* 43:264–268.

Loewenstein, R.M. (1958). Panel on Psychoanalytic Theory of Thinking, reported by J.A. Arlow. *Journal of the American Psychoanalytic Association,* 6:143–153.

Mahler, M., Pine, F., and Bergmann, A. (1975). *The Psychological Birth of the Human Infant.* New York: Basic Books.

Melges, F.T. (1982). *Time and the Inner Future.* New York: John Wiley & Sons.

Piaget, J. (1953). *The Child's Construction of Reality,* translated by M. Cook. London: Routledge and Keegan Paul, Chapter 4.

Schilder, P. (1936). Psychopathology of time .*Journal of Nervous and Mental Diseases,* 83:530-546.

Spitz, R. (1955). The primal cavity. *Psychoanalytic Study of the Child,* 10:215–240.

Stein, M. (1953). Premonition as a defense. *Psychoanalytic Quarterly,* 22:69–74.

Whitehead, A.N. (1920). *The Concept of Nature.* Cambridge: Cambridge University Press.

Whitrow, G.J. (1980). *The Natural Philosophy of Time.* Oxford: Oxford University Press.

Yates, S. (1935). Some aspects of time difficulties and their relation to music. *International Journal of Psycho-Analysis,* 16:341–354.

Chapter 13

The Superego
Notes and Problems

Jacob A. Arlow, MD

Commentary: Kimberly L. Kleinman, MS, LCSW.

Arlow re-examines the concept of the superego. He provides clarification and also keeps the door open to greater and clearer iterations. He erases the misconception that the superego springs whole from the oedipal phase and instead emphasizes that the superego began its development before the oedipal phase and continues throughout life. He demonstrates how one's ideal and one's moral positions are a constellation of fantasies and identifications that shift and assemble fluidly. He agrees with A. Freud's marker of the structurization of the superego (the capacity to see one's faults) *and* he emphasizes that the superego could hardly be a structure per se.

Arlow's overview of the formation of the superego contradicts theorists who think that Arlow adhered to a one person psychology. The "real" parent, the fantasy parent, the interaction of the parent's unconscious and the child's innate characteristics create a continually evolving collage.

He rejects the idea of lacunae on that basis, it conveys the idea of a static configuration, and this does not comport with his idea that the superego cannot be typified with global labels like rigid or punitive. It is also important to note that throughout his entire discussion of superego, it's formation and function, he does not mention castration.

The Superego
Notes and Problems

Jacob A. Arlow, MD

In light of developments of the past 20 years , a reexamination of the superego concept seems to be in order. In 1960, Sandler noted the difficulty that workers at the Hampstead Clinic had in extracting from their clinical data material easily recognizable as derivatives of superego functioning. He also noted the danger of what he called "the apparent conceptual dissolution of the superego." By this he referred to the difficulty in differentiating superego function and content from the activities of the rest of the psychic apparatus, and he related this development to the confusion surrounding the understanding of the genetic roots of the superego. In large measure these difficulties have persisted to the present time. If anything, they appear to have been aggravated. Perusing our literature, one is struck by the fact that while the superego concept is mentioned frequently in contributions dealing with many subjects, the concept superego itself rarely appears as the central topic of a clinical or theoretical contribution.

Perhaps the most significant influences affecting the superego concept stem from several trends in psychoanalysis that in our time have come to occupy the center of attention. Among these are the emphasis on preoedipal factors, especially very early object relations, together with a concomitant, relative diminution of the role of conflict, particularly of the vicissitudes of the oedipal phase and its resolution. Certainly these developments reflect contemporary concern with the psychopathology of the narcissistic character disorders and of the self. Since the proponents of the theories covering these entities trace the origin of the respective, specific psychopathologies to disturbed object relations during the earliest months of life and/or to a miscarriage of the primordial empathic interaction between mother and child (Kohut, 1971), their concern for that relatively late-developing agency of the mind, the superego, is proportionately attenuated. Instead, archaic idealizations, first of the self and later of the parents, have to a considerable extent replaced the importance previously accorded the role of the superego in symptom and character formation. It is not an exaggeration to say that analysis of superego function has been shunted to one side by the current preoccupation with the persistence or the regressive reactivation of archaic idealizations. These are often confused with the precise concept of that superego component which is known as the ego ideal.

Development of the Superego

The term superego itself is somewhat misleading. It tends to evoke a somewhat closer connection to the mode of functioning of the ego than perhaps Freud had intended to suggest. Among the considerations Freud apparently had in mind in selecting this particular term were the following: as a word superego testified to the process by which this agency of the mind originated, namely, out of identifications effected in the ego with the principal figures of the oedipal constellation at the time when the conflict was being resolved. The term, accordingly, expresses in dramatic form the newly established relationship of the self, being observed and judged by an intrapsychic agency, an agency that has come to take the place of a previously existing set of interpersonal relations wherein the individual was observed from the outside by parents and surrogate parent figures.

It is, however, only in the limited sense of this aspect of the ontogenesis of the superego that we may speak with confidence of the transition from outer conflict to inner conflict, which is one of the most popular ways in which the genesis of the superego is formulated. Clinical experience and conclusions drawn from developmental studies all bear witness to the extremely complicated evolution, nature, and functioning of the superego. From the time he conceived of the superego as an independent agency, Freud warned against oversimplified approaches to understanding its functioning. He noted that the significant identifications on which the superego was based were not only with the parent of the same sex, and Anna Freud (1936) added that detachment of superego functioning from the actual parents is far from complete even at the passing of the oedipal phase.

Concerning the quality of superego functioning, Freud (1923) observed that in any individual the superego is not necessarily a replica of the behavior of the parents. The latter were not simply internalized, incorporated, or introjected. The severity or harshness of the superego may instead reflect the process of projection of the individual's own aggressiveness, and/or it may indicate how the individual misperceives the dangers of retaliation in terms of his own hostility. Hartmann and Loewenstein (1962) suggested that the severity of a child's superego may be quite independent of the actual behavior of the parents toward the child. It may have its origin in the relative economics of the instinctual situation characteristic of the child's reality. Feeling helpless and impotent in the face of the more powerful, restricting and frustrating adults, the child may turn his pent-up aggression against the self in the form of a harsh superego. Some observers, notably Johnson and Szurek (1952) noted that the nature of the child's superego may be determined not so much by the parents' actual behavior as by the nature of the parents' superego. Some parents unwittingly seduce their children into expressing their own forbidden impulses, thus attaining unconscious, vicarious gratification through the antisocial behavior of their children. I cite all of these as examples of a set of object

213

relations in which neither the overt, external behavior nor the spoken "do's" and "don'ts" correspond to what the child utilizes in constructing the guidelines for inner regulation. In a series of carefully observed cases at the Yale Child Study Center, Ritvo and Solnit (1958) pointed out how difficult it is to predict from the parent-child interaction what aspects of the parents' personality will serve as the basis for identification. In connection with the superego, Ritvo (1972) reported how it was impossible to predict from the vicissitudes of experience, particularly from the relationship to the parents, what would be the nature of the child's superego. The message that is transmitted from parent to child goes by way of very subtle forms of communication, not very different perhaps from the way unconscious content is communicated by the patient to the analyst during psychoanalytic treatment (Freud, 1900; Loewenstein, 1956; Arlow, 1979).

Although many additional pertinent observations could be adduced in this connection, only one more will be noted. Each child brings to the perception and assimilation of the meaning of his experience with the objects in his environment the influence of his own, particular, preexisting wishes and conflicts and of his persistent, unconscious fantasies. These create the mental set in terms of which the external object is perceived, organized, and apprehended (Arlow, 1969). Object representations, according to Sandler (1960), Hartmann and Loewenstein (1962), have to be considered part of the inner world, and they affect the process of identification as well as the relations with real objects (Sandler, 1960). If identification is to be described in terms of a fusion of self representation and object representation, then we must conclude that, in the process of differentiation and structuralization of the superego, instinctual elements play an important role from the very beginning. Examination of the data of regression of superego functioning, which will be discussed later, demonstrates that superego demands can be as imperious, as peremptory as any of the primary-process-dominated impulses of the id.

Although this quality of the superego does not appear anywhere in its official name, it is a quality which Freud underscored many times.

Not all the energic investment of the superego, we should note, is aggressive. There is a benign, loving aspect of the self-superego relationship, as was emphasized by Freud in his study of humor (1927), by Schafer (1960) in regard to the loving superego, and by Furar (1967) in his concept of the superego as comforter.* It should also be noted that there is a certain minimum level of psychic development that must take place before the superego emerges as an effective participant in intersystemic conflict. On the side of the ego, a certain advance in defensive function is essential. The turning of the drive against the self seems to be a forerunner of the superego's turning aggression on the self. Concerning the other ego defenses, the role of identification with the aggressor, if not explicitly stated, has been implied. Jacobson (1964) stresses the importance of the mechanism of reaction formation, but she points out that it operates not only against the aggressive impulses of the id but also against oedipal and narcissistic strivings.

In addition, there are important functions of an autonomous nature that must attain a certain development before the organization of an effective superego becomes possible—advances in intellectual ability, the mastery of language and understanding, a capacity for self-observation and for sublimation (Hartmann and Loewenstein, 1962). Anna Freud (1936) defined what may be considered the culmination of the process of superego structuralization when she said, "True morality begins when the internalized criticism, now embodied in the standard exacted by the superego, coincides with the ego's perception of its own fault" (p. 119). It takes very little to remind us how difficult it is to perceive, much less to acknowledge, one's own fault. Experiences of that sort run counter to the prevailing principle of mental life, the pleasure principle. To be sure, then, a high degree of maturation and autonomy are required to approach the attainment of such a level of both ego and superego functioning.

To summarize this part of the paper, the purpose was to demonstrate first that the path from outer conflict to inner control and conflict is not simply a matter of a set of coherent identifications; and second, that the vicissitudes of the instinctual drives and the maturation and development of the ego are essential precursors and contributors to the process of superego development. These factors are influential before, during, and after the resolution of the oedipus complex. A precise transition point marking the emergence of the superego as an independent agency, I believe, is almost impossible to delineate.

Superego as a Structure

Problems of ontogenesis direct attention to both the contents of the superego and how it functions. Piaget (1927) to the contrary notwithstanding, the young child can hardly be thought of as an accomplished logician, much less a moral philosopher. When we confront manifestations of the individual's superego activity in the clinical setting, we find that the psychological concept of good and bad is far removed from the philosopher's concept of ethics. The superego is by no means a uniform, coherent, integrated, harmonious structure. It is a mass of contradictions, fraught with internal inconsistencies, or, as we say in our technical language, intrasystemic conflicts. Its functioning is neither uniform nor reliable, and it is in this respect that the idea of a superego representing the policeman of the psyche holds up best. Like the policeman in real life, the superego is hardly around when needed most.

The superego is a conglomeration of many identifications derived from experiences with objects, from fantasies and imagination, and stemming from almost all levels of development, not necessarily exclusively those of the oedipal or the post-oedipal period. To speak of the survival of primitive idealizations within the structure of the superego as if they were isolated entities seems to me to dodge the issues. It is a fact that the persistence of archaic idealizations of the self and/or the parents may interfere with the development of later desirable types of idealization, but we should not lose sight of the fact that, during the oedipal phase, these elements are transformed and merged into the structure of the developing superego as part of the ego ideal (Hartmann and Loewenstein, 1962). Not only in narcissistic psychopathology but regularly in dreams and in fantasies, however, the regressive reemergence of representations of primitive idealizations can be observed. Perhaps we should speak of fixation points of idealizations in the superego in a manner comparable to the way we speak of fixation of instinctual components in the id or of defects or developmental weaknesses in the case of the ego. In my event, the superego functions in a very dynamic, that is, changeable way, interacting with the other components of the psychic apparatus according to how events of the individual's life stimulate conflicts and fantasies.

Moral judgment, whether directed against the self or others, and the form of punishment to be exacted are not applied uniformly and regularly. The superego is very discriminating in its treatment of the self. Like any judge in real life, it can be corrupted, seduced, deceived, beguiled, distracted, and sequestered. It is possible that the tendency we have to characterize the quality of a particular individual's superego in global terms with the deft application of a few appropriate adjectives originated from the special clinical material from which we learned about the functioning of the superego. I refer to the examples of severe abnormal operation of superego activity, as observed in depression, paranoia, severe obsessive-compulsive neurosis, etc. It is inaccurate to think of the superego as having a uniform structure, with scattered lacunae of extraordinary, incompatible functioning standing out like foreign bodies in a matrix of morality. The lacunae image is much too static a metaphor for the subtle and complex interplay between the superego and the rest of the psyche. Furthermore, what the metaphor implies is that the superego of individuals in a particular society tends to be or should be relatively the same, but we know that this is true only in the grossest way. The moral code one espouses is more a reflection of his personality than the other way around, and moral code, of course, should not be regarded as identical with one's superego.

It has been noted how the superego is built of many different experiences with objects leading to identification. Just as the object concept is capable of regressive dissolution into its antecedent representations connected with specific experiences—a regressive dissolution that takes place in consequence of conflict—so the superego is capable of regressive dissolution into its antecedent representations and experiences. Superego regression need not be uniform or complete or involve all levels of superego function equally. Some aspects of superego function may be involved without others. In this respect, one can establish a parallelism to the fate of ego functions, namely, referring to those functions that remain immune to reinstinctualization as a result of conflict and those that are vulnerable to such regressive transformation (Arlow and Brenner, 1964). It has been suggested, furthermore, that in the course of development, regression of superego functioning may occur as a precursor to the reorganization of the superego, effecting a new integration, one that leads to a more adaptive mode of superego activity. Kris (1955) described a comparable form of regression of ego function, which takes place as part of normal development and which eventuates in a more adaptive, more sublimated, ego.

There have been several attempts to split the superego as a structure, sharply separating the elements into ego ideal and superego proper respectively, the former emphasizing the "do's" and "ought to," the latter representing the "do not's" and "must not's" (Nunberg, 1926; Piers and Singer, 1953; Lampl-de Groot, 1962). On the basis of such a delineation of function, specific affects like shame and guilt could be assigned roles as regulatory agents of superego functioning, evoking specific dangers associated with prototypical, developmental encounters. While such efforts would be welcome as an attempt to simplify and clarify clinical observation, the data refuse to fall in line. The all-pervasive principle of multiple function (Waelder, 1936) works against such efforts. Besides, the idealizing "ought to" is the other side of the coin "must not." For example, someone who pursues a narcissistically grandiose ideal of perfection may experience failure in terms of an inner voice commanding, "You must not be less than perfect." A more primitive level of the same experience, reflecting perhaps stages in the development of the precursors of the superego, could be the type of self-accusatory, auditory hallucinations that Freud (1917) described in connection with melancholia. Here the reproaches against the self are once again experienced as being heard—heard, however, in the voice of some parental figure or educator who once really had admonished the patient in that fashion. How far back one wishes to extend this hierarchy of regression of superego function will depend upon one's theoretical orientation, particularly on one's concept of what the limits of reconstructing unconscious fantasy are.

In this part of the presentation, the purpose has been to emphasize two points: first, that our concepts of superego regression presuppose certain lines of development moving along a path toward a superego characterized by a noninstinctual mode of energic investment and by qualities of operation that are divested of specific object representations; and second, that the clinical phenomenology of patterns of superego functioning are usually comprehensible in terms of very specific, very concrete unconscious fantasy. This should come as no surprise, because the superego is such a latecomer in the structuring of the psyche.

The concept of the unconscious beating fantasy determining the phenomena of moral masochism can be confirmed quite readily in clinical investigation. At the same time, unconscious fantasies play an important role in how the fundamental aspects of superego theory and phenomenology are articulated. This trend recurs in such phrases as "the relationship between a sadistic superego and a masochistic ego"—a definitely anthropomorphic and concrete representation. Even Freud's mythopoetic, anthropological version of the origin of conscience in <u>Totem and Taboo</u> (1913) represents a reduplication of patients' fantasies derived from unconscious wishes of parricide and oral incorporation, followed by remorse. The ego-superego interaction originally described in melancholia is often explicitly expressed in the clinical data from certain mildly depressed cases of anxiety hysteria, where the injured lost object was imagined to have been incorporated, reconstituted, and reexperienced from within as a representation of the superego. Two clinical illustrations come to mind. The first one is from a man who had lost his twin brother during a period when they were engaged in sharp academic competition; this patient had recurrent attacks of abdominal pain, during which he would address his abdomen as if he were talking to some internal persecutor, demanding, "Why don't you let me be? Don't you think I've suffered enough?" I have presented the data pertaining to his symptomatology elsewhere (Arlow, 1960, 1976), but they demonstrated how his internal persecutor was the realization of a fantasy of the dead twin brother, personifying the patient's conscience, punishing from within the abdominal cavity. In the second case, the patient also complained of abdominal symptoms, only here they took the form of mild intestinal distress. The symptoms appeared when the patient, a Jewish ex-GI, was about to marry a German Christian girl. Several years before, on the day he left service, the patient had an automobile accident in which his wife was killed. She had been a German Jewish refugee, whom he had rescued. In celebration of his forthcoming marriage, he gave his fiancée a string of pearls. The following day he came to the session complaining of abdominal discomfort. He said he felt it was due to something that be had eaten the night before, and then he related two dreams. In the first dream, he and his fiancée passed by a store window. In the window was a portrait of his former wife, looking at him reproachfully and wearing the string of pearls he was just about to give his fiancée. In the second dream, he saw a ship that had been torpedoed. Many people were escaping, and his first wife was floating by on a dinner plate. I think the data speak for themselves.

Even more complex interrelations between superego functioning and unconscious fantasy may be demonstrated in the material of patients who suffer from criminality out of a sense of guilt, specifically criminality out of a borrowed sense of guilt. In at least half a dozen cases of this sort that I have been able to follow, it was more than a shared sense of shame that activated recurrent patterns of self-inflicted punishment. What was involved as well was an elaborate, acted-out fantasy, in which the patient identified himself with the erring parent and managed to bring upon himself the punishment that he felt should have been meted out to the parent. This theme was elaborated along many lines, through complicated scenarios often involving public humiliation and scenes of ultimately exposing the culprit to the legal and moral condemnation that he had managed to avoid in reality. What he fantasied others should have done to the parent but did not, he was acting out doing to himself.

Defenses Motivated Primarily by Supergo Anxieties

One of the striking features of superego functioning as observed in the clinical setting is the rich and subtle shifts of defense in the context of quick, facile, regressive alteration of superego function. The concept of defense used here applies to both ego and superego functioning and follows Brenner's (1981) suggestion, namely, "defense can be defined only in terms of its consequence or function: the reduction of the unpleasure aroused by a drive derivative or by some aspect of superego functioning" (p. 568). Reduction of unpleasure aroused by some aspect of superego functioning covers a most comprehensive set of experiences. Among other things, these include the unpleasure connected with what is called guilt, as well as peer disapproval, fear of punishment, etc.

Sometimes in the data of a single session, one may discern the many levels of transformation that occur in the mode and content of superego activity. Rather than describe one such session in complete detail, I shall demonstrate briefly the mechanisms employed in the course of one session in the context of the clinical material. The issue concerns the patient's conflicted feelings toward his mother. He had gradually came to understand that, without being aware of it, he was very angry with his controlling, frustrating, and rejecting mother. That the hostility had been displaced onto his wife became clear in a session in which he reported how an impulse to choke his wife to death intruded into his mind when he was beginning to make love to her. At the next session, he reported that he had had trouble falling asleep. He thought perhaps he would dream of the contents of the previous hour, but then he forgot what he had been talking about. After a while he thought he remembered. Hadn't we been talking about angry thoughts? But he did not recall any ideas of murder specifically. So here in quick succession one can observe the mechanisms of avoidance (that is, not going to sleep), repression (he forgot the idea of murder), and copping of a lesser plea (that is, confessing to the lesser charge of angry thoughts rather than murder). In an isolated, intellectualized fashion characteristic of this patient, he substituted generalized thoughts of violence for his specific wish to murder the mother (the wife, manifestly). He became overly concerned and felt extremely guilty about the possibility that he had slighted his daughter by some idle remark, and he successfully, although unconsciously, solicited, by way of displacement and exaggeration, reassurance from his wife that he need not feel guilty. When a close friend asked how the analysis was going, the patient replied that he had had a breakthrough, and he received in response from his friend congratulations for being a good subject for analysis and making progress in the session. (He did not tell him what the breakthrough was.) The patient then recalled a very upsetting telephone conversation with his mother. At the end of the conversation, after his mother had hung up, he found himself shouting into the receiver, "I hate you. I hate you. I wish you were dead." This was followed by pain in the precordium and in true observance of the lex talionis, he had a conviction that he would die. Toward the end of the session he developed a headache, which he associated with an earlier fantasy of bushing in his mother's head. Finally the session concluded with a set of testimonials to placate his conscience. He reviewed for me his recent contributions to the advancement of his community and his efforts on behalf of the common good, which in reality were considerable.

In this material one can observe the tremendous range of superego interactions, from the most primitive to the most advanced, from the primitive lex talionis thrust toward self-destruction to the sense of moral justification that comes from the performance of good deeds. In this connection, some passing note should be made of how considerations of ego interests may subvert the superego in pursuit of id gratification, the kind of problem that Rangell (1976) has emphasized in connection with public political morality. I refer, for example, to the inner advice that an individual may give himself—"Be realistic. Everybody cheats on examinations. You want to get ahead."—or the psychological morality used to justify masochistic misadventures—"Don't let them push you around. Be a man. Fight back."

Conclusions

Current trends try to emphasize an individual's earliest relations to objects in the formation of the superego. The classic view emphasized a sharp transition connected with the resolution of the oedipus complex. Clinical and developmental studies, especially postoedipal data, indicate that the superego continues to develop past the phase immediately following the resolution of the oedipus complex. The process of internalizing the environmental prohibition and rewards and the consolidations of values, ideas, and morality, it would seem, is a continuous one, with all phases of development contributing their influence. The events of the oedipal phase have been said to play the predominant role in the process. This is a proposition which perhaps has to be reexamined by closer scrutiny of the clinical data.

As examined in the clinical encounter, manifestations of superego function are highly refined, subtle, variable, and to a great extent not predictable in a very reliable way. Accordingly, an individual's superego functioning really cannot be characterized in any global way, as harsh or permissive, sadistic, severe, etc. Such characteristics come to the fore primarily when we are dealing with certain special problems of symptom formation and character traits, but they may not be applicable to all superego functioning, especially in other contexts. The nature of the individual's specific conflicts is more significant in determining what aspects of superego function come to our attention—and the analytic situation is, of course, so skewed as to bring to the surface derivatives of the conflict in a specific way. As far as symptom formation is concerned, fear of retaliation far outweighs the fear of the superego. In fact, both Freud (1913, 1923) and Waelder (1967) emphasized that guilt rarely plays an important role in symptom formation, except when them has been real, that is, actual misfortune in the individual's life. Then the individual feels abandoned by fate or by God, and takes his misfortune as a sign that he should feel guilty.

This is far from a complete catalog of the problems of the superego that remain to be examined. How the superego participates in artistic creation in a period of changing morality represents one of the sociological applications of psychoanalytic insight into the process of historical transformation. In this regard it would also be timely to reconsider psychoanalytic ideas about the differences between male and female superego. The clinical data are at hand; yet they do not seem to have been exploited sufficiently in order to resolve this ever-recurring problem. We can conclude that the superego remains a rich realm beckoning for further exploration and investigation.

References

Arlow, J.A. (1960), Fantasy system in twins. *Psychoanal. Quart.,* 29:175–199.

——— (1969), Unconscious fantasy and disturbances of conscious experience. *Psychoanal. Quart.,* 38:1–27.

——— (1976), Communication and character. *Psychoanal. Study Child,* 31:139–163.

——— (1979). Metaphor and the psychoanalytic situation. *Psychoanal. Quart.,* 48:363–385.

——— & Brenner, C. (1964), *Psychoanalytic Concepts and the Structural Theory.* New York: Int. Univ. Press.

Brenner, C. (1981), Defense and defense mechanisms. *Psychoanal. Quart.* 50: 557–569.

——— (1982), *The Mind in Conflict.* New York, Int. Univ. Press (in press).

Freud, A. (1936), The ego and the mechanisms of defense. *S.E.,* 2.

Freud, S. (1900), The interpretation of dreams. *S.E.,* 4 & 5.

——— (1913), Totem and taboo. *S.E.,* 13:1–165.

——— (1917), Mourning and melancholia. *S.E.,* 14:237–261.

——— (1923), The ego and the id. *S.E.,* 19:3–66.

——— (1924), The economic problems of masochism. *S.E.,* 19:157–170.

——— (1927), Humor. *S.E.,* 21:159–166.

Furer, M. (1967), Some developmental aspects of the superego. *Int. J. Psychoanal.,* 48:277–280.

Hartmann, H. & Loewenstein, R.M. (1962), Notes on the superego. *Psychoanal. Study Child,* 17:42–81.

Jacobson, E. (1964), *The Self and the Object World.* New York: Int. Univ. Press.

Joenson, A.M. & Szurek, S.A. (1952), The genesis of antisocial acting out in children and adults. *Psychoanal. Quart.* 21:323–343.

Kohut, H. (1971), *The Analysis of the Self.* New York: Int. Univ. Press.

Kris, E. (1955), Neutralization and sublimation—observations on young children. *Psychoanal. Study Child*, 10:30–46.

Lampl-De Groot, J. (1962), Ego ideal and superego. *Psychoanal. Study Child*, 17:94–106.

Loewenstein, R.M. (1956), Some remarks on the role of speech in psychoanalytic technique, *Int. J. Psychoanal.*, 37:460–468.

Nunberg, H. (1926), The sense of guilt and the need for punishment, *Int. J. Psychoanal.*, 7:420–433.

Piaget, J. (1927), *The Child's Conception of Physical Causality.* New York: Humanities Press, 1951.

Piers, G. & Singer, M.B. (1953), *Shame and Guilt.* Springfield: Charles C. Thomas.

Rangell, L. (1976), Lessons from Watergate, *Psychoanal. Quart.*, 45:37–61.

Ritvo, S. (1972), Outcome of predictions on superego formation. In: *Moral Values and the Superego Concept in Psychoanalysis,* ed. S. C. Post. New York: Int.. Univ. Press, pp. 74–86.

——— & Solnit, A.J. (1958), Influences of early mother-child interaction on identification processes, *Psychoanal. Study Child* 13:64–85.

Sandler, J. (1960), On the concept of superego, Psychoanal. Study Child, 15:128–162.

Schafer, R. (1960), The loving and beloved superego in Freud's structural theory, *Psychoanal. Study Child*, 15:163–188.

Waelder, R. (1936), The principle of multiple function, <u>Psychoanal. Quart.</u>, 5:45–62.

——— (1967), *Progress and Revolution.* New York: Int. Univ. Press.

Chapter 14

Development and Pathology of the Oedipus Complex

1987
Jacob Arlow, MD

Commentary: Kimberly L. Kleinman, MS. LCSW

Arlow begins the chapter by acknowledging the tendency of our field to have trends. He wondered if he was invited to participate in the 1987 Mahler symposium in order to give a polite nod to Oedipal issues, perhaps even drive theory. He goes on to remind us that whatever is in fashion, theory is the description of data, and our data begins with the mind of the child. He reminds his audience that Freud's various theories of pathogenesis were added perspectives, not replacements of previous findings. He states that the drive and object are different aspects of the same experience. This is a common Arlowian perspective, he is implicitly stating that new theories are new perspectives, not new truths. Arlow describes how an (internal) object is a representation of a persistent experience. He specifically mentions hypothesizing "two sets of memories of sensory impressions" as another way to describe the split between the good object and bad object Kleinian theory emphasizes. He goes on to say that Kernberg's description of splitting could be described as a "regressive

227

reactivation" of the time when objects were perceived as good or bad. Arlow goes on to say that just as drive and object cannot be considered separately, neither can self and object be considered stand alone concepts. His next statement seems to imply that just as he can look at other theories in a flexible way, so too must we consider the Oedipus Complex in a more flexible way. Yes, it can be conceded that the vicissitudes of the drives have been written about in a way that implies that the proponents of this theory insist on the phases occurring in a rigid time sequence. This would be a problem of the signifier, not adequately representing the signified. He states "Development is an uneven process." I think he is saying that sometimes developmental theory is misunderstood and he is also saying that sometimes developmental theory is not sufficiently complex in its exposition.

In the second half of this paper Arlow gives a succinct overview of the Oedipal Conflict. He begins by explaining that concepts of development are not linear nor are they significantly predictive. He then states that the psychoanalytic situation uncovers the unconscious fantasies that were prominent in the life of the patient when the patient was between 3 and 5. To quote: "The polarities of creative loving versus aggressive destruction, of phallic versus castrated, are preeminent." He goes on to bring up that narcissistic injury and low self-esteem have many sources. Transference interactions cannot be seen as generating from a specific phase when treating an adult. There has already been a synthesis, many other experiences. So too trauma. The effects of impingements cannot be predicted. Oedipal disappointment is a neglected source of narcissistic injury and low self esteem. This seems like an implied dispute with Kohut: Pre-Oedipal issues are not the only source of narcissistic injury. Fantasy is the cornerstone of our work, but fantasy is always idiosyncratic, individual, and this is most likely an argument aimed at Melanie Klein. Arlow's description of his understanding of the effects of fantasy, as well as mentioning merger, incorporation and transferential wishes align well with the concept of Kleinian Positions from my perspective. I imagine that Arlow would not agree with me about that.

Arlow's last paragraph is clearly an argument against the idea of the nurturing corrective emotional experience. We have to pay attention to the disavowed guilt and aggression, to the entire spectrum of the patient's communications.

Development and Pathology of the Oedipus Complex

Mahler Symposium
Albert Einstein College of Medicine
January 16, 1987Jacob A. Arlow, MD

From both psychoanalysis and aesthetics, we learn of the intimate connection between form and content. The formal structure of a dream, for example, often enough is related to its latent meaning. From the analysis of such clinical entities as the déjà vu experience, depersonalization, and disturbances of the sense of time, one discovers how the formal structure of experience may express the fulfillment of wishes or defense against painful affects.

Accordingly, when I first saw the program for today's symposium, I pondered the significance of its formal structure. From the developmental point of view, one would expect that the emergence of the self, the mastering of the separation-individuation process, and the delineation of gender identity, all of which more or less antedate the evolution of the so-called Oedipus phase, would precede discussion of the Oedipus complex. But clearly this is not the order of the day. I assume the program was arranged in keeping with the historical development of psychoanalysis, rather than the psychological development of the individual. Nonetheless, certain suspicions began to arise. Was consideration of the Oedipus complex put first so that one could piously dispose of it, in order to get on to newer, more meaningful, more relevant issues? After all, we have been assured by eminent authority that the Oedipus complex has waned. But is it totally dead? Like Mark Anthony, I have not come to praise the Oedipus complex. It is an old friend, one that served us well. On the other hand, I do not come to bury it. The conflicts from that phase are alive and well and living in all of us — well, nearly all of us.

In a set of widely ranging questions, Dr. Pine has articulated many of the theoretical problems facing psychoanalysts today. As he points out, these are issues of immediate practical consequence. We are, after all, practitioners dedicated to helping our patients. Our theories of how the mind works and why people fall ill determine, in large measure, how we understand what the patient is saying and what we do about it. It seems hardly necessary to state that, at the present time, analysts differ with each other concerning many of these issues.

There is one matter, however, on which, at least for the time being, there seems to be practically universal agreement, and that is the use of the psychoanalytic situation. The fundamental feature of the psychoanalytic situation is that the patient speak with complete candor and, as far as possible, report uncritically whatever thoughts come to his mind, as they come to his mind. From the therapeutic and investigative point of view, the purpose of free association is to obtain a moment-to-moment record of the functioning of the individual's mind, as free as possible from external influence. The other features of the psychoanalytic situation — the physical setting, the arrangements of time and fee, and the benevolent neutrality and nonjudgmental attitude of the analyst — all serve to buttress the fundamental goal of the technique, namely, to obtain, as far as possible, a record of the patient's thoughts, minimally influenced by external intrusions, except in the form of interpretations. Information obtained in this manner serves, or should serve, as the data from which interpretations are formulated, cases are conceptualized, and generalizations and theories are built.

To my mind, devising the psychoanalytic situation was the most creative and most original of Freud's contributions to the study of the mind, It is not necessary to repeat the history of the evolution of this fundamental aspect of psychoanalytic technique. In his "Autobiographical Study" (1925), Freud made it clear that the goal of the psychoanalytic situation was to facilitate the emergence into consciousness of all sides of the derivatives of <u>pathogenic unconscious conflicts</u>. A dynamic view of human personality, a concept of contending, interacting factors, some conscious, some unconscious, was for Freud the very essence of the psychoanalytic theory of the mind. Several times in the course of his writings, he changed his views about the nature and the origin of the forces in conflict, but never once did he swerve from this fundamental vision of the role of conflict in human nature. This approach, the essence of psychoanalysis, was formulated more recently by Kris (1950) in an aphoristic way, when he said that psychoanalysis is human nature seen from the vantage point of conflict.

In the psychoanalytic situation, the analyst is privy to the vicissitudes of an ongoing debate taking place within the patient's mind. There are many participants in this debate and many conflicting viewpoints. Some of the voices raised speak for considerations of the present. Others express hopes or fears from the past. Some speak not in their own voice, but express sentiments and attitudes of some long forgotten individual from the patient's early life. Some of the voices bring to mind unpleasant memories and considerations which the others do not wish to hear. It is a never-ending debate characterized by shifting alliances, bitter assaults, and compromises. Essentially what the analyst does is to permit each voice to be heard, to expose the nature and the origin of the various alliances and compromises, and to help the participants in the debate achieve a satisfactory, i.e., a workable, livable compromise, one that is better than the old arrangements that did not work so well. How we designate the participants in this debate, what names we give them, and where we think they came from is of secondary importance compared to the fact that, taken together, the unworkable compromises they arranged have brought symptoms, inhibition, and anxiety, as well as a host of other difficulties to the patient. At the same time, we learn that some compromises are most felicitous in their outcome. In fact, they may contribute to life-enhancing pursuits and adaptive character traits. It is not conflict that is pathogenic. Intrapsychic conflict is an inexorable dimension of the human condition. What brings the individual to grief is the failed nature of some of the compromises he has effected and their persisting influence on his mental life.

Why the individual fails in this endeavor, in other words, the nature of the process of pathogenesis, has been considered by analysts from the very beginning of psychoanalysis. Freud changed his views on the subject many times as new observations compelled him to confront his theories afresh. Originally, he had emphasized the factor of sexual seduction at an early age. When observations concerning the sexual drive were the center of his interest, he emphasized the role of fixation as a consequence of excessive stimulation or inadequate gratification. He saw an additional factor in the actual threats of physical injury made to the growing child by adults. At another stage in his work, Freud emphasized the economic factor, namely, the noxious effects of excessive accumulation of sexual drive energy. These various theories did not necessarily run in series, with one supplanting the other in time. For the most part, they ran in parallel. Freud even left room in his theories of pathogenesis for a phylogenetic factor, making room for the inherent effects of the ancient experiences of the race. Perhaps his final contribution to the problem of pathogenesis is to be found in the dual instinct theory, which he enunciated in "Beyond the Pleasure Principle" (1920). In this work, he felt it necessary to assume that certain forms of psychopathology and some aspects of all psychopathology must be ascribed to some inherent, fundamentally repetitive process that leads ultimately to self-destruction. If nothing else, Freud set the stage for his followers to consider a multiplicity of theories of pathogenesis, and, in the by now almost fifty years following his death, such theories have multiplied indeed.

But no matter how numerous the vicissitudes of early development, the conflicts that appear to arise during the Oedipus phase, Freud felt, were crucial not only for the process of pathogenesis but also for the total development of the individual. To a large extent, he felt that the manner in which the individual resolved his oedipal conflicts determined the course of his life. This conviction on Freud's part may be traced to his materialist biological approach to psychology, as well as to the way he interpreted his clinical experience. It was not that Freud was unaware of preoedipal influences. The evidence of his sensitivity to such issues is abundantly clear. He was, however, deeply committed to the biological concept of an ontogenic unfolding of stages of development, a theory of biological transformation that was dominant at the time he received his education. By introducing the structural theory, which emphasizes the role of the ego in integrating and resolving the contradictions among the various elements in conflict, Freud made it possible to explore in greater detail the factors, inherent or experiential, that determine the ego's capacity to effect appropriate compromise formations. The implications of structural concepts for developmental theory and pathogenesis were enormous. To quote Shapiro (1977),

> "... ego psychology provided new opportunities to expand the scope of psychoanalytic application to include the possibility that faulty ego functions influence secondarily the form of conflict, just as conflict may influence autonomous ego functions. Ego psychology also provided the theoretical possibility that there is a constant interplay between the status of object relations identification and body image consolidation and that this interplay may influence distortions and create uneven functioning among specific ego functions." (page 562)

It is not necessary to document for this audience the knowledge that has accrued from this interest in the development of the ego. One need only note that, in recent years, a major focus of psychoanalytic investigation has centered on this topic. Pertinent findings have emerged from studies by analysts of infant and child development, from long-term observation and, from within the psychoanalytic situation, from daring reconstructions of childhood trauma, extending to the very earliest phases of the individual's existence.

This interest in the very early psychological experience of the infant is by no means purely academic. As I have attempted to make clear in an earlier presentation (Arlow, 1981), much of this concern grows out of practical necessity. It derives from efforts to achieve better results in treatment as analysts have encountered more difficult therapeutic challenges with the widening scope of psychoanalysis (Stone,). These observations, however, have often been used to buttress certain theories of pathogenesis. In some of these theories, a specific feature of the developmental process may be emphasized as the specific major etiological factor in pathogenesis. A practical consequence of such theories is that they appear to simplify problems of technique. Whether intended or not, the consequence of certain object relations theories is such as to make it appear that an early interaction between mother and child may constitute a relationship that has an unconscious dynamic thrust of its own, causing that relationship to recur repetitively and inappropriately in new situations with individuals other than the primary object. One result of such theories may be seen in the tendency in current psychoanalytic theory to juxtapose drive versus object relations in conceptualizing development and pathogenesis.

A related issue concerns the role of the Oedipus complex. Is it merely a side issue, parallel to and/or superseded by the persisting reemergence of latter-day expressions of the distorted earliest object relations? To me, this too appears to be a spurious issue. Is it really possible to conceive of perceptual experience devoid of feeling tone? Is it possible to summon up a mental representation devoid of affect? It seems to be a fundamental of psychoanalytic theory that drive and object are different aspects of the same experience. It is a reasonable assumption, presumably adopted by both analysts and non-analysts, that the infant's earliest perceptual experiences are registered as either pleasurable or unpleasant. This is the first and the fundamental categorization of experience, a tendency that must be related to survival value in the evolution of the human species. From the point of view of survival, noxious events, as a rule, generate pain and therefore are to be avoided. The contrary holds true for pleasurable experiences. It is according to these criteria that the perceptual experience is processed and organized. What is later recognized as the need-gratifying object originates out of memories of repetitive sensory impressions accompanied by pleasurable feelings of gratification. It seems to me that the cognitive aspect has not been accorded the attention it deserves in psychoanalytic theories of development.

Object seeking is predominantly oriented by the need to try to achieve an identity of pleasurable perceptions, remembered but not independently attainable by the infant. Since they are linked to need gratification, finding and refinding the object are activities intimately connected with pleasure. Here the second criterion for categorizing or processing information enters, namely, the assimilation of perceptual experience in terms of what is familiar or unfamiliar. Subsequently, the memory traces of pleasurable sensory impressions connected with the external sensory stimulus become organized into a coherent memory structure, a mental representation of a person, which we call an object. The term "object," therefore, represents a concept pertaining to a persistent, structured experience. In a complementary fashion, a coherent organization of memory traces of representations connected with pain may serve as a basis for another kind of object representation, connected with the same set of sensory impressions. Thus, it may happen that two sets of memories of sensory impressions may he organized as mental representations, one associated with pain, the other with pleasure. The pleasant representations of such memories may be labeled as good and the unpleasant ones as bad. It is in this sense that I can understand what the Kleinians mean when they talk about good objects and bad objects, in referring to the psychic events of the earliest months of life.

It is also in this sense that I can understand Kernberg's concept of splitting, as a regressive reactivation of this primitive stage of organization of the object concept.

Strictly speaking, the term "object" refers to the mental representation of a person. It is built up of many discrete memories of interactions with that person. Especially in dreams, but also in the patient's associations, one observes that specific memories, articulating particular aspects of the relationship with the object, appear. The object concept is an organized integration of the experiences and fantasies connected with a particular person. It is by no means a logical or coherent structure. I think it is misleading to think of an object being internalized or even of object relations being internalized. What comes into being in the mind of the individual as the object concept is a more or less organized generalization of one's experience with a particular person, a concept that is readily prone to regressive dissolution into its component parts.

Just as drive and object cannot be considered independently of each other, so self and object have to be understood as different aspects of the same developmental (as opposed to maturational) process. As the infant delineates inner from outer experience, he also begins to distinguish between himself and the object world. As the object concept is constructed gradually out of pooled representations of earlier interactions, so is the self concept built up out of pooled self representations of earlier experiences (Jacobson, ; Spiegel,), out of memory traces gradually integrated into a reliable, relatively consistent sense of self. As in the case of objects, we do not always understand our self, nor do we always like it, but we feel secure in the knowledge of its history, which we conjure up in the form of re-presentations, which constitute the memory of an organized past, of a continuity of identity. In the case of the self, what can be re-presented to the mind as a record of past experience is not only the record of past perceptions, but also representations of inner experience — memories, thoughts, theories, concepts — a good portion of which constitute the exclusive property of the self.

The self is a timebound concept. The sense of continuity and permanence of the self concept is stoutly maintained. There is an inwardly acknowledged conviction of self-identity and continuity that parallels but remains forever stronger than the sense of continuity and permanence pertaining to an object. Earlier representations of the self may have been repudiated or disavowed, but the sense of connection is hardly ever sundered in an absolute way, except in very severe forms of psychopathology.

The early literature on the evolution of the self tended to emphasize the steps in learning to distinguish inner from outer, stressing particularly the vicissitudes of anal drives in relation to the fecal mass and to the caretaker as intermediary in the process. In recent years many observers have added enormously to our knowledge of this process. In exquisitely detailed observations, Mahler ( ) described the steps leading to the emergence of the individual as a self-conscious, separate identity. With this developmental achievement, the individual advances to the threshold of the so-called oedipal phase.

It is indeed an unfortunate historical fact in the evolution of psychoanalytic nomenclature that the various developmental phases were originally labeled in terms of the major vicissitudes of the drive organization (Arlow and Brenner, 1964). Such designations placed almost exclusive emphasis on the transformation of the drives in rigid time sequence. In fact, the various phases of functional development overlap and merge subtly one into the other. The attainment of the psychological attributes characteristic for a particular age is by no means uniform. Development is an uneven process.

Progress towards the oedipal phase and within the oedipal phase is by no means the sum of the advances of the previous phases. Psychological growth is characterized, most observers inform us, by periods of progression and retrogression and of hierarchical reorganization at later levels which, in a new context, endow functions with a different role and significance. This was a point that Hartmann ( ) called to our attention when he discussed the genetic fallacy. In addition, as Beres and Obers ( ) indicated many years ago, the effects of early traumata and the influence of certain defects may be overcome at later stages of development as a result of beneficent object relations. An inadequate, very early mother-infant relationship, for example, does not necessarily presage irreparable psychic damage nor absolutely interfere with the ability to effect adequate transference in the treatment situation. Later beneficent relations with helpful adults may obscure or obliterate earlier trauma. Of course, these are not the patients who ordinarily come to treatment, but often enough we come upon such observations in our clinical experience. I cited one such case in detail in a study of a child raised by deaf-mute parents (Arlow, 1976).

The fact is that the psychoanalytic concept of trauma is a retrospective one. Except for very extreme cases of deprivation or injury, the "trauma" is not inherent in the specific event or relationship. The psychoanalytically trained observers of child development advisedly have been cautious indeed in making predictions about long-term sequelae of events observed in early childhood. Take, for example, the situation of two girls born with identical birth injuries to the brachial plexus, resulting in withered and practically useless right arms. That they would both have problems in the course of development no one would dispute; neither can anyone predict in advance whether the ultimate response to this physical insult would necessarily lead to maladjustment, symptom formation, or severe character deformation. I am quite certain that we have all had the experience of observing how differently things can turn out in such circumstances.

It is within the psychoanalytic situation that we get the evidence of the inadequate mastery of the vicissitudes of development, in effect, of the failed compromise formations. As mentioned earlier, the psychoanalytic situation is tilted to facilitate the appearance of derivatives of unconscious conflicts. These derivatives appear as secondary expressions of persistent unconscious fantasies, organized in childhood, as far as the evidence seems to indicate, roughly between the third and fifth years of life. The themes of these fantasies are familiar enough. They pertain to desires to love, possess, master, excel, supersede significant others, some of the primary objects in the child's life. These wishes may be very aggressive in content and primitive in form. They are magical, irrational and fantastic. Other considerations, however, appear in opposition to these desires, chiefly the fear of punishment by physical mutilation, but not exclusively so. Other anxieties, stemming from earlier periods, also enter, such as fear of abandonment and loss of love. These conflicts take place in the context of advances in the delineation of the sense of self and others, together with an appreciation of sexual identity and differentiation. The polarities of creative loving versus aggressive destruction, of phallic versus castrated, are preeminent.

It must be stressed that the unconscious fantasies are not merely vehicles of biological wishes, as we had been led to believe earlier in the course of psychoanalysis. The unconscious fantasies are in themselves compromise formations. They have a genealogy of their own; they are linked to the experiences of the preoedipal period, experiences that are now integrated in keeping with a totally changed psychological configuration. The specific features of the psychopathology evolving out of the conflicts of the Oedipus chase are determined by the nature of the compromise formations that the ego is able to effect in the derivative expressions of the unconscious fantasy. In the psychoanalytic situation, we learn not only of pathogenic compromise formations, but also of successful ones. It is striking and yet, at the same time, quite commonplace to observe various, sometimes seemingly contradictory, compromise formations that may eventuate out of the same unconscious conflict. in our clinical, work, we observe often enough situations in which a valuable interest or skill, a neurotic symptom, a perverse practice, and a perverse character trait, all originating out of the same unconscious conflict, coexist side by side in the mental life of an individual. It is the kind of compromise that can be effected, rather than the nature of the unconscious wish or the attendant anxiety, that determines the evolution and nature of oedipal pathology.

Translating the surface manifestations of derivatives of the patient's unconscious fantasy is the principal task of the analyst during treatment. The unconscious fantasies of the Oedipus phase represent a distillation and integration in a dynamic way of the significant, lasting, early experiences of the individual. Whether every event that occurred in the early history of the individual leaves some dynamic trace on mental development is a difficult proposition to prove. The relationship to pain and pleasure, however, is fundamental and colors our mental experience from the very beginning to the very end. This point has special bearing on problems of self-esteem and narcissism and their relationship to certain oedipal phenomena. I refer to the sense of worthlessness, the loss of self-esteem, and the narcissistic rage that follow the oedipal defeat, a subject that has been relatively neglected in the literature. The consequences of this inevitable frustration are protean in their manifestations. A broad range of normal and pathological phenomena grow out of fantasies the individual generates in response to oedipal disappointment.

In considering pathology of the Oedipus complex, considerations of injured narcissism must be reckoned side by side with castration anxiety. Experiences of unpleasure or pain, connected with what is ultimately understood as the self, are present from the beginning of life and persist. There is an unbroken line of evolution from the painful tensions of the hungry child, to the toddler who cannot master the world, control his own body functions or do what adults do, to the frustrated oedipal child, who feels inferior, inadequate, unloved and unlovable. All painful states diminish self-esteem, each one resonating and reverberating with the memory of other humiliations. Specific forms and experiences in object relations may attenuate or intensify the effects of such assaults upon one's narcissism. They are not, however, the sole cause of the propensity to narcissistic injury.

Each individual distills his early experience in terms of a set of unconscious fantasies that are peculiar, one can say idiosyncratic, for him. These persistent fantasies establish the framework within which experience is perceived, interpreted and responded to. In this manner, the impact of the past is transmitted to the present and the future.

Ordinary relationships, neurotic symptoms, and the transference during psychoanalytic treatment are influenced by derivatives of unconscious fantasies. It is really not quite accurate to say that transference represents a repetition of earlier relationships or experiences with important objects of the individual's past. What we observe in the transference is an unconscious attempt on the part of the patient to foist upon the treatment situation a scenario which is a derivative of an unconscious fantasy. Transference is not a compulsive repetition of the past. It is an attempt to actualize in the present, in the treatment situation, a derivative of an unconscious fantasy based on childhood conflict. Some transference patterns represent relationships that never existed, as, for example, the transference onto the analyst of wishes and anticipations concerning a father whom the patient never knew or saw. Certain transference wishes, by their very nature, could never have been real experiences, as, for example, the wish to merge or to devour and incorporate the object. What occurs in the transference is an attempt to actualize a derivative of the unconscious fantasy, much in the same way as earlier certain object relations represented actualizations of derivatives of such fantasies.

Making such distinctions may sound like hair-splitting. The fact is that they have very important implications for both theory and practice in psychoanalysis today. I refer to the tendency to interpret certain phenomena encountered in the treatment situation as if they were direct translations, unchanged from earliest childhood, of certain experiences and object relationships. By virtue of similarity of phenomenology, an etiological, genetic connection is presumed to exist between the two phenomena. Illustrations of this tendency abound, and I have referred to some of them in previous communications. Positing a necessary connection between the transitional object and the fetish on the basis of phenomenology alone would be one such example. Interpreting the patient's resistant independence of the analyst's efforts as a necessary derivative of failure to resolve the rapprochement crisis would be another. It is not that such connections may not exist. What is lacking is the intermediate, associative, supportive material, most particularly the influence of unconscious factors. In such interpretations, a developmental vicissitude is seen as remaining unchanged and unchanging, repeatedly reasserting itself, not out of inner conflict, but as a consequence of some externally imposed event. It is not, as some people think, that the significance of the Oedipus phase is minimized. What is in question is the role of conflict in mental life.

The net effect of this mode of phenomenological interpretation constitutes an attempt to substitute a non-dynamic, developmental etiology for a dynamic, i.e., conflictual, view of development and its relationship to etiology. Technically, during treatment, such approaches minimize the role of insight into unconscious conflicts. Instead they concentrate on the element of miscarried development, emphasizing rather how the analyst functions as a nurturing, sustaining, holding environment. As I indicated in other connections, this enables the analyst to be comfortable in his role as healer and rescuer. The patient also finds it appealing. He can view himself as the innocent victim of mistreatment at the hands of his caretakers during a period in his life when he had only needs and no responsibilities. There can be no doubt that, treatment, such an approach is much more satisfying than confronting guilt-laden, fear-ridden derivatives of the Oedipus phase.

The issue is not an either/or proposition. For all its twistings and turnings, mental development is a continuous process, all phases of which have to be taken into account and placed in their proper perspective. To determine how all of these factors align themselves presents a difficult problem of methodology. The most reliable data that we can obtain issue from the detailed examination of the patient's associations within the analytic situation. What is essential is a meticulous examination of the data from the point of view of logical and cogent criteria for interpretation. Psychoanalytic treatment is a form of discourse. We have to pay greater attention to how meaning and inferences evolve out of communication. Accordingly, the intuitions that grow out of our empathy and experience have to be tempered by careful examination of the context, contiguity, configurations, metaphors and other criteria which should govern our assessment of the data in a rational way. This is a segment of psychoanalysis which, in my opinion, is only in its infancy, but it is one that it behooves us to develop for the purpose of resolving in some disciplined way the many different, and often contradictory, approaches that are emerging concerning development, pathogenesis and treatment.

Chapter 15

Contribution to Panel on THE INFLUENCE OF SOCIAL, CULTURAL AND HISTORICAL FACTORS IN FREUD'S WORK

American Academy of Psychoanalysis
December 6, 1984, Jacob A. Arlow, MD

Commentary: Kimberly Kleinman, MS, LCSW

Arlow's thesis in this paper revolve around the concepts of "genuis" and the question how do people who are in the same cultural and historical matrix distinguish themselves? What is fascinating in this article is the introduction of Ahad Ha'am (Asher Ginzberg) and his ideas. Concepts that we still consider part of the psychoanalytic canon are also the subject of Ahad Ha'am's essays. Arlow emphasized intrapsychic conflict and the superego in this paper.

Arlow describes intrapsychic conflict as a foundational concept, culminating in fundamental revisions of Freud's concept of the mental apparatus. What is also interesting is that Ahad Ha'am also has a prescient description of how the mind works that describes compromise formation: the psychological life takes a definite middle course from which it cannot be diverted by the sudden revolt of any of its powers, each of which is forcibly kept within bounds." (Ahad Ha'am, page 127)

Interestingly the passages Arlow quotes demonstrates that Ha'am was thinking about several other dimensions of how people think. Ha'am muses about how society influences the individual. Ha'am description of 'hypnotic agents" seems analogous to Jung's collective unconscious. He goes on to describe how people who are influenced by societal effects will imagine that they act of their own free will. The idea that one creates a narrative to explain thoughts at behavior in a way that is sytonic is similar to rationalization.

Arlow synthesizes the connection between Freud and Ha'ams approach to moral development. He points out that Ha'am wrote this 30 years before the Ego and the Id. Returning to the concept of genuis, Arlow points out that Freud was the one who made these concepts a coherent whole and made them useful.

Contribution to Panel on
THE INFLUENCE OF SOCIAL, CULTURAL AND HISTORICAL FACTORS IN FREUD'S WORK

American Academy of Psychoanalysis
December 6, 1984
Jacob A. Arlow, MD

Trying to reveal the hidden sources of genius remains a never-ending challenge, at once fascinating and, it would seem, ultimately disappointing. Freud, who revealed the secret roots of so many mysteries of the human mind, was equally intrigued by this challenge and in the end had to admit defeat. He said, in effect, that before the mysteries of art and creativity psychoanalysis must lay down its arms. Yet volumes have been written and continue to be written trying to explain how Freud developed his revolutionary insights into the nature of man. Typical of such efforts was a panel that I chaired at the 1969 meeting of the American Psychological Association, entitled "The Ideological Wellsprings of Psychoanalysis" (Published in the <u>Psychoanalytic Quarterly</u>, 1974), from which emerged a set of excellent scholarly studies of the intellectual and cultural ambience of Freud's formative years. The panel today clearly continues in the spirit of that earlier enterprise. We did not unlock the secret of Freud's genius then. I doubt we will do any better today.

My major contribution this afternoon, therefore, may seem a bit off the goal of the panel. I propose to describe how two major concepts of psychoanalytic thought appear in the work of a contemporary of Freud's, a man from a vastly different background, who, in comparison to Freud's worldwide renown, must be regarded as a relatively obscure figure.

The person I refer to is Asher Ginsberg, better known by his Hebrew pen name, Ahad Ha'am. He was a figure who loomed large in Zionist circles at the turn of the century because he represented spiritual or intellectual Zionism as opposed to political Zionism. He was born in 1856, the same year as Freud, and died in 1927. There is no evidence to suggest that they ever knew each other. Neither one is ever mentioned in the writings of the other. It can be safely assumed that their influence on each other was nil.

Far from the worldly intellectual stimulation of Vienna, Ahad Ha'am was born in a provincial town in the Ukraine into an orthodox Chasidic family. Except for the traditional Biblical and Talmudic education he received from private tutors, he was essentially self-educated. He never attended the university, but read widely on his own in Jewish studies, moral philosophy, psychology, history and sociology. He studied Russian, German, French, English and Latin independently. He was acquainted with the positivism of Comte and the metaphysical and ethical ideas of the British moralists and empirical philosophers from Locke to Hume to John Stuart Mill and Huxley. He was particularly interested in the work of the French psychologists Taine and Paulhan (Simon, 1912, Encyclopedia Judaica, 1972). (I should mention in passing that a reference to an 1894 paper by Paulhan entitled "Concerning the Anxiety of the Psyche in Dreams" appears in the biography of Freud's "Interpretation of Dreams [1900], although there is no reference to this work in the actual text..)

Ahad Ha'am was a "feuilletonist," that is, an essayist or newspaper columnist. His main work was that of editor of Ha-shiloah. It was a Hebrew periodical of limited circulation, in which Ahad Ha'am published his essays.

It is more than a safe conjecture to say that Freud never read any of Ginsberg's articles. Although there is no evidence, it is possible, in the fervent and excitement that surrounded the emergence of the Zionist movement in the beginning of the 20th Century, Freud may have heard of the name of Ahad Ha'am.

I propose now to examine what Ahad Ha'am had to say about two concepts that were central to Freud's thinking, intrapsychic conflict and the superego. Intrapsychic conflict is an all-pervasive concept in Freudian theory. It is intimately connected with his formulations concerning the basic drives and the dynamic unconscious. Intrapsychic conflict, eventuating in compromise formation, underlies Freud's understanding of normal and abnormal psychology, of dreams and symptoms, and culminated finally in his fundamental revision of the mental apparatus in terms of the structural theory. The notion of intrapsychic conflict and compromise formation has been discussed and elaborated from many points of view, the most recent example being Brenner's book on The Mind in Conflict (1982).

Writing in 1893, two years before the publication of "Studies in Hysteria" (1895), in an article entitled "Priest and Prophet," Ahad Ha'am said:

"We learn from the science of mechanics that the impact of two forces moving in different directions—one eastward, for example, and one northward—will produce a movement of intermediate direction. At a time when men were accustomed to attribute all motion to a guiding will, they may have explained this phenomenon by supposing that the two original forces made a compromise and agreed that each should be satisfied with a little so as to leave something for the other. Nowadays, when we distinguish between mechanical and volitional motion we know that this 'compromise' is not the result of a conscious assent on the part of the two forces; that on the contrary each of them plays for its own hand and endeavors not to be turned from its course even a hair's breadth; and that it is just this struggle between them that produces the intermediate effect, which takes direction not identical with either of the other two... (Ahad Ha'am, page 125)

"Modern European scholars who investigate the mind from a very different point of view find in it many more than two forces; but they describe the working of those forces in much the same way. A French thinker, Paulhan, regards the human psyche as a large community containing innumerable individuals; that is to say, impressions, ideas, feelings, impulses and so forth. Each of these individuals lives a life of its own and struggles to widen the sphere of its influence, associating with itself all that is akin to its own character and repelling all that is opposed to it. Each strives in short to set its own impress on the whole life of the mind. There is no mutual accommodation among them, no regard for one another. The triumph of one is the defeat of another, and the defeated idea or impulse never acquiesces in its defeat, but remains ever on the alert, waiting for a favorable opportunity to reassert itself and extend its dominion. And it is just through this action of the individual members of the psychological community...that human life attains complexity and breadth, many-sidedness and variety. It may happen in the course of time, after tossing about in different directions, that the mind reaches a condition of equilibrium. In other words, the psychological life takes a definite middle course from which it cannot be diverted by the sudden revolt of any of its powers, each of which is forcibly kept within bounds." (Ahad Ha'am, page 127)

The parallels to psychoanalytic theory are clear enough. Ahad Ha'am describes the life of the mind in terms of a persistent and continuing conflict between opposing forces and impulses. The conflict is relentless and unremitting until some compromise can be arranged, a compromise which sometimes takes on a fixed and stable appearance, i.e., it becomes, as we would say, structuralized, a permanent, relatively stable attribute of the personality.

I will not recapitulate at this point the essential features of the superego concept, except to remind you that Freud said that the superego retains the character of the father as a result of the repression of the Oedipus complex under the influence of authority, religious teaching, schooling and reading (Freud, 1923, page 34). "The differentiation of the superego from the id is no matter of chance; it represents the most important characteristics of the development of both the individual and of the species; indeed, by giving permanent expression to the influence of the parents it perpetuates the existence of the factors to which it owes its origin. (p. 37). And finally, in his classic description of the superego in "The Ego and the Id," Freud states:

> "The experiences of the ego seem at first to be lost for inheritance, but when they have been repeated often enough and with sufficient strength in many individuals in successive generations, they transform themselves, so to say, into experiences of the id, the impressions of which are preserved by heredity. *Thus in the id, which is capable of being inherited, are harboured residues of the existences of countless egos; and when the ego forms its superego out of the id, it may perhaps only be reviving shapes of former egos and be bringing them to resurrection.*" (Freud, 1923, p. 38, emphasis added.)

To summarize, in 1923 Freud put forward the salient features of the superego concept. It is a determining dimension of all human behavior, a constant element in psychic life. It operates unconsciously. It may be fended off by various mechanisms of defense including rationalization, and it is founded on a multiplicity of identifications reaching back into the life of the individual but also into the cultural and historical evolution of the group and its leaders and lawgivers. Further, in "Group Psychology and the Analysis of the Ego (1921), Freud said "the primal father is the group ego ideal."

Now let us see what Ahad Ha'am had to say about the origin and function of morality in men. In an essay entitled "Two Masters," Ahad Ha'am wrote:

"Familiar as we now are with the phenomenon of hypnotism, we know that under certain conditions it is possible to induce a peculiar kind of sleep in a human being, and that, if the hypnotic subject is commanded to perform at a certain time after his awakening some action foreign to his character and his wishes, he will obey the order at the appointed time. He will not know, however, that he is compelled to do so by the will and behest of another. He will firmly believe (according to the evidence of expert investigators) that he is doing what he does of his own freewill and because he likes to do so, for various reasons which his imagination will create, in order to satisfy his own mind.

"The phenomenon in this form excites surprise, as something extraordinary; but we find a parallel in the experience of every man and every age, though the phenomenon is not ordinarily thrown into such strong relief, and therefore does not excite surprise or attract attention. Every civilized man who is born and bred in an orderly state of society lives all his life in the condition of the hypnotic subject, unconsciously subservient to the will of others. The social environment produces the hypnotic sleep in him from his earliest years. In the form of education, it imposes on him a load of various commands, which from the outset limit his movements, and give a definite character to his intelligence, his feelings, his impulses and his desires. In later life this activity of the social environment is ceaselessly continued in various ways. Language and literature, religion and morality, laws and customs—all these and their like are the media through which society puts the individual to sleep, and constantly repeats to him its commandments, until he can no longer help rendering them obedience.

"Society, however, which this influences the individual, is not a thing apart, external to the individual. Its whole existence and activity are in and through individuals, who transmit its commands one to another, and influence one another, by word and deed, in ways determined by the spirit of society. It may, therefore, be said with justice that every individual member of society carries in his own being thousands of hidden hypnotic agents, whose commands are stern and peremptory. 'Such and such shall be your opinions, such and such your actions.' The individual obeys, unconsciously. His opinions and his actions are framed to order. At the same time, he finds cogent arguments in favor of his opinions, and sound reasons for his actions. He is not conscious that it is the spirit of other men that thinks in his brain and actuates his hand, while his own essential spirit, his inner Ego, is sometimes utterly at variance with the resulting actions, but cannot make its voice heard because of the thousand tongues of the external Ego (what a French philosopher, Bergson, calls the 'verbal Ego') in which society enfolds him.

"We may go further. Society does not create its spiritual stock-in-trade and its way of life afresh in every generation. These things come to birth in the earliest stages of society, being a product of the conditions of life, then proceed through a long course of development till they attain a form that suits that particular society, and then, finally, are handed down from generation to generation without any fundamental change. Thus society in any given generation is nothing but the instrument of the will of earlier generations. The arch-hypnotizers, the all-powerful masters of the individual and of society alike, are the men of the distant past. The grass has grown on their graves for hundreds of years, it may be for thousands; but their voice is still obeyed, their commandments are still observed, and no man or generation can tell where lies the dividing line between himself and them, between his and theirs.

"When, therefore, we hear people talking loudly about their 'inner consciousness,' by which they pronounce judgement on truth and falsehood, good and evil, beauty and ugliness, we have a right to remember what we should find if we could analyze this 'consciousness.' We should find that the elements of which it was compounded were almost entirely the different commands of different hypnotic agents in different ages, which, through a complex chain of causes, had become united in this particular body of men, and had found its manifestation in their individual Ego..." (pp. 91–94)

Ahad Ha'am wrote this essay in 1892, thirty years before "The Ego and the Id." In this essay, he elaborates a concept of moral functioning which operates largely unconsciously and the moral forces of which exert a dynamic influence on behavior and thought. Furthermore, these influences are operative from early life, and they are historically determined. They reflect the vicissitudes of the experience of the individual's forbears, of the lessons learned from the ideal images of the community's past. Early in life identifications are made with such individuals and their teachings, and these identifications continue to exert an unconscious, i.e., hypnotic, effect upon each member of the community. These are identifications that compel obedience. The group experience through its cultural institutions, the family, schools and religion, perpetuates the influence of the leader and transmits that influence from generation to generation. All of the features of the psychoanalytic concept of the superego may be recognized in these elements, with, of course, the very notable exception of the relationship to the passing of the Oedipus complex.

It is not necessary to belabor the point. Both Freud and Ahad Ha'am drew nourishment in common from the wellsprings of 19th Century European

254

thought. So did hundreds of others of their contemporaries in whose works subsequent authorities have found ideas strikingly parallel to those enunciated by Freud. Similar social, cultural and historical factors applied to all these authors. To be sure, certain influences from the external world may have been more significant in the case of some authors as opposed to others. Certainly Freud's experience as a Jew in anti-Semitic Vienna was important. The question is: was it decisive? It is, I believe, almost impossible to demonstrate which of the elements that played upon Freud's development proved to be the germinal factor of his genius. To pursue this line of thought would force us to face the Marxist banality that Freud, Ahad Ha'am and the rest of them were products of their times. Ahad Ha'am and many others like him reaped the benefits of the more beneficent elements of the social, cultural and historical forces of 19th Century Europe, and consequently were able to see and to understand many things in a new light. It remained for Freud, however, to be able to benefit from all of these elements, to see beyond what others were able to perceive, and to integrate his knowledge and his insights into a new conception of man and his mind. How he did it, I do not know.

Chapter 16

Technique and the Analytic Relationship: Contemporary Views from Classical Perspective

Jacob A. Arlow, MD

Commentary: Kimberly L. Kleinman, MS, LCSW

Arlow walks us through psychoanalysis's theoretical arc from "lifting repression" to understanding the mind. In his personal psychoanalytic journey, ego psychology was just beginning to be applied. The analyst no longer waits to reconstruct a singular trauma. Trauma is not an event nor is it a relationship, trauma is the sequelae of events and relationships. He describes his analytic stance as a vacillation between passive listening and active intervention. The patient too has to actively evaluate the products of his or her mind. When Arlow describes the passive phase of listening, it is impossible not to think about the analytic use of projective identification. To my mind, he is explicating his response to Kleinian technique making full use of his talent for specificity. He uses empathic identification. He refers to his 1974 article about empathy where he and Beres wrote: "empathy is mediated by the communication of unconscious fantasy shared by the patient and the analyst. The cues for this communication are both verbal and nonverbal: they emanate from words, gestures, and behavior." The patient is attempting to influence the analyst.

Arlow uses one of the terms that has been misunderstood by some in reference to his work. He refers to the community of daydreams. In essence he is saying that the symbols, social representations etc. are clues to the unconscious. Unconscious fantasy is the backbone of Arlow's theories. I have socially heard people say that Arlow is just concerned with daydreams. Clearly this is a misunderstanding. Arlow goes on to describe how he uses analysis of the narrative to decipher unconscious fantasy. When the patient asks a question, he thinks of the question as a statement. The beginning of the session is the theme or thesis of the session, and the rest of the session is a variation on that theme. Arlow also describes his use of narrative contiguity. Elements of the patient's narrative that may on the surface seem to be a change of subject are connected by some unexpressed element.

I hear a contrast with Self Psychology technique at the end of this paper. The analyst is not a mirror, agreement is not the aim of interpretations. Interventions that upset the patient's equilibrium are useful sources of information.

Finally, Arlow describes his use of narrative anomaly as a clue to unconscious fantasy. This idea is a cornerstone to perceiving the "footprints," the unconscious mind creates as a clue to its contents. The use of narrative inconsistency is a cornerstone of Ainsworth's attachment research.

[Handwritten designation: B22]

Technique and the Analytic Relationship: Contemporary Views from Classical Perspective

Jacob A. Arlow, MD

The participants in this panel have been charged to focus on the evolution of their psychoanalytic technique as it has interacted with their conceptualization of the psychoanalytic relationship over the years of their clinical experience, and it is towards this specific goal that I have directed my thoughts.

My psychoanalytic training began in the early 40s when ego psychology was first beginning to be applied to the clinical situation. It was not until the final year in training that we read Anna Freud's "The Ego and the Mechanisms of Defense" (1936) and Hartmann's "The Problem of Adaptation" (1938). The instruction in technique which we received articulated the views expressed in Freud's classical papers on the subject between 1896 and 1912.

Obviously principles of technique must correlate with the theory of pathogenesis. The theory of pathogenesis which we were taught was based on the "Studies on Hysteria" (1893). Since psychopathology was felt to result from the effects of a repressed memory and affect, which acted like a foreign body in the psychic apparatus, the goal of treatment was to get the patient to recall the repressed memory. Accordingly, we tended to sit by very patiently, doing very little, while the analysand associated freely. We hoped that somehow the repressed memory or an associated screen memory would pop out from the

Unconscious. We tried to help the patient overcome the infantile amnesia, so we listened for the material, not to the material. Even as late as one of Freud's last papers, "Constructions in Psychoanalysis" (1937), you will find that he subscribed to recollection as the goal of treatment. But it was not just that the repressed memory had to be recalled; it was also necessary for the associated affect to be discharged. Our difficulty in achieving this goal was sometimes painted over with the expression, "The patient has intellectual insight, but not emotional insight." (In this connection, I often wonder to what extent we may have encouraged our patients to act out by subtly approving of affect-laden experiences.) Defense analysis was still in the future.

Because the patient could not always recollect the forgotten experience, Freud recognized that it was often necessary to reconstruct the forgotten traumatic event. I suspect that, in clinical practice, reconstructions far outnumber actual recollections. It is notable, as I have pointed out, that even a most credible, internally consistent reconstruction rarely leads the patient to recollect the traumatic event. From my experience, I have learned, first, how much more common it is to find traumatic relationships rather than single traumata as a source of psychopathology. Second, and more important, I came to understand that what constituted trauma was not inherent in the nature of the event or the relationship, but rather in the nature of their psychological consequences.

With the introduction of the structural hypothesis, the concept of intrapsychic conflict eventuating in adaptive or maladaptive compromise formations clarified the issue of pathogenesis and consequently the theory of technique. Now what I try to do is demonstrate to the patient how his or her mind works, something of how it got to be that way, and the analysand's responsibility for choosing compromise solutions that are personally congenial.

My understanding of the nature of the patient/analyst relationship has been a continuing process, extending even into the present time. I never felt comfortable with the metaphor of the telephone Freud used to explain how the analyst came to understand the nature of the patient's unconscious mental life, nor was I satisfied with Isakower's concept of the analyzing instrument, which essentially seems to me to be a modified version of the telephone metaphor. What I found more helpful were the ideas Sterba (1934) presented in his paper concerning the split of the ego in the analytic process. We instruct our patients, he noted, to serve as passive reporters of their mental presentations, to exercise no critical judgment of what is or is not to be reported, what is or is not to be regarded as important. But sooner or later, we intervene and, in effect, ask the patient to change his role; to consider, to pass judgment, to evaluate, to subject one or another aspect of his productions to critical examination. We induce a split in his functioning from passive reporter to active observer. This facilitates the patient's identifying with the analyst and his mode of functioning.

At the same time, however, a parallel process takes place in the analyst, as he oscillates from passive recipient of the patient's productions to active intervener. As recipient, the analyst's conscious experiences, i.e., his mental representations, are the patient's productions. For a moment or so it is as if the analyst were himself the patient. In effect, he has identified with the patient. He thinks and feels as the patient and may sometimes go so far as to dream along with the patient. An example of this last process I described in a paper on empathy which I wrote with Dr. Beres (1974). In it I reported how, in the course of an analytic session, while listening to a patient relate his dream, I had a quick dream of my own which paralleled in content and also in form the elements of the manifest dream the patient was reporting. It was an experience of consummate empathic identification. From similar experiences, not always as dramatic, I came to realize how much one can understand and learn from one's own reactions while listening to a patient. I concluded that, except when the analyst is completely distracted by some personal, practical concerns or is suffering from some acute physical discomfort, every thought, every feeling that occurs to him is some commentary on the patient's conflict. I emphasize "commentary" to distinguish the experience from total identity. It is only a clue, suggesting specific areas to be investigated further.

The process of identifying with the patient leads to empathy, which is the first stage in the development of insight. Without really consciously intending to, the patient organizes and shapes his productions in a way that influences the analyst very much as the artist, the poet or the creative writer employs selected techniques of communication in order to influence his audience to the end that they share with him derivative representations of his unconscious fantasies and the defenses against the wishes contained therein.

I am more circumspect in what I have come to consider countertransference. If, in the case of the patient, transference consists of an unconscious foisting upon the person of the analyst of a scenario, a derivative of one of the patient's unconscious fantasy wishes, then the same should be true in the opposite direction in countertransference. In true countertransference, the patient serves as the object of some unconscious wish on the part of the analyst. Perhaps the most common example of this mechanism to be observed is the wish to rescue the patient. The patient's productions stimulate in the analyst derivative representations of his own unconscious wishes and fantasies, but the patient is not necessarily always the object of those wishes.

[Page 5 of the original paper ends here. Pages 6, 7, and 8 are missing, and the paper resumes in mid-sentence at the top of page 9.]

of his father's aberrant sexual behavior. One can cite many other examples of the guilt and the wish to undercut his father's position sexually, financially and morally. The process of working through essentially represents the analysis of the manifold derivative representations of the unconscious fantasy.

I take a stricter approach to the understanding of transference in the treatment situation. To be sure, transferences are ubiquitous and, to a certain extent, all human interactions are infused with their influence. To me such an approach represents a tautology, since it expresses nothing more than the idea that all behavior is influenced by experience from the past. Transference in the treatment situation, I feel, must be specific and pertinent.

As derivative representations of unconscious fantasy, character traits and symptoms may be placed in the same category. They represent compromises of the various forces that participate in the process of fantasy formation. I found such an approach to illuminate the meaning of the specific details characteristic of symptoms and character traits.

This approach has rendered me sensitive to the significance in the patient's associations of what might be called social representations of unconscious fantasies or, to use Hanns Sachs' term, "the community of daydreams." Because certain aspects of religion, mythology, politics, and literature, in particular, represent derivatives of unconscious fantasies that can be shared in common, they appeal to the individual and therefore may offer invaluable clues to the nature of the patient's unconscious fantasies. Accordingly, if a patient mentions some novel, movie, play, myth, religious ritual or legend, I suspect we are dealing with a derivative of an important unconscious conflict, and accordingly I pay special attention to the context in which associations arise. I find it valuable to elicit fuller description of the particular creative work the patient mentioned, and when I am not aware of the contents of the particular movie, play or novel, I do not hesitate to ask the patient for a fuller description. Like dreams, all of these art forms are highways to the unconscious mind.

Essentially the appeal of all of these art forms is dependent upon their metaphoric quality. In effect, they speak in words that do not literally mean what they say, or in media whose manifest representations articulate something quite different. Accordingly, I have come to take special note of the metaphors the analysand uses and I often find it useful to treat the metaphor literally and to get associations to it. I have come to regard metaphors as outcroppings of unconscious fantasy. In this sense, I have also come to regard dreams as visual metaphors, conveying in pictures messages that are not literally apparent in their concrete presentations. In fact, one could even say that the systems of our unconscious fantasies represent a metaphoric apprehension of the psychological experiences of childhood.

The spoken language, of course, is the basic medium of the interchange during analytic treatment. Just as metaphors are unconsciously determined, so are many of the most ordinary, seemingly practical uses we make of words. Freud pointed out that a negation represents a method by which a declarative statement may be introduced into consciousness. In my practice, I have expanded that principle to include the interrogatory, the subjunctive. the conditional, etc. Just as every negation implies a declarative statement, so also does every interrogatory, subjunctive or conditional statement. For the purpose of understanding what the patient is defending against, I find it useful to hear for myself all of these sentences as potentially declarative statements.

Finally, I have come to view the analytic situation as articulating a special form of discourse. The real circumstances that brought analyst and analysand together are always operative, no matter how subtle. Somewhere the patient is always aware that he is coming to treatment for the purpose of getting help by talking to another person and, whether he decides upon it intentionally or not, whatever he expresses is influenced by the notion that he is here to get help. In this spirit, I place special emphasis on the first thing that the patient says at the beginning of the session. It is the leitmotif, or shall we say the coda, of what is to follow, and it is especially true if the first production relates to the analyst. The rest of the session, like a musical sonata, represents repetition and variation on the theme and, in many sessions, especially if the importance of the underlying transference mode has been overlooked, the patient will return to the opening theme at the very end of the session. This is a good clue to the fact that something important has been overlooked or that the patient is still fending off the insights that have been transmitted to him.

In any communication, meaning is determined heavily by context. This is especially true in the psychoanalytic situation. The context and order in which the elements of the patient's productions appear and their contiguous relationship to each other define the nature of the unconscious processes operative at the time. It is as if each element is connected to the next one by some implied but unexpressed element, a connection apparent to the analyst but not to the analysand. As I listen to the patient, I try to supply the missing element that the contiguity of the productions defines.

I have come to regard technique as consisting primarily of intervening on one side or the other of the unstable equilibrium between impulse, defense and guilt that has been established in the patient's mind. Accordingly, I render less weight to whether the patient agrees or disagrees with the observations I make. Instead I listen and analyze the responses to my disequilibrating interventions.

If anything, my experience has taught me how powerfully the principle of determinism operates in the patient's productions. In that spirit, I have become particularly sensitive to repetitions, similarities, differences and opposites, figurative language of any sort, especially metaphor, and the use of unusual or strange words or expressions. Anything that would not fit into the dynamics of an ordinary conversation arouses my special curiosity.

I do not mean to suggest that these changes in technique are all original with me, but they do represent my awareness of some of the changes that have taken place in how I come to understand my analysand's difficulties and how I can advance the process of therapeutic insight.

References

Arlow, J.A. (1995). *The Structure of Memory.* The Victor Calef Memorial Lecture, San Francisco Psychoanalytic Institute.

Beres, D. & Arlow, J.A. (1974). Fantasy and identification in empathy. *Psychoanalytic Quarterly,* 43:26–50.

Freud, A. (1936). *The Ego and the Mechanisms of Defense.* New York: International Universities Press.

Freud, S. (1912). The dynamics of transference. *Standard Edition,* Vol. 12, p. 108. London: The Hogarth Press.

——— (1937). Constructions in psychoanalysis. *Standard Edition,* Vol. 23, pp. 255-269. London: The Hogarth Press.

——— & Breuer, J. (1893). Studies on hysteria. *Standard Edition,* Vol. 2. London: The Hogarth Press.

Hartmann, H. (1938). *Ego Psychology and the Problem of Adaptation.* New York: International Universities Press.

Nunberg, H. (1925). The road to recovery. In: *The Practice and Theory of Psychoanalysis.* New York: Nervous and Mental Disease Publishing, 1948, pp. 75–88.

——— (1951). Transference and reality. *International Journal of Psycho-Analysis,* 32:1–9.

Sterba, R. (1934). The fate of the ego in analytic therapy. *International Journal of Psycho-Analysis,* 15:117–126.

Strachey, J. (1934). The nature of the therapeutic action in psychoanalysis. *International Journal of Psycho-Analysis,* 15:127–159.

Chapter 17

Some Historical Observations on the Origin of the Psychoanalytic Curriculum

Jacob A. Arlow, MD

Commentary: Kimberly L. Kleinman, MS, LCSW

Not many psychoanalytic papers have a surprise ending, but this one does. For that reason, I won't spoil the ending by discussing it in detail. Arlow was intensively involved in issues around training, and this paper is an outgrowth of his hard earned wisdom about the politics and pitfalls of training psychoanalysts. A clinician applies to become a member of a psychoanalytic institute and isn't admitted. Arlow discusses why.

I think that it highlights some of the current difficulties we have with approving current candidates' clinical work and allowing them to progress to membership. Many psychoanalytic educators have commented on how we expect less experienced candidates to sound like peers prior to graduating. Many feel this supports good standards for our field. Others feel it is stultifying. Arlow illustrates his point of view in a witty manner that is a fun read.

Some Historical Observations on the Origin of the Psychoanalytic Curriculum

Jacob A. Arlow, MD

Some 30 years ago, before I was Chairman of the Board on Professional Standards and before I served for five years as Chairman of the Committee on Psychoanalytic Education (I include this to establish my credentials as a psychoanalytic educator), I was President of the American Psychoanalytic Association. As one of the prerogatives and responsibilities of my office, I used to visit the various committees of the Board and Council in order to observe how their members were fulfilling their duties to the Association. One such visit was to the Membership Committee, a body which at that time served the function which at present has been allocated to the Committee on Certification. Their function was roughly identical and their decisions, as today, were based primarily on the examination and evaluation of case reports of patients treated by the applicant.

There was one applicant who remained indelibly in my memory. He was clearly a most talented man, with an extraordinary gift for lucid presentation. In his covering letter to the Membership Committee, he expressed himself in part as follows: "When it comes to evaluating my case write-ups, I would like to direct the attention of the Membership Committee to the following considerations. I am a beginner in the field and I live and work in a city where very few people have ever heard of psychoanalysis. Those who do know about

268

it are mostly hostile to it. Under the circumstances, as you can well imagine, it has been difficult for me to get a good analytic case, although I feel confident that, properly applied, psychoanalysis would be of benefit to most patients.

"The first case that I am presenting is that of a young woman still in her teens. She was caught up in the family intrigues all too common in our upper middle class suburban society, but she was a person who was not easily fooled and, not surprisingly, was bent on revenge against those who wronged her. In my description of the case, I have focused on a particular dream and its implications for the transference, implications which dawned on me only slowly. It was for me, however, a most illuminating experience, and I trust the committee will agree.

The second case is that of a young man with artistic leanings who suffered from severe obsessive-compulsive symptoms, centering primarily about religious themes. He was the scion of a well-to-do family, whose fortunes in recent years had taken a sharp decline. The understanding of this case which, as I have indicated in my report, I have followed for a very long period of time, also centered around the interpretation of a crucial dream. On the basis of my understanding of this dream, we were led in the analysis to the unraveling of the patient's infantile neurosis and the recovery of a traumatic event from his earliest years. As you will see, I have taken great pains in my description of this case to supply the necessary process details, which serve to validate the preoedipal reconstruction.

"My next two cases may perhaps be regarded as problematic in both instances, I have used the psychoanalytic approach meticulously. The former derives from the realm of child analysis. I understand that at the present time there is considerable controversy among analysts and in the Board on Professional Standards itself concerning the admissibility of experience from child analysis for qualification for membership in the American Psychoanalytic Association. I do appreciate that the method of treatment diverges in large measure from standard psychoanalytic procedure, inasmuch as children are unable to associate freely and also because they cannot form a real transference, in light of the fact that they are still in a relationship with their primary objects. Nonetheless, I feel that the material that I have to present is so revealing about the nature of childhood sexuality and so illustrative of the genesis of anxiety that the case warrants presentation for purposes of admission to the American Psychoanalytic Association.

"The fourth case represents a venture which is rarely undertaken even by more experienced analysts, to say nothing of a beginner. It is a meticulous psychoanalytic investigation of the productions of an undeniable case of psychosis. The patient was a highly successful individual, married, with no children. He appears to have suffered several breakdowns of a paranoid nature. Although I admit that this was a rather daring undertaking, I have reached the conclusion that my analysis of this patient's productions enabled me to elucidate, in a way that probably has not been done before, the psychodynamics of certain types of psychoses. I trust that the members of the committee will not find this last assertion too brash and immodest but will take it in the spirit of honest inquiry with which I approach the material of this fascinating individual."

Intrigued as the members of the committee were by the exemplary case reports the applicant had submitted, after much debate and controversy, they voted to reject the applicant's request for admission to membership in our association. The reasons for rejection were given to the applicant in a letter from the Chairman of the Committee on Membership, a straightforward and, as I would regard, rather hard-nosed person. He said in part: "The Committee on Membership read your case reports with great interest. You are unquestionably an unusually perceptive observer, with a most enviable capacity for lucid and convincing exposition. There are, however, a number of difficulties with each of the cases you presented for consideration. While Case No, I holds together in a most remarkable fashion and is as engrossing as a novel, the fact remains that the patient was in treatment only a very short period of time. it is not clear from your report whether she was in analysis nine weeks or eleven weeks. In any event, the treatment ended abruptly and one-sidedly when the patient decided to discontinue. Apparently the transference implications of much of her behavior, as you yourself admit, had been missed by you until it was too late. The fact that you refused to take her back into treatment sometime later, when she appealed to you, puzzled several members of our committee. Could this have been the residue of some hostile countertransference feeling? Perhaps you felt frustrated that she left just at the point where you thought you had solved the problem of her neurosis.

"This brings up some issues in connection with Case No 2 as well. Did the patient really enter a termination phase? The rules of the Board on Professional Standards do not require that the patient go through a successful termination, but the drastic method of imposing a deadline one-sidedly seemed to some of the members of the committee as ill-conceived. Perhaps the patient was sicker than you appreciated. Unfortunately, we do not have a supervisor's report on this case. Some members of the committee felt that the patient could be characterized as suffering from a borderline disturbance with a potential for paranoid compensation. Others thought that the therapeutic achievements of this case may have reflected an idealizing transference. As you can appreciate, there are differences of approach to theory and technique among the members of the committee as well. Accordingly, there was some disagreement about the validity of the reconstruction of the preoedipal trauma but, by and large, the majority of the committee sustained your interpretation. Many of them considered it to be quite brilliant. In sum, however, there was sufficient uncertainty about the severity of the pathological process and the prognosis for the patient to invalidate the case for purposes of membership.

"Your observations on the case of the five-year-old patient with the phobia were striking indeed and your interaction with him impressed especially those members of our committee who have some experience with child analysis. Leaving aside the controversy about admissibility of child analysis experience for purposes of membership certification, this case could hardly be called one of child analysis. You saw the patient very infrequently, two or three times perhaps. Most of the work was done by the father under your guidance. We assume that he is either a colleague or someone with previous experience in analysis. In any event, in spite of the splendid outcome for the patient, we could not accept that case either.

"The final case that you presented could not be considered a case. Your report constitutes a brilliant application of psychoanalytic concepts to the phenomenology of the paranoid psychosis, but what you have given the committee is an exercise, albeit a brilliant one, in psychoanalysis applied to data not obtained within the standard psychoanalytic situation. While conceivably this might be the kind of material obtainable in direct working with the patient, the fact is that no such involvement ever took place. Some of your interpretations were felt to be rather dogmatic, not taking into account the possibility of alternative explanations. Accordingly, we had to conclude, brilliant though your analysis was, it could not be considered a case study for purposes of membership.

"All the members of the committee were greatly impressed by your insights and exposition. You are the kind of person that the Association eagerly seeks but never finds. So we ask you in the meantime to continue with your analysis. Your analyst seems to be doing an excellent job. He has helped you clear up the crippling symptoms that appeared in consequence of your father's death. We are sure that further self-exploration will help you overcome certain countertransference difficulties that we have detected in some of the case reports. Please let us hear from you very soon.

"In the meantime, my committee and I have a very unusual and delicate request to make of you. We have found your exposition of psychoanalytic process and interpretation so lucid and convincing that we would like to use this case material for purposes of teaching candidates in psychoanalytic training. We realize that this raises certain issues of confidentiality vis-a-vis the identity of the patients, but there are ways in which these difficulties, we are sure, may be circumvented. The most difficult situation would arise in connection with your first case, the patient whom you called Dora. She seems willful and angry and has already caused enough grief and trouble to her parents and others The case of the charming little Hans with the horse phobia should present no problem. You achieved an exemplary result and his family is well disposed to you on that score. The third case, whom you labeled the Wolf Man, also seems to present no problem. We gather that be is quite an exhibitionist. He is, after all, an artist. He struck us as the kind of man who would revel in having his case published to the entire world. It might even make him a celebrity. Finally, of course, the memoirs of Senate President Schreber, published by him, are part of the public domain. Our lawyers state that we would hardly even have to ask his permission, although it night be the better part of wisdom to get in touch with him.

"We hope we have not been too disappointing to you, Dr Freud. We look forward to accepting you into membership the next time and we hope that you will consider our request to use your case material for purposes of student indoctrination as the compliment it is intended to be."

Chapter 18

Some Analytic Reflections on the Problem of Morality in the Therapeutic Setting

Jacob A. Arlow, MD

Commentary by Kimberly L. Kleinman, MS, LCSW

We learn about professional ethics during training. Are issues of morality the purview of philosophers and theologians? At the time of this writing, issues around the COVID 19 pandemic and vaccines against it effect how we practice on a daily basis. What about patients who either wittingly or unwittingly have become prey to propaganda promoted by groups who have multiple agendas? Issues of oppression cannot be imagined to be outside the door of the consulting room, whether the oppression is related to race, class, identity or gender. Arlow offers a rubric for thinking about this issue, based on thinking about compassion.

Arlow provides clinical examples of cruelty towards women. These examples could apply to all forms of cruelty such as cruelty towards children, towards employees as just some of the examples. In one of my classes, a clinical vignette was presented. A daughter called her mother during a session. She called to tell her mother she was having an asthma attack. The mother screamed at the daughter.

Arlow implies that in some cases our interventions may also be an accusation since our focus will be drawn to issues that conflict with our morality. In addition, it is Quixotic to think that we are perceived as judgmentally neutral by our analysands.

Some Analytic Reflections on the Problem of Morality in the Therapeutic Setting

Jacob A. Arlow, MD

In this beautiful setting on an early summer morning, we have assembled to grapple with questions whose solutions have eluded philosophers and theologians for centuries. So in the 25 minutes allotted to me for this presentation, you should expect and will probably receive very little. At best I can offer some few reflections on how some problems of good and evil impinge on the thought and the technique of the psychoanalyst.

In the course of his work, the practicing analyst becomes more or less comfortable with issues of good and bad, and right and wrong. For the most part, he manages such problems intuitively. Evil, however, is an issue of somewhat different dimension. It is more dramatic, more intense, more destructive. What burden of judgment we place upon it depends upon the magnitude of the pain and damage that ensues and the degree to which the perpetrator had consciously intended and enjoyed what he had wrought? In the therapeutic context, every confrontation with evil impinges on our own value system and serves to dispel the illusion of a completely non-judgmental stance towards what we hear from our patients. Without some sense of our own values, we would be at a loss regarding what technical procedures to employ.

The tendency towards evil is an inexorable component of man's very nature. As the Bible tells us, it took God only a few generations of experience with mankind to conclude that "the imagination of man's heart is evil from his youth." And in the same spirit, Machiavelli wrote, "Whoever takes it upon himself to establish a commonwealth and prescribe laws must presuppose all men naturally bad and that they will yield to their innate evil passions as often as they can with safety," and, in terms that almost parallel the psychoanalytic theory of drives, the *Ramayana* states, "There are three all-powerful evils; lust, anger and greed."

In order to establish domestic tranquility and to further the principles of its ideology, society establishes rules and regulations to foster the principles that constitute the ethical base of the society. Kluckahon ( ) notes that, while such codes may differ in many respects, what is common to all of them is the interdiction of the infliction of pain, damage or murder, together with the taboo of incest. Beyond that, cultural ideals may differ markedly, as can be attested from the experience of both ancient and recent cultures. In this context, Beres ( ) emphasizes the distinction between ethics and morality. Ethics comprises the rules, regulations and the principles of the community, as arrived at as a basis for social cohesion. Laws represent the codification of ethical regulations, while morality indicates the relation of the individual to those ethical principles. Beres reviews the historical development typical of various countries over time and the manner in which psychological pressures are brought to bear on the developing individuals in a society to create a character structure consonant with its ethical principles.

In Freud's view ( ), this process involves a progressive renunciation of the gratification of those instinctual impulses that lead to pleasure, but these selfsame impulses, under specific circumstances, may become the fountainhead of evil. He noted in this connection that "the more civilized one is, the more energy one devotes to the avoidance of pain rather than to the pursuit of pleasure." (p.) One should note that it was part of Freud's genius that he could tolerate and study objectively, not only the good and bad in man, but also the evil. He quoted the Latin phrase, "nihil humanum mihi alienum est." For analysts, this serves, as it were, almost as an article of faith.

Moral issues, i.e., those involving judgment concerning right or wrong, are part of the inevitable experience of analysts and are usually comprehended in terms of derivative representations of early identifications and persistent conflicts. On the other hand, situations involving conflicts between good and evil pose a much more difficult task. Under what circumstances does one choose merely to interpret, to point out the consequences, or perhaps to issue a prohibition? As a rule, people who are thoroughly evil do not come for treatment by psychoanalysis. They are not overly inclined towards looking within themselves for the causes of their difficulties. Evil in the analytic situation challenges our neutrality, demands that we face our own value system and even re-examine or challenge the principles of technique we have been taught. It is important, therefore, to examine, however inadequately, what elements enter into the analyst's reaction to his perception and response to evil.

Our notions of good and evil stem from our developmental history and from biology as well. Gratification and pleasure are good and are easily assimilated; intensely painful experiences become identified as evil. Developmental and analytic observations have demonstrated how painful sensations may be disavowed, projected outward, to reappear as the demons that torture us in our dreams and our imagination. To jump ahead, during the vast transformations of ethical concepts that take place during adolescence and even later, the proponents of what is considered evil have foisted upon them the demons of our early years. But to return to the genesis of our concepts of good and evil, they are rooted not only in the experiences of the pleasure/unpleasure continuum but of the authoritative commands taken as objective information of what constitutes right and wrong. These influences play upon the mindset of the young child, namely, the capacity and the need for compassionate identification. I came to appreciate the full force of this mechanism when my oldest son was about four and a half years of age. The night before the incident

279

I had been injured while ice skating, sustaining abrasions and contusions on the right side of my face. In the morning, my son entered my bedroom, took one look at my face and, without a word, went back to his bed and returned to cover me with his blanket, an item to which he had a very fond attachment. He identified with me in my pain but (and?) with his mother in his efforts to assuage my suffering. He enfolded me in the comforting blanket, as he himself had been comforted on many previous occasions.

It is not only the element of identification, which is important here, but also the notion of compassion. The word is derived from two Latin roots: cum, with, and passion, to feel, but also to suffer. Much of our concepts of right and wrong and morality have their beginning in the capacity of the child to experience in fantasy an identification with the other in a painful situation, an identification that leads to a wish to spare others and to alleviate pain. A logical extension of this psychology is the golden rule expressed in its negative form, that is, what is unpleasant (unacceptable to you) do not do unto others.

The capacity for compassionate identification is not just learned or taught. More than any other mammalian offspring, the human child is completely helpless at birth and cannot survive without the protective intervention of adults. From infant observation we have learned of the rich capacity for communication of signals of distress, as well as pleasure, that pass between child and adult, of affective states that are shared in common. Thus, we note the capacity and the tendency toward compassionate identification derived from several different sources in early life. Of these, identification with the caring mother is probably the most important.

How the mechanism of compassionate identification enters into the generation of ethical principles may be illustrated by this example in the Old Testament. The text reads: "There shall be but one law in your land, one law for the native-born and the stranger who dwells in your midst." For the purpose of assuring domestic tranquility, this is a perfectly logical notion, sensible and pragmatic. But the text continues with a psychological, not a legal or pragmatic, justification for this principle. It reads: "For remember that you too were once strangers in the land of Egypt." What buttresses the principle of equality before the law is the evocation of the sentiment of compassionate identification.

In the therapeutic situation, the capacity for compassionate identification constitutes an essential element of the ability of the therapist to be empathic. Countertransference acting outs are essentially miscarriages of compassionate identification and they can lead to moral dilemmas and serve to compound right and wrong. The technical rules that pertain to the handling of the transference buttress and sustain the ethical principles of treatment. They help preserve the moral stance of the therapist.

In our clinical work the tendency towards compassionate identification, as well as identification in general, expresses itself in manifold ways. Paramount among these is the evocation of an impulse to rescue, the so-called rescue fantasy. As the analyst identifies with his patient, he becomes sympathetic, but remaining fixed at this stage interferes with the process of developing empathy and insight and enhances the potentiality for countertransference acting out of the rescue fantasy. Every situation of intense countertransference raises the potential for boundary violation and a compromise of moral integrity.

To what extent the element of compassionate identification plays a role in the genesis of moral masochism is difficult to say, but clearly it must play some role. In the genesis of this character trait, a powerful identification with the suffering individual, usually characterized by a passive, feminine, erotic quality, seems to play a significant role. As Spiegel ( ) has pointed out, such an identification may be adopted as a defense against castration anxieties stemming from oedipal conflicts. The patient uses morality as an instrument with which to torture himself.

Guilt, self-punishment and morality lead quite directly to the analysis of religious observance as seen in the course of clinical work. For many analysts, dealing with religious themes and observance is most problematic. In part this stems from the rational, materialistic tradition out of which psychoanalysis emerged. If religious observance is the equivalent of an obsessional neurosis, then it must be analyzed away during treatment. On the other hand, there are those who feel that such an approach is an assault upon the patient's integrity and may undermine one of the foundations of the individual's moral behavior. As far as the validity of an analysis, Waelder ( ) said, it makes no difference whether the analyst is or is not a religious person. This is a view that is not universally shared in our ranks. It is inconceivable that religion, often an important aspect of the individual's life, should not at some point interlock with the persistent unconscious conflicts that bring him to treatment. At issue is to what extent certain religious ideas and commitments constitute a maladaptive compromise formation of the patient's neurotic conflicts. In pursuit of the therapeutic goals, the analyst perforce must make some judgment of the role and the power of the analysand's religious imperatives and how they affect his morality. All too often we are confronted by surprising contradictions. This is particularly striking when there exists an extreme contradiction between the analyst's and the patient's moral stance regarding political issues.

Gaining insight into the nature of the patient's developmental history and unconscious conflicts, the analyst may come to understand why the analysand may incline towards one or another political view or social philosophy. The analyst has his own moral principles which incline him to certain conclusions concerning good and evil and political and social rights. Respect for the patient's integrity, however, is by far the weightier principle. There are situations, however, where the analysand's behavior, growing out of his social philosophy, is so repugnant to the analyst that therapeutic collaboration becomes impossible.

Waelder ( ) pointed out that, in the course of political life, the ideal of real justice and equality is impossible to attain. This is not necessarily the result of a conflict between good and evil, but rather a conflict between varying forms of goodness. When confronted with the good and evil in the world in which we live, what about the analyst's moral stance? In 1974 the American Psychoanalytic Association sponsored a symposium at the American Association for the Advancement of Science on the subject of "Ethics, Moral Values and Psychological Interventions." The influence of the spirit of the times was decisive. The agenda of the moral issues concerned such items as unjust wars, racial discrimination and inequality, poverty, governmental snooping into the private and political lives of the citizens. In a word, the analysts came down hard on the side of liberal policies. It was the kind of agenda that people at the opposite end of the political spectrum would characterize as typical of "bleeding hearts" liberals. Such a characterization implies that the compassion felt by liberals must stem from some masochistic trend, perhaps an identification with the unfortunates in our social order. It would seem that, as a rule, the moral and political stance of analysts is deeply influenced by a compassionate identification which is an essential part of the analyst's mental set.

If compassionate identification plays an important role in the development of a moral sense, its abrogation is an essential feature for the perpetration of evil. It has been noted that there were many instances of officers of death camps during the Holocaust who were gentle, tender husbands and fathers to their families, but at the same time were capable of the most heinous atrocities against Jews and gypsies. An essential element in making this evil possible was the withdrawal of the sense of identification and its attendant compassion for their victims. In Erikson's term ( ), a process of despeciation, a regarding of Jews and gypsies as less than humans, non-humans, was a necessary condition to enable the murderers to carry out the Nazi policies. It is also the process that makes indifference to evil possible. Certain racist theories convey the same message. (During delicate diplomatic negotiations, Talleyrand was informed of an atrocity that French troops had committed. "It was a crime," his adjutant said to which Talleyrand is reputed to have replied, "It was worse than a crime, it was a mistake."]

There are situations in which the impulse to help, based upon a compassionate identification, may have an opposite effect. What seems good from one point of view may be bad from another, although not necessarily evil. A case in point may be culled from Sinclair Lewis' *Arrowsmith,* a scientist who, out of compassion for the suffering patients, violated scientific protocol and administered the vaccine to the members of the control group as well. Out of compassion for the experimental subjects, a good motive, the experiment was ruined, which was bad. It was not, however, evil. This is a literary character. In the case of our patients, we take into account the underlying unconscious motivation when we can perceive it. This, however, is not always the case. Concerning such situations, Nunberg ( ) once stated, "If you have doubts about the motivation for a certain parapraxis, you can safely judge the unconscious intent by the consequences that the parapraxis brings about."

Sometimes it is difficult to ascertain whether a particular act represents something good or evil, even when we are fully aware of the unconscious motivation. The memorable incident in Victor Hugo's *Les Misérables* may be used to illustrate this point. The police return Jean Valjean to the Bishop's residence because, having found the Bishop's silver candelabra in his possession, they accuse him of theft. To spare Valjean, the Bishop says the candelabra were a gift and, in fact, he reproaches Valjean for not having taken the silver goblet that the Bishop had presumably given him. All three participants in this episode know this is a lie that now permits Valjean to go free. This is the playing out of the rescue fantasy on a grand scale. Actually, however, the Bishop committed a criminal act. He was an accessory after the fact. He assisted in a theft. We are touched by the nobility and the self-sacrifice of the cleric, Was his act moral or immoral? Was it good or evil? One cannot predict the consequences of the act. Valjean could use his ill-gotten gains to rehabilitate himself, which in the novel he did, or he possibly could have used the money he got from the sale of the silver to buy a pistol or a sabre and to embark more proficiently on a career of crime. Nunberg's dictum concerning the consequences of the ambiguous action seems particularly apposite at this juncture. In our daily work there are many occasions when we find ourselves precisely in this kind of situation. Will a "good" motive, conscious or unconscious, give rise to evil?

Judging the moral quality of our patient's behavior represents a difficult balance between our understanding of the dynamics, conscious and unconscious, and the relative degree of our identification with the patient. How much sympathy or antipathy is mixed with our empathy? According to our own values, we are influenced by the nature of the patient's unconscious dynamics and the vicissitudes of his interpersonal relations. Let me illustrate the problem through the following vignettes, each of which pertains to a similar problem, namely, the pain perpetrated by a man upon a woman by breaking off a longstanding relationship with her, thus bringing her pain and grief.

Case No. 1. The patient has done this several times now in his life. He feels frustrated and guilty about it. He had a cruel and threatening father. His problem involves castration anxiety. His relationship to women is influenced, among other things, by the idea that marriage or a permanent relationship represents a trap from which he will never be able to extricate himself. He has an unconscious fantasy of a dentate vagina or a life and death encounter within the claustrum, struggling with a representative of the father or his phallus.

Case No. 2. This patient has broken off relations with women several times under similar circumstances. He feels guilty for the pain he causes the woman, but somehow cannot avoid repeating the pattern. The dynamics of the case reveal a classical revenge motive of the primal scene. Like patient No. 1, he is disturbed by the turn of events. He had a mother who was alternately seductive and rejecting. He realizes the pain that he has caused and feels sorry for his victims. Psychologically he can share the pain.

Case No. 3. His problems were preoedipal in origin. When he was less than two, a brother was born and the mother had a psychotic break, which kept her away for several months. When she returned, she was far from completely well. She was by no means an adequate or caring mother. She had a similar

285

break when the patient was four. Throughout his life, this patient has repeated a pattern of abandoning women, in ways that were not only painful to them but also objectively disadvantageous. He caused then real pain and damage. He justifies his behavior by detailing the hurtful things that his wife and other women have perpetrated upon him. He feels no remorse. Whatever regret he experiences is for the inconvenience that followed upon his changed position in life. Concern for his victim, so-called, is minimal.

Case No. 4 is an essentially psychopathic character, a Don Juan who abandons women after having robbed them of their money. Evidence of compassionate identification is completely lacking. He had a disastrously deprived childhood. Some of the features mentioned in Case No. 3 can be discerned in this situation.

Here are four individuals who caused pain and even damage, somewhat similar in nature if not degree. Are they to be pitied or scorned? Does the hurt they experience outweigh the pain they cause? Does the fact that, in several of the cases, the basic motivation was not easily discernible by the patient mitigate our judgment of their behavior? In a word, do we regard them as perpetrators or victims? Good or evil? In his reaction to such situations each analyst's own morality is put to the test.

To think that the analyst's technical procedures, no matter how carefully expressed, are experienced by the analysand as judgmentally neutral is completely illusory. In practically every instance when the analysis of a set of defenses against an impulse is persistently pursued, some implication of moral judgment is involved. It is as if the analyst were saying, "I'm not going to let you get away with this. Why did you do it?" When a child hears the question, "Why did you do it?", he perceives it as an accusation. In a certain sense, the same is true with patients when their defenses are being whittled away. When a patient feels that he is being repetitively confronted with evidence of motives or behavior that he considers morally unacceptable, he confuses interpretation with accusation. Why be reminded of something that he himself had already rejected in the past? For the patient, the persistent application of analytic technique, because it produces pain, is at the same time considered immoral. Furthermore, the things the analyst picks up to interpret imply, usually quite correctly, the application of the analyst's moral values. We reassure ourselves with the idea that such values are adaptive, integrative and ultimately helpful to the patient.

As I mentioned at the outset of this presentation, the subject is much too large to be treated under these limited conditions. If, however, I have given you a point of departure to explore the intricacies and ramifications of this problem, I shall feel justified in my effort. Thank you.

Chapter 19

Training for Psychoanalysis and Psychotherapy

Jacob A. Arlow, MD

Commentary: Kimberly L. Kleinman, MS, LCSW

Arlow was deeply involved in issues concerning psychoanalytic education. He brings up an issue that has not yet been resolved by psychoanalytic institutes. Should we teach Freud? Arlow points out that Freud did not write for didactic purposes. Many of the classic texts like Dora, Little Hans and the Interpretations of Dreams, are all very distant from how we practice now. He said: *"They should be appreciated for what they are, namely, milestones on the pathway to great discoveries, but not texts for modern psychoanalytic theory or practice."*

Arlow also notes that candidates have difficulties separating observations and interpretations. I have had the same experience when showing videos of mothers and toddlers interacting. My students will comment on how instructive or distance a mother is. But they cannot describe exactly what the mother did and then trace the thinking involved with the conclusions they espoused. Interestingly, I don›t have the same experience when teaching in China. I find my Chinese students to be enthusiastic and exquisite observers.

Arlow feels that it is most helpful to teach the historical development of psychoanalytic ideas. He feels one should learn all the psychoanalytic approaches. He feels this will help the candidate develop a detached view of psychoanalysis, as opposed to taking up a theoretical orientation the way one might take up a political cause.

Arlow also takes up how clinical learning takes place. He advocates for greater exposure to the clinical work of experienced analysts. He implicitly cautions us about what metaphors we use to teach, as they can take on a life of their own. He also explores the problem of stilted listening, something he has written about elsewhere and here. Arlow also clarifies that the idea that all that is mutative in a psychoanalytic treatment happens in the transference is actually a reflection of Strachey's Kleinian point of view. *«Is it even possible for all of the unconscious, instinctual conflicts relating to certain fantasy wishes to be worked out in connection with the analyst? Some of them, by their very nature, run counter to this supposition.»*

He ends his paper on a note that is dear to me as a child analyst. Psychoanalysis is a developmental psychology. He states it is of utmost importance that analysts be fully versed in the many vicissitudes of development and impingements on development.

Training for Psychoanalysis and Psychotherapy

Jacob A. Arlow, MD

It would be well to begin by acknowledging that we are discussing preparation for the practice of what has been termed "an impossible profession," the practice of which concerns not only the infinite vagaries of the human mind, but also the fact that our own psychology and personality are so much involved in the pursuit of our technical tasks. Furthermore, the integration of the knowledge and skills acquired during training demands a long period of seasoning, one that comes only from experience. The best planned, the best organized training program cannot preempt the new learning that comes from experience. Nonetheless, the training program is an organized experience that we wish our candidates to go through to prepare them in the best way for the work ahead.

The weight of the past is a heavy burden on current programs of psychoanalytic training. By and large, psychoanalytic education today rests on a philosophy and a set of practices inherited from the earliest days of its history. Over the years, reflecting upon my own experience as a student and as a teacher and having listened to many hours of supervision and consultation, I have been impressed that there are recurrent difficulties that students trained even in the best of Institutes demonstrate and in a number of ways I believe these difficulties may be alleviated through improvement in the training program, particularly the curriculum. I have noted, for example, how often students are confused as to what constitutes data in psychoanalysis, how they mistake observations for interpretation and vice versa, their misunderstanding of such basic concepts as transference and the role of countertransference reactions. Above all, one may observe the difficulties students have in arriving at interpretations, confusing analogies with identities, making interpretations outside of context, listening in a stilted fashion, and so forth. The list could be extended at great length. There are many ways in which the current curricula fail to meet the needs of today's candidates.

Therese Benedek once told me how, in Vienna, during the pristine days of our science, most of the learning was done around the coffee tables of the favored café. The candidates-in-training would wait patiently for the next paper by Freud to appear, and, when it finally came into their hands, they would discuss it at great length. She said, "He was our Prometheus. He brought us the fire from the gods." That was the curriculum.

In a certain sense, this model has persisted to this very day. Although classes are more formal and take place in the less romantic but probably more comfortable ambiance of the Institute's classrooms, the systematic study of Freud's papers in seriatim became the core curriculum of psychoanalysis. Depending upon where one wishes to begin to count, psychoanalysis is about a hundred years old. During this time it has spawned a vast literature that even now is in a stage of dynamic growth. Central to this literature is Freud's impressive corpus of contributions, a vast body of knowledge to which analysts will refer for the rest of their careers. Freud was a prolific writer but, above all, he was a very dynamic and original thinker. Only on a few occasions did he write directly for didactic purposes, as in the "Introductory Lectures to Psychoanalysis." For the most part, he was making new and revolutionary disclosures, and his writings are more a record of his thinking about these discoveries. As a result, he kept changing his views in time and only rarely went back to correct earlier articles or to append footnotes. Even a most superficial reading of Freud's writings will reveal how he kept changing both the theory and technique of psychoanalysis as he confronted fresh problems in the course of his therapeutic research. He was aware of the need for change. It is, indeed, a fact that since his time both the theory and practice of psychoanalysis have changed enormously. But has psychoanalytic education changed in equal proportion? Has psychoanalytic education kept pace with the new realities?

The social and professional setting of psychoanalysis has changed enormously. Originally psychoanalysis grew out of medicine. In those early days, the symptoms from which most patients suffered—hysterical paralyses, sleep disorders, fugue states, somnambulism, somatic conversion phenomena— all resembled physical disorders. Then as now, the medical practitioner represented the first source of relief to whom the patients turned. With the comparatively limited diagnostic means available to the practitioners of those days, it was no easy task to distinguish psychological from organic illness. But how the times and the techniques have changed! The flamboyant, hysterical phenomenology of the late 19th Century has all but disappeared. This is particularly true in the case of those people who nowadays might turn to psychoanalysis for help. Today, not only does medical science possess a range of diagnostic capability undreamed of even 50 years ago, but the very nature of medicine has changed. A deeper understanding of the physics and chemistry of bodily processes and cellular activity has revolutionized medicine and has made possible dramatic new methods for diagnosing and treating illnesses. Perforce the physician today must rely more and more on the objective, technical data which the laboratory can furnish. This objective laboratory stance of modern medical training militates strongly against the developing of those skills and qualities so necessary for empathic interaction with patients in the case of psychoanalysts, the efforts of medical schools to counteract this tendency to the contrary notwithstanding. For the purpose of our discussion it becomes clear that medical training today has little relevance and leaves very little room for preparing one for the study of psychoanalysis. I suspect that most practitioners of psychoanalysis today do not possess a medical degree. The idea of requiring a medical degree of candidates who enter training is long past. For the future psychoanalyst, the time spent in acquiring a medical degree can be expended more profitably in other pursuits.

There are some advantages that the medically trained candidate brings to the study of psychoanalysis, namely, a knowledge of the anatomy and physiology of the brain and nervous system, clinical neurology and psychiatry, an acquaintance with neuroscience but, above all, the tremendous advantage of at least a years' residency in a mental institution for the treatment of the insane. Only this last kind of experience can impress upon the future non-medical analyst a sense of conviction of the depth and the reality of unconscious wishes and fantasies, and of their derivative expressions in behavior and thought that we find in so-called neurotic and normal individuals. Nowadays, however, it is possible for PhDs in psychology and psychoanalysis to obtain a parallel experience. On the other hand, the non-medical candidates come from an educational program rich in the humanities and languages, with some knowledge of folklore, philosophy, mythology, religion and art. These are important categories of educational experience that we have a right to expect in the background of future psychoanalysts.

The division of psychoanalytic training into three parts—the personal analysis, the curriculum and supervised analysis—is a natural one. I shall omit consideration of the personal analysis. It is too big and too difficult a subject to grapple with while we are contending with the more formal aspects of psychoanalytic training. In what follows I propose to direct our examination primarily to the curriculum, and to view it from three perspectives: the historical, the methodological and the developmental. To me these comprise the three essential areas of experience that form the basis for learning psychoanalysis and they are as much a part of the supervisory experience as they are part of the curriculum.

The Historical Overview

Psychoanalysis is now almost 100 years old. It has spawned a vast literature that even now is in a stage of dynamic growth. I like to remind my audience that we are living in what I call the post-apostolic period of psychoanalysis. With the death of Anna Freud and the members of her generation, there is no one around today who can lay claim to authority derived from direct contact with the fountainhead of psychoanalytic knowledge. There is no true holy writ in psychoanalysis.

Freud's writings, however, are treated in exactly this spirit. His writings constitute the major reading in the curriculum of almost every training institute. Freud was a prolific writer and also a very dynamic and original thinker. Only on a few occasions did he write directly for didactic purposes, as in the "Introductory Lectures to Psychoanalysis" and his papers on technique. His writings are more a record of discoveries and his thinking about his new findings. As a result he kept changing his views in time and only rarely did he go back to correct earlier articles or to append footnotes. Nonetheless, his papers are all too often taught uncritically, without reference to historical perspective and some are studied in much too great detail. Psychoanalysis is perhaps the only scientific field that employs textbooks that are almost 100 years old. The beginning analytic candidate gets his first exposure to principles of psychoanalytic technique from the chapter on therapy in the "Studies in Hysteria," in spite of the fact that the techniques employed there do not resemble anything that we do nowadays. As we know, there is a universal tendency to linger at our early experiences. I suspect this may be true as well of learning psychoanalysis. What we learn first seems to stick with us longest, even when it is no longer useful. For example, when I was a student, we spent an entire semester on the study of Chapter 7 of "The Interpretation of Dreams." It is still an important segment in current training, despite the fact that the concepts contained therein have long since been abandoned. I learned, for example, that in one institute the candidates finally objected when they were asked for a third time to read "The Project for a Scientific Psychology," all this in spite of the fact that Freud himself never intended to publish that work. The classic case histories, originally records of discovery, still form the core of the first-year instruction in most institutes. What do we make of the fact, as Dr. Horowitz ( ) recently reminded us, that more than a thousand papers have been written on the Dora case? All these contributions are nothing more or less than discussions of a clinical case and a set of theories where the author is not present to give additional material which may or may not be at his disposal or to counter with ideas or interpretations that he had entertained but had dismissed for various reasons. For what purpose is so much intellectual effort expended? Do any of these contributions represent a reliable addition to our knowledge? In the case of Dora, Freud discovered transference. That is what is important. From Little Hans he was able to demonstrate <u>in statu nascendi</u> those representations of the Oedipus complex and castration anxiety that he had reconstructed or interpreted from the treatment of adults. He also tried to use the data of Little Hans' experience to debate his theory that pent-up libido was the cause of anxiety, an idea which he abandoned subsequently. The case histories should be discussed specifically in terms of historical perspective, but not read intensively. They should be appreciated for what they are, namely, milestones on the pathway to great discoveries, but not texts for modern psychoanalytic theory or practice.

A related issue, although somewhat peripheral to our immediate concern is the idealization of Freud as the folk hero of the psychoanalytic movement. All too often idealization and denigration go hand in band, as I have indicated elsewhere (Arlow, 1972). In this process Freud nay be transformed into an icon serving as a container for the residue of unresolved transferences in the personal analysis. If I have already mentioned the innumerable papers that have grown out of Freud's case studies, just think of the perhaps even much larger literature written by members of the psychoanalytic community on Freud's life and psychology. I recall sitting in on a course on "The Interpretation of Dreams," where the instructor repeated, as so many others have, the idea that the book represented the record of Freud's personal analysis. Accordingly, in this course, Jones' biography of Freud and the Fliess letters constituted literary adjuncts to the study. All this was done in spite of the fact that, at many points in "The Interpretation of Dreams," Freud states quite explicitly that he breaks off further associations because they are too personal. If historians of psychoanalysis wish to play psychological detective, they are welcome to do so, but it should not be part of psychoanalytic training. What difference does it make if we learn the real identity of Freud's patients? Does it matter to us what Freud and his friend Silberstein wrote to each other in their adolescent years, or whether Freud really dropped the seduction theory in order to protect Fliess? All of this would make an interesting elective in a course on the history of the psychoanalytic movement, but it has no place in the curriculum for psychoanalytic training.

In the same spirit, Freud's political and moral philosophy could be the subject of a fascinating elective, but it is not truly a part of the training of a psychoanalyst. What is essential in the Leonardo da Vinci paper is the fact that in it Freud described the genesis of a certain type of homosexuality. The relation of these ideas to the actual life and experience of Leonardo is really irrelevant. If anything, the pathography of Leonardo detracts from Freud's important discovery. Preoccupation with such issues nay be confusing to the candidate and interfere with his taking an objective stance on the issues of psychoanalysis and the psychoanalytic method.

My first suggestion, therefore, would involve an educational experience for the candidate that would afford him an overall view of the historical development and evolution of psychoanalytic thought, both theory and practice, beginning, of course, with Freud's seminal contributions and continuing on to the study of the subsequent extension, elaboration, challenges and divergences that arose. I am not proposing a track study devoted to the history of psychoanalysis and certainly not to its institutional squabbles. What I have in mind is a consistent examination of the interplay between observation, theory building and technique, centering first and predominantly on Freud's ideas and how they were elaborated or challenged on other grounds, a study of issues, not of personalities or of movements. At the end of his training, a student should be able to appreciate the evolution of Freud's psychoanalytic concepts, how they were tied to crucial findings and challenges from the material obtained within the psychoanalytic situation. Freud did change his ideas on many occasions. Not all of his papers are of equal relevance, valuable as each one may be. A well-trained candidate should be able to appreciate the contribution of each one of Freud's papers in terms of its historical context.

In that spirit, such a track of instruction should include a sampling of the so-called divergent and dissident views from the early days of psychoanalysis down to the present. What are the scientific issues, not the personal ones? What were they in the past? What are they today? What are the crucial issues in developmental psychology, object relations theory, interpersonal, subjectivist, transactional, semantic, Kleinian, Laconian? In a word, an attempt has to be made to disengage ourselves from the historical drag of psychoanalysis as a movement in order to concentrate on psychoanalysis as a science, its inner logic, its contradictions and its development.

Certain practical problems would attend the organization of this aspect of the curriculum. Fresh judgments would have to be made about the amount of time and emphasis placed on certain parts of the literature that in the past have been the subject of concentrated and extensive study. Choices will have to be made. I imagine one could spend much less time on "The Studies in Hysteria," on the papers on the actual neuroses and on the case histories. Many survey articles have appeared in recent years that could be used with profit, provided we overcome a certain antipathy to employing contributions by living colleagues.

Methodological Perspective

In any science the validity of the conclusions one can reach depends upon the nature of the investigative instrument and the method used to analyze the data. In psychoanalysis our instrument is the psychoanalytic situation; the data, the productions of the patient obtained through the technique of free association. There are certain assumptions that are built into the psychoanalytic situation. These serve as the rational basis for the technique of free association. These assumptions constitute the essential principles of psychoanalysis as a psychology. They are determinism, dynamics and topography. Determinism articulates the principle that mental events are not random but causally related to each other. Dynamics indicates that mental life is characterized by an interplay of forces in conflict, and topography draws attention to the inescapable conclusion that much of mental life is not immediately apparent or available to consciousness but can be inferred from the manifest elements reported by the analysand. As applied to theories of pathogenesis, the genetic approach is a corollary of the aforementioned principles. A mode of investigation that deviates or is not based on these principles cannot be considered psychoanalytic.

With these principles in mind, we can appreciate how the text of the patient's associations, including how he or she responds to the analyst's interventions, constitutes repetitive samplings of how the analysand's mind works. By monitoring the flow of the patient's thoughts and by observing the connections that the analysand makes, the analyst comes to understand the nature of the analysand's difficulties. In a sense every observation or intervention by the analyst represents an intrusion into and a dynamic influence upon the stream of the analysand's associations. Whatever the analyst says, together with the adventitious events that occur, serves to destabilize the unsteady equilibrium of psychic forces that the patient has been attempting to maintain. How the patient responds to the analyst's intrusions into the flow of his associations mirrors the way in which at some time in the past the patient had responded to the same thoughts or impulses when he confronted them on his own. Thus, every interaction with the analyst tends to recapitulate a bit of the patient's psychological history. What was once an intrapsychic event of the past becomes during treatment an interpersonal interaction with the analyst. But the analyst's observations and interventions are by no means the only evocative powers acting upon the analysand. Depending upon the nature of the individual's psychological constitution, evolving out of his idiosyncratic historical development, reflecting his persistent unconscious conflicts, almost any element of experience can affect the text of the associations during the analytic session. At any particular moment they may represent the evocative power of such moving instruments as literature, cinema, religion, or on the other hand, some evanescent, hardly noticed sensory event—a particular shape or color or smell. Any one of these may constitute an intensely dynamic stimulus to a stream of associations, of memories or fantasies.

How to understand this fundamental dynamism and what to do about it is the essence of psychoanalytic methodology, on one hand, and of technique, on the other. From my experience, I have become convinced that few graduates of psychoanalytic training programs have a firm grasp of psychoanalytic methodology and a clear idea of how it should be applied. I know of very few courses in training programs that center on the precise, methodological analysis of process notes. Much more attention gets focused on a parallel process, perhaps equally important, namely, the monitoring of the analyst-candidate's intuitive response to the patient's material. That inner process is a nebulous one, its examination most difficult to pursue, whether in the supervisory situation or in the classroom. Nevertheless, in most training programs the latter is emphasized at the expense of the former. The intuitive response of the analyst represents a commentary on the patient's associations, but it is not necessarily identical with the unconscious meaning of the patient's thoughts (see Arlow, 1979).

If anything, recent developments in the profession and in the literature have aggravated the trend of according increasing significance to the analyst as a participant, who should monitor his inner processes and try to analyze them, and then bring them into the interpretive sphere, rather than recognizing that, practically all of the time, the analyst's personal reactions, the so-called countertransference, represent a commentary on the patient's material, a developing insight that the patient's associations have stimulated within the analyst. Preoccupation with countertransference feelings and thoughts, as well as with countertransference enactments, inevitably diverts the analyst's attention away from the patterning of the patient's associations, from the role of context, from the significance of the contiguity and the coherence of the elements in the patient's productions. How to use one's empathic, intuitive countertransference reactions is an important part of psychoanalytic methodology. It has to be understood as a consequence of the dynamic interaction between analyst and analysand, something akin to the mutual stimulation that occurs in ordinary conversation. The analyst's reaction is not necessarily, and in my opinion only on occasion, an example of so-called projective identification. What has been happening in the field, however, is that the relationship aspect of treatment is being emphasized at the expense of the characteristically analytic aspect of technique. In doing so, I believe we have come a long way from what psychoanalytic methodology is fundamentally about.

With these thoughts in mind, let us consider how the student is introduced in a practical way to the workings of the psychoanalytic situation and the dynamic principles that pertain to the treatment effort. Disregarding the experience of one's personal analysis, we realize that, by and large, the candidate's first encounter with actual psychoanalytic data consists of the material of his first supervised case. As a rule, he has no model of concrete clinical experience to guide him—only a set of general principles based, for the most part, on Freud's early papers on technique. The effect of these papers upon the candidate is telling. The impact of Freud's genius endows these technical precepts with imponderable authority and influence in spite of the fact that it is well known that many of Freud's early technical precepts have been discarded. Using his great literary gift, Freud was able to create a number of powerful metaphors concerning technique, metaphors which have affected subsequent generations of candidates. Metaphors are excellent teaching devices but they are evocative and tend to expand and even to take on a life of their own. There are several metaphors of technique that have influenced generations of candidates, directing them how to listen, and how to interpret the free associations of patients.

Let us examine a number of Freud's leading, and perhaps most powerful, metaphors as they pertain to the psychoanalytic situation and to the technique of interpretation. I will refer to the following: the metaphor of the surgeon, the mirror, the telephone, the train and the two-room model of the mind. I will only mention the most salient consequences upon the technique of the developing candidate that flow from each of these metaphors.

From the metaphor of the surgeon, we must learn "to put aside all feelings, even human sympathy, so as to perform the operation as skillfully as possible" (Freud, 1912, p. 115).

From the metaphor of the mirror, we learn that the analyst should "show nothing but what is shown to him" (Freud, 1912, p. 118).

From the metaphor of the telephone, the analyst is directed to "turn his own unconscious, like a receptive organ, towards the transmitting unconscious of the patient so that the analyst's unconscious can, from the derivatives of the patient's unconscious, reconstruct that unconscious which has determined the patient's free associations" (Freud, 1912, p. 115). This last metaphor, as we know, formed the basis of Isakower's concept of the "analyzing instrument," a vague and ill-defined concept which presumes that, if one is well analyzed, he would understand the patient's material correctly. Rational, cognitive assessment of the nature of the patient's free associations, the configurations that the material assumes, the significance of context, contiguity and metaphor are completely secondary or omitted as far as the concept of the analyzing instrument is concerned. It is from the beginning a contradiction of terms to think that one can "turn his own unconscious, like a receptive organ." We have no conscious control over our "unconscious."

From the train metaphor emerges the concept of the analysand as the passive transmitter of the material of the system Ucs (Freud, 1913),

And finally, the two-room model of the mind places major emphasis on getting the repressed material into consciousness as the goal of treatment (Freud, 1915-16). It reflects Freud's theory of mental functioning according to the topographic system, before the emphasis on the defensive transformations and compromise formations, to which analysts today pay, or should pay the most meticulous attention.

Such conceptualization of the psychoanalytic process very often eventuates in a passive, indiscriminate equating of each item in the patients productions, an overly formal, technically intellectualized, unrealistic type of responding to the patient's productions, which results in what I call stilted listening. Pursuing the image of digging to uncover some forgotten event of the past and waiting patiently for some bizarre fantasy to emerge, the candidate loses sight of what really should be the goal of technique, namely, to demonstrate to the analysand how his mind works. As a result, the candidate accepts with equanimity the most irrational sequences of thought that the patient produces. He disregards the lapses in continuity of communication, the use of unusual or striking or irrelevant words and metaphors. He overlooks the seemingly unmotivated breaks in communication, etc., etc. The most bizarre statements proffered by the analysand, which would never go unnoticed and unremarked in ordinary conversation, are allowed to pass, as the analyst continues to listen with unruffled equanimity and waits patiently for the correct interpretation to pop into his mind from the depths of his psyche.

Much of this stilted listening could be avoided if, at the very beginning of the analytic training, process notes of actual sessions, conducted by a skilled and experienced therapist, not by a fellow candidate or tyro, were used to demonstrate to the candidates the method of psychoanalytic listening and the basis for interpretation. Instead, in current training for the most part, candidates are encouraged to speculate, primarily on the basis of analogy to what they have read, in order to determine the unconscious import of the patient's productions. There is nothing wrong with this approach provided these speculations are brought into context with the actual productions of the patient, to see to what extent they are valid in the precise text that is being examined. Unless one does this, one encourages the candidates to commit what I call the phenomenological error, i.e., interpreting unconscious content on the basis of manifest content alone. I recall one instructor many years ago who told his candidates that any dream can be interpreted at three levels—the phallic, the anal and the oral. But what about the context in which the dream appeared, the day's events, the transference, the associations that the patient gave to the precise material? Don't they serve as constraints upon a global, multi-level interpretation?

What the candidate has to learn is that there is a method that is peculiar to psychoanalytic investigation. There is both an art and a science to doing analysis. Some people have intuitive gifts, but therapeutic analysis cannot survive on art alone. The students must be taught a rational, more objective way of dealing with the data of observation. Only such an approach will make the theory of technique and the criteria for interpretation scientifically meaningful to the candidate. The student should be able to demonstrate a drive derivative, a defense, compromise formation, etc., in the text of process notes. If graduates of training programs have not accomplished this, then scientific discourse concerning differing theories and practices of psychoanalysis becomes impossible. If every man's theory is as good as any other man's theory, no theory is any good. A thorough appreciation of the methodology of psychoanalysis should be a *sine qua non* of any training program.

It should be conceptualized early on in course work based on material presented by experienced analysts and realized, in the course of supervision, from the candidate›s own experience.

There is a hidden controversy contained in these considerations. It concerns the therapeutic effect of psychoanalysis, an important debate very much in the forefront of current psychoanalytic discourse. How does psychoanalysis work? When it is effective, is it because of understanding or because of a special relationship to a special person? Only a methodologically precise examination of the clinical data, i.e., process notes rather than histories, can serve as the base on which such issues can be resolved.

A special and very important aspect of this problem is the teaching concerning the significance and the technical management of transference phenomena. The received wisdom is that only transference interpretations are mutative and, second, that as far as possible, everything should be brought into the transference. The formal idea was most definitively articulated by Strachey (1934) at the Marienbad Congress. It reflects his Kleinian orientation. Listening to the transference interpretations, the analysand comes to appreciate the difference between the introjected, destructive mother image contained in his superego, in contrast to the reasonable, rational image of the analyst. In piecemeal fashion over the course of the analysis, the bad, internal superego introject is extruded and the good, reasonable, psychoanalytic introject now becomes ensconced in the superego. The theoretical and technical background for these ideas is in another one of Freud's powerful metaphors, namely, that one cannot undo an infantile, instinctual fixation on an object in effigy. To make it effective, one must have a real, concrete, current-day, substitute object, namely, the analyst. The question is: does actual clinical observation confirm these ideas? Is it true that only transference interpretations are effective? Is it even possible for all of the unconscious, instinctual conflicts relating to certain fantasy wishes to be worked out in connection with the analyst? Some of them, by their very nature, run counter to this supposition. In my experience, close examination of the details in the psychoanalytic process demonstrates how most often transference appears as a defense, precisely in the setting when derivative expressions of a forbidden wish threaten to involve the primary object in the patient's thoughts. It is at such a juncture that transference material begins to appear. Freud originally stated that transference appears in the analysis as a resistance. In keeping with the theory of pathogenesis that he held at that time, he meant that transference appeared in lieu of recollection. Instead of remembering what has been repressed, the patient unwittingly relives it with the analyst. Current concepts of the ubiquitous nature of transference challenge such a notion. The process of transference is going on all the time, inside and outside of the analysis, before treatment as well as during treatment, and it will persist after treatment as well. Only precise study, methodologically meticulous, can resolve such issues. This is only one example of how psychoanalytic training and teaching can change and, I believe, advance in an appropriate scientific fashion.

The Developmental Perspective

Psychoanalysis is a developmental psychology. Psychoanalytic theories of pathogenesis all articulate the notion of disturbances of development, emphasizing particularly the vicissitudes of childhood experience. The study of all aspects of human development thus becomes a major area of interest in the psychoanalytic curriculum. This is one of the areas of psychoanalytic interest that has grown more rapidly in recent years than perhaps any other. Many observations have been accumulated and competing theories have been put forward concerning how different developmental vicissitudes affect the process of normal growth as well as pathogenesis. It becomes a matter of utmost significance, therefore, for future analysts to be able to judge critically which observational theories are relevant and valid. A consistent syllabus, beginning with the findings of infant observation and proceeding through the development of self and object differentiation, the crystallization of psychic structure, the organization of the drives, together with consideration of all functions that have been relatively neglected, such as the development of language, thinking processes and intellectual development in general, has yet to be realized. These rich observations should become part of a broad, overall perspective of human development, expressing both normal and pathological forms. At one point in such a curriculum, considerations of the process of educability and the influence of social forces enter. Issues of character formation, personal identity and moral imperatives remain dynamically significant long past the so-called resolution of the Oedipus conflicts. The main point is that the development of the human individual, its normal and pathogenic potential, must be considered in the spirit of the basic psychoanalytic principles of determinism, dynamics, topography and genetics, as mentioned earlier.

To conclude, I would say that we have to take a new, hard look at where we stand in the development of psychoanalysis as a science. As we do so, we must recognize our responsibility to provide the coming generation of psychoanalysts with the appropriate conceptual and methodological instruments to become effective practitioners and at the same time to enhance our common goal of advancing our science.

References

Arlow, J.A. (1972). Some dilemmas in psychoanalytic education. *Journal of the American Psychoanalytic Association,* 20:556–566.

———— (1979). The genesis of interpretation. *Journal of the American Psychoanalytic Association,* 27, supplement, 193–206.

Freud, S. (1912). Recommendations to physicians practicing psychoanalysis. *Standard Edition,* Vol. 12, pp. 109–120.

———— (1913). On beginning the treatment. *Standard Edition,* Vol. 12, pp. 123–144.

———— (1915-16). Introductory lectures on psychoanalysis. *Standard Edition,* Vol. 16, pp. 295-296.

Strachey, J. (1934). The nature of the therapeutic action of psychoanalysis. *International Journal of Psychoanalysis,* 15:127–159.

Abstract

Most curricula of psychoanalytic education repeat with little change principles and practices inherited from the past. The core of the instruction is often founded on reading and discussion of Freud's papers. All too often this is clone in an uncritical fashion and without regard for the historical perspective, namely, the consistent evolution of Freud's theorizing as he made new discoveries in his clinical work. In this contribution, it is suggested that the psychoanalytic curriculum be organized according to three perspectives: (1) the historical development of psychoanalytic concepts and technique; (2) psychoanalytic methodology and (3) psychoanalytic developmental psychology. The need for a fresh approach to the curriculum becomes apparent in the difficulty that analysts have in establishing a common frame of reference for discourse concerning controversial issues in psychoanalysis. A proper grounding in basic psychoanalytic principles and methodology is a fundamental need in resolving these difficulties.

www.ingramcontent.com/pod-product-compliance
Lightning Source LLC
Chambersburg PA
CBHW060221030426
42335CB00015B/1801